Lutiapik

Lutiapik

Betty Lee

McClelland and Stewart Limited

ISBN 0-7710-5225-1

The Canadian Publishers
McClelland and Stewart Limited
25 Hollinger Road, Toronto

Printed and bound in Canada
by
John Deyell Company

To all of the
northern nurses
who did the same thing

Author's Note

This book began as a question. "Why," I asked my friend, Dorothy Knight, two years ago, "don't you talk into a tape recorder and tell everything you can remember about your tour of nursing duty in the Arctic? You never know. You might come up with something interesting."

Dorothy seemed surprised. "Do you really think so? After all, I was only doing my job."

Precisely. This is the true story of how a city-born nurse with the Canadian Indian and Northern Health Service did her job in one of the most remote areas of the world. It is a story about loneliness and boredom. It is a story about fear and self-doubt. It is a story about a naïve kind of courage which, even today, Dorothy Knight does not realize she possessed.

More important, it is a story about a woman alone with her own sense of responsibility. And how loneliness can shape and influence a life just as effectively as can the experience of being constantly with others.

No names in the story have been changed. It would be difficult to do so. There was only one small settlement ninety miles west of Frobisher Bay in 1957, and that was Lake Harbour. There were few inhabitants, either white or Inuit. This, of course, is their story too. I thank them for their frankness and co-operation.

Betty Lee

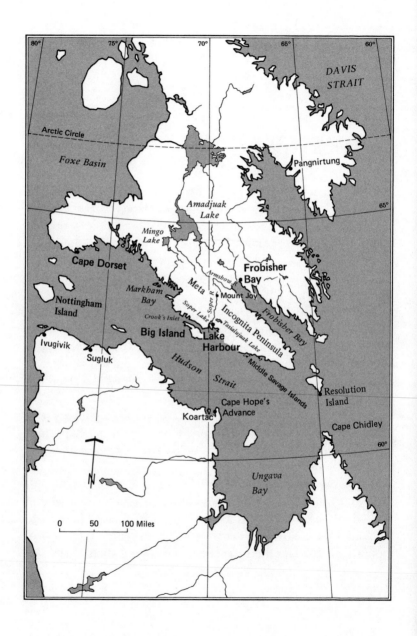

1

She knew it was a death camp the moment the peterhead boat passed the Islands of God's Mercy and chugged slowly into the inlet. Eskimo settlements were always noisy with the howls of sled dogs the instant visitors appeared. This place was silent, its three white canvas tents ghostly against the slate-grey of the Arctic rock. There were no sealskins stretched to dry, no racks of meat or animal entrails set out in the bright August sun.

No one in the peterhead spoke. Akavak, the special constable from Lake Harbour, and his wife, Pitsulala, sat impassively, their flat brown faces turned towards the deserted shore. Ishawakta, the young nursing station employee, stood in the bow, ready to jump as soon as Gerry Heapy, the RCMP officer found a spot to land. Gerry was at the wheel, remembering perhaps that he had tried to dissuade her from coming. "The Eskimos say there's a sick camp down near Markham Bay?" he had grinned at her. The grin, of course, was meant to remind her that Markham Bay was at least 100 miles down the Baffin Island coast from the settlement. "Okay, you're the nurse, Dorothy Knight. But it could be just another case of constipation, you know. It's a long trip to pass out laxatives."

Just a year ago, in August 1957, when she had arrived in Lake Harbour from Toronto as the new Northern Health Service nurse, she might have agreed with him. That afternoon, though, Dorothy shrugged at Gerry's grumbles and replied that if the RCMP couldn't help, she would rent an Eskimo boat and go with Ishawakta to check out the story. Gerry walked out of her house, and she heard him kicking at stones near the porch door. She was packing instruments and a fresh supply of drugs into her medical bag when the officer came back to say he had decided to make the police peterhead available next morning.

Dorothy grabbed the black bag as the boat scraped to a stop against a rounded rock. Ishawakta secured the line, then reached out his hand to help her over the side. It was a steep climb to the camp; her sealskin *kamiks* slithered as she fought to find footholds. She looked back down the slope. Gerry was following, his service cap pushed back on his head. Akavak and Pitsulala were close behind. Ahead of her, Ishawakta had reached the nearest *tupik* and was peering inside. He emerged, shaking his head.

"*Agai*," he said. "No, nothing."

"So what have we got here?" Gerry asked. He mopped his forehead with the back of his parka sleeve.

"Nothing," repeated Ishawakta. "Maybe all gone now."

"Maybe they have," said Gerry. "Looks pretty quiet to me."

Dorothy started to walk. "Let's see."

She headed across the accumulation of bones and decaying blubber that seemed to be a part of most Inuit encampments in the Arctic. The she stopped and pointed to a flat area a few yards away from the tents. "Akavak," she called.

The Eskimo padded up behind her. "*Kingmil*," he grunted. Dogs. There were at least a dozen carcasses, swarming with flies. Some of the animals, she saw, were no more than puppies. All had been shot in the head.

"Good God!" said Gerry. "Why that?"

Dorothy kept walking towards the second tent. She opened the flap, looked inside, then called to the others. "Over here. It's a woman and a young boy." She crouched to enter the dim *tupik*. It was chilly and a little damp. There was no familiar blubber lamp. An empty powdered milk can lay on its side. There was a wooden sleeping platform at the back of the tent, but the woman was sitting, stockinged legs stretched out before her, on the rough stone floor of the shelter. The boy sat facing her. Both were emaciated. There were no greetings. When Gerry and Akavak came through the tent opening, the woman carefully closed a book she had been cradling in the lap of her *amouti* and placed it on the stones. Dorothy saw it was a Bible printed in Eskimo syllabics.

She took the woman's wrist to check her pulse as Akavak began his questioning. "*Shengeeto*," she heard the woman say softly. Weak. The boy stared blankly as Dorothy lifted his limp hand. She looked up at Gerry. "Their pulses are steady enough. It looks as though they're both starving. Would you tell Akavak to have Pitsulala mix up some oatmeal?"

Gerry talked with the Eskimo constable, then followed Dorothy out of the *tupik*. "The woman says there's a body in the other tent. Her brother-in-law, I think. She tried to bury him but had to quit. Too weak to finish the job."

Dorothy turned her face to catch the sea breeze that suddenly ruffled the calm water of the inlet. She could smell the rotting bodies of the dogs. She noted gratefully that Ishawakta had brought a primus stove from the peterhead and was brewing tea. "Only one body?" she asked. "But there are three tents, Gerry. There must have been other people here."

"There were. Probably three or four men from what I could hear. Akavak is asking about them." He frowned. "Do you think it's something infectious?"

She thought about it as they stooped to enter the far *tupik*. The dead man was lying on a red Hudson's Bay blanket, dressed in pants, *kamiks* and a duffle-cloth parka. There were some sealskin thongs on the ground near his head, but no attempt had been made to lash the shroud into place. Gerry knelt on one side of the body, opening the parka to find the Eskimo's numbered identification tag. Dorothy knelt on the other side of the corpse. There was no sign of measles, one of the deadly killers of the Arctic. She dismissed thoughts of tuberculosis. Disaster had apparently hit the members of the camp at about the same time.

Perhaps the man had died of diphtheria. There had been some epidemics near Lake Harbour during the past few years. The swollen neck and a bloody discharge from the mouth were typical. But then, she remembered, didn't victims of diphtheria bleed from the nose?

"Botulism?" she asked herself aloud. "Or trichinosis?"

11

Gerry copied the tag number into his notebook, then tucked it into his pocket. "Trichinosis?" He sat back on his heels, staring at the dead Eskimo.

"You get it from eating raw pork," said Dorothy. "Or bear and walrus in this part of the world. That edema, the swelling around the face, is a possible clue. So is the bleeding. He could have died from other complications, of course. Probably pneumonia." Trichinosis, she thought, could also explain why the woman and the child seemed to be unaffected. It was sometimes the custom for Eskimo men to eat the muscle meat of animals and leave the entrails for the women and children. Muscle meat was where the trichinosis roundworm lodged.

She considered cutting into the flesh of the corpse for an autopsy specimen to send to the Department of National Health and Welfare in Ottawa, but decided against it. She had no formaldehyde to preserve the material, and it was a couple of weeks yet before the government ship, *C. D. Howe*, would get into Lake Harbour on its annual Eastern Arctic medical patrol. She stared wordlessly at Gerry. There was nothing more she could say. She drew the blanket over the dead man's face and went out into the sunshine.

Down near the first tent, she saw Akavak, Pitsulala, and Ishawakta bunched around a figure lying on the rocks. Gerry came out of the *tupik* behind her. "I think," she said to him, "they've found another body."

Akavak began explaining in Eskimo as they walked across the campsite. "They found him just behind the tents," Gerry told her. "It's the woman's husband. She says the man knew she was too weak to drag him out of the tent after he died. So he went away by himself."

The second corpse looked very much like the first – facial edema, frothy blood around the mouth. Dorothy listened as Akavak continued to tell the story. Although she knew many of the Inuit words, Gerry occasionally interrupted to interpret. The four men of the camp had become very sick about twenty sleeps ago. There had been swelling of the eyelids and much pain in the body. There had been no hunting because of the terrible illness, though the boy had once caught some fish in a nearby lake.

Two men had died four sleeps ago, and the woman, the child, and the two weakening male survivors had trussed the bodies into blankets and buried them under stones. A boat loaded with Eskimos had sailed near the inlet; the woman called from the shore that there was sickness and death in the camp and they should tell the nurse in Lake Harbour. The boat sailed away and the camp was alone again. Another man died three sleeps ago. When the hungry dogs had tried to eat the body, the woman drove them away with a whip, then shot them. She rolled the corpse into a blanket and that was all she could do. Then her husband went out to die. There was continuing hunger.

Dorothy glanced at the faces of the three Lake Harbour Eskimos. Expressionless. *Ayonamut,* she thought. Even after a year in this harsh land, it was difficult for her to accept the implacable Eskimo philosophy – it can't be helped; the pattern of life and death can never be altered. Akavak finished what he had to say, then folded his arms across his Grenfell cloth parka. That, he was indicating, is what has happened in this place. *Ayonamut.* Numbly she watched as Ishawakta walked across to the primus stove and brought her a mug of hot tea.

"Lutiapik," he said softly. It was the name chosen for her by the Eskimos when they had seen the new nurse was even shorter than them and as spare as a sled dog in July. Dorothy, it was decided, would be known as the little person who eases pain.

"Lutiapik," Ishawakta repeated. He grinned the crooked grin she had come to know so well. "Woman in tent say she knew you would come." His grin widened. *Knew she would come!* She held the mug tightly in both hands. Was this what her year in the Arctic had been all about? Was this the end of uncertainty, her nagging sense of inadequacy in the North?

Gerry, she was aware, had heard what Ishawakta had said. She avoided his eyes, taking a long swallow of tea. The constable was silent for a moment, then shoved his hands into the pockets of his pants. "Well, we'd better take a look at the other two bodies," he said. "I'll need the identification numbers. Then we'll bury the four men and burn the camp. The woman and the kid will have to come back with us, anyway."

Knew she would come.

"You think it's okay to get them down to the boat now, Dorothy?"

"I'll see."

Inside the cheerless *tupik*, the woman and child were sitting as patiently as when she first found them. The bowls of soft food Pitsulala had brought lay empty on the stones. The Inuit looked up at her. There was still no greeting, no smile, no attempt at the handshake that was so important to the Arctic people. But she could see they would be strong again and that they also knew it. *"Peoyook,"* she nodded. Good. The woman nodded back. Life for her here was finished, but she and the boy would be quickly absorbed into another Eskimo community. Shelter would be offered without question; food would be shared.

When she went outside, Akavak and Gerry were piling tent canvas and rubbish around the bodies of the dogs. Pitsulala had found a threadbare blanket and was wrapping the woman's husband in the simple shroud. Ishawakta had begun lifting stones from the burial cairn built further around the slope. Dorothy stood, her black bag at her feet, looking across the quiet inlet. According to a radio report they had received, her successor at the Lake Harbour nursing station would be arriving on the *Howe.* Dorothy would stay until the nurse was briefed and settled, then hitch a ride to Frobisher Bay on one of the planes that dropped into the settlement every now and then at this time of the year. From there, she would fly to Montreal and home.

She felt a sharp stab of regret at the thought of leaving. *I've changed,* she realized. *I'm so very different from what I was when it all began. Am I really the same person who sat talking with Heather McDonald that night at the Silver Rail in Toronto?*

What was it she had once read about the Arctic? She had never really understood what it meant until that summer. She fumbled in her pocket for a cigarette, remembering the words.

"No one can live for long in the North without being profoundly influenced by both its complexity and simplicity. All that is superficial, superfluous, and unnecessary is forever eliminated from your life. The Arctic, in fact, changes your destiny."

She watched the men moving about the doomed campsite. Pitsulala and Ishawakta entered the *tupik* to fetch the woman and the child; then Akavak pulled at the ropes until the tent collapsed. The woman did not look back at the heap of grimy canvas that had been her home. All she took with her was her crescent-shaped knife and her Bible.

"We've never sent a *single* woman to a one-nurse posting in the North before now," said Heather McDonald, delicately extracting meat from a lobster claw. "It's not a strict rule, but it's simpler that way. We look for a married couple. A nurse whose husband has been trained as a teacher or a welfare worker, usually. But they're not always easy to find." The tall, thin-faced nursing supervisor of the Indian and Northern Health Service glanced down at her dinner plate. "How old are you again, Dorothy?"

"Twenty-eight." She was still somewhat stunned to realize she had landed the job advertised in the *Canadian Nurse Journal*. She had really wanted to work in the wilderness with the Indians, of course, and it had been a shock to learn she was expected to go to the Arctic. Odd that the advertisement had not made it clear that the Indian and Northern Health Service included the Arctic.

Even in the Toronto restaurant, she could visualize her dream of the wilderness. Silent lakes and big-bellied rivers. Streams rich with trout. And giant trees. There had been that nurse she had known at the Children's Hospital in Detroit who told her tales about the time she had worked in the Northwest Territories as a teacher. Stories about living in a log cabin and teaching the Indian kids to read from an Eaton's catalogue because there were no textbooks.

"I'm twenty-eight this month, Miss McDonald," she repeated. Somewhere, she had heard there were no trees in the Arctic.

"Well," sighed the supervisor. "It *is* 1957 and I can see you're a pretty sensible person. You know it's possible to take a companion along with you. Perhaps a nursing assistant. There'll be other whites in Lake Harbour, of course. The men at the RCMP detachment, the Hudson's Bay manager, the Anglican missionary and his wife. But you'll be alone in your house. Completely alone for a year."

"Oh, I won't be lonely," said Dorothy. She smiled across the table. What she had really meant to say was that privacy had always been a luxury. The news that she would have her own home in the North pleased and excited her. Her mind flickered back to the crowded house on Waverley Road where she had grown up with her four brothers and young sister. Was there a time any of them could be really alone? Privacy on Waverley Road was withdrawal behind a book, sitting in a corner of the basement, or pulling the sheets over one's head.

Later, in nurse's training, the sleeping figures of her fellow students cluttered the apartment in Sarnia. She could still hear the snores. She could still hear the grunts and moans when the alarm clock summoned the unwilling back to consciousness for the seven-to-seven night shift. Her mouth tightened a little at the thought of those days in Sarnia, but it prompted her to say: "It was interesting that you felt I had the right qualifications for the job."

"Qualifications?" Miss McDonald sipped from her water glass. "Well, you're a registered nurse with five years' experience. Right? You're in good health. You're clearly very interested in a northern posting. I'm sure you'll handle the assignment very well."

Dorothy waited for the supervisor to go on. What kinds of things would she be expected to do in Lake Harbour? Make beds in the small hospital she had been told was there? She suppressed a giggle. Miss Rahno Beamish, director of nursing at Sarnia General, had made sure she could do that job well enough. *Those corners aren't quite as tight as they should be, Miss Knight!* She could see the disapproving mouth and the eyes behind the no-nonsense glasses. Dedication, deference to authority, and you're absolutely right, Miss Beamish. She wondered how many beds there were in the Lake Harbour hospital.

The nursing supervisor switched to another subject. "There have been other nurses in Lake Harbour. Since the thirties, actually, though the federal station has only been there for five years. It's a well set-up post, I believe."

Believe?

"I've never been there. The settlement is quite small and out of the way. You can look it up on a map, if it's marked. You'll find it on the southern coast of Baffin Island, about ninety miles west of Frobisher Bay."

Dorothy clasped her hands in her lap, one over the other. It was a gesture she had picked up from the nuns at the convent high school she attended as a teenager. This was all ridiculously easy. No briefing sessions. No lectures about rules and procedures. God, how she loathed rules. Sometimes they were a comfort, though, like the reassurance of doctor's orders on a chart. But what, precisely, were the rules for an INHS nurse? Didn't the supervisor even know? Was it just to behave oneself? To bind wounds and give advice? Or just to be there because the government said so? She bit her lip, wondering whether it would be out of place to ask.

But Miss McDonald was talking cheerfully about salary. Dorothy would receive $3,120 for the twelve-month contract, plus $1,200 northern allowance. The money would be deposited to her account in the Bank of Nova Scotia in Frobisher Bay. "If you need to buy anything special in Lake Harbour, of course," the supervisor added, "you can pay the Hudson's Bay manager by cheque. I hear that always works out all right." There was a short pause. "You really want this job, don't you Dorothy?"

She thought, trying to shut her ears to the clatter of the restaurant. Yes, she did. She wanted it the same way she wanted to go where the train was travelling that day she heard it wailing in the distance. She wanted it the same way she wanted freedom and independence. She wanted it as she wanted a place of her own to furnish the way she liked. She wanted it the same way she wanted to love and be loved. "I want it," she told Heather McDonald.

"Why exactly?"

"Because I'm curious!" she said. She felt a flush of guilt. Well, it was true. It wasn't some missionary zeal to improve the health of the northern people or save them from disease that had prompted her to answer the advertisement. Curiosity had led her into those three grim years of training, into the exhausting routine of the ward, into the antiseptic atmosphere of the operating theatre. Curiosity had sent her tagging along with her brothers when they went on bird-nesting expeditions into the Scarborough woods. Curiosity had kept her from fainting at her first autopsy.

Miss McDonald signalled for the check. Dorothy stared across the room, forcing herself to think selflessly about Miss Beamish in Sarnia, about nursing dedication, and about all the northern natives who needed to be helped. But all she could see was a house in a place called the Arctic. And her own possessions beside her bed.

2

Dorothy was impatient for the ship to sail. Health and Welfare wrote to say the *C. D. Howe* would leave for the Arctic in the last week of June. But when she arrived in Montreal, she found the vessel still taking on supplies. She was the first passenger to report on board. After unpacking her cabin luggage in the quiet passengers' quarters, she went on shore to explore the city. Montreal, though, was a bore. Since she knew no one in town, there was no one to visit, no one to telephone. She called Toronto twice, eager for the sound of familiar voices.

The black-and-white, chunkily built government icebreaker fascinated her. She was glad she could be alone to explore its corridors, its decks, the intriguing flights of metal steps that led to secret places. Miss McDonald had already explained something about the annual INHS Eastern Arctic Patrol. The ship toured northern settlements to unload supplies, deliver personnel, and to check the health of the Eskimos. "There'll be one or two doctors on board," the nursing supervisor had said. "There'll be a dentist, a radiologist, and a nurse to keep an eye on the Eskimos going home from TB sanatoriums. She'll be on duty with the patrol when the ship is in port."

"I'd like to help with the patrol work," Dorothy had said that evening in Toronto. But how? While the crew worked noisily in the hold among the accumulating crates and bundles, she stood in the empty sick bay and wondered again what she really needed to know about the Arctic. Ottawa had sent her no literature about the North. She had received no information about the people she was being sent to work with. She knew nothing about their way of life. Come to think of it, Health and Welfare had forwarded no further instructions about what they expected her to do.

She had already discovered that the captain of the *Howe* was not an easy man to question or approach. Sombre and grim-faced in his black uniform, Paul Fournier grated out orders, waved his arms impatiently if something went wrong, then vanished until another emergency occurred. He chatted with her briefly at the dinner table but it was clear he had other matters on his mind.

Dorothy once looked up from her soup and asked: "Is it very cold?" Fournier tore at a bread roll then reached for the butter.

"No," he answered vaguely. "Is yours?"

My God, she thought, wanting to giggle. He thinks I mean the soup. "The Arctic," she explained. "I was wondering how cold it gets in Lake Harbour."

Fournier stared across the dining salon. "It gets pretty cold," he said. "Pretty cold indeed."

She silently spooned her soup. She had wanted to remind the captain that it got pretty cold in Toronto as well. Sometimes, in January and February, the ice would freeze twenty feet high against the pebbly beachfront at Kew, and it would be so frigid, her nostrils would be sticky with frost. She remembered the agony as circulation returned to her fingers on winter mornings after she came home from mass. So how much colder was the Arctic than a two-below morning in Toronto?

A day or so later, she returned from a morning in the city to find she had acquired fellow passengers. Suddenly, there was laughter and chatter and the slamming of cabin doors. The bulky man with the thinning hair and owlish glasses was Dr. H. B. Sabean, the chief medical officer of the patrol. There was Dr. Jack Hildes, a researcher. Dr. Paul Hutchinson, the dentist. Fred Lee, the X-ray technician who found it somewhat amusing that she had never been north before.

She flattened herself against the bulkhead as a steward panted by, carrying suitcases. Somewhere in the crowded corridor she was introduced to Glenn, the ship's helicopter pilot. She shook hands with a bearded priest with gentle eyes who told her he was Father Franz VandeVelde, a Belgian Oblate, and that he was "going home" to Pelly Bay. There was Lyle Faulkner, an officer with the Royal Canadian Air Force, and a cheerful public health nurse named Heather Matthews who was joining the INHS nursing station staff at Frobisher Bay after the patrol. There was a small woman, who said she was an interpreter and that her name was Mary Paneegoosho. It was only after Mary had disappeared into a cabin that Dorothy realized she had met her first Eskimo.

She escaped to the open deck, feeling shy and a little awkward among so many strangers. She had never managed to make friends easily. She stood hesitantly for a moment, watching the ship's crane swing over the side with another net-load of crates, then walked towards the prow.

The sight of the *Howe's* Eskimo passengers was unexpected. She was sure the natives had not been there when she had gone ashore earlier, but now there were at least forty of them on the lower deck. She peered curiously over the rail. These were the kinds of people who would be her patients during the coming year. *Who are you?* she thought. As far as she remembered, she had never seen a picture of an Eskimo, though she had heard they were intrepid people who hunted animals for food. Primitive independence like that was awesome to someone brought up in the city. How could she be of help to individuals who knew more about themselves and their environment than she had ever learned?

The Eskimos ignored her. Perhaps they could not see her on the upper level. There was some laughter and bursts of talk that seemed dominated by the gutteral sound of k . . . k . . . k. But there was no shouting, even among the children who scurried about the deck. She looked for differences between the Arctic people and herself. There seemed to be few, though the Eskimos were shorter than the average Canadian, and their eyes were slanted above high Oriental cheekbones. Most were dressed in ordinary pants, shirts, and cotton dresses. But some of the women wore long, swallow-tailed robes. There were babies cradled comfortably in the baggy hoods.

Several Eskimo women were sewing at hand-powered machines. Sounds floated up to her in the still June air. The whirr of the machines. The staccato sentences. The low laughter. She was aware of an aura of self-containment and content. She would have liked to have joined the Eskimos in the prow, but standing at the high rail, she felt as though she were staring down a long tunnel into another, private world. The longing to enter the tunnel and reach the other side lingered with her for the rest of the day and far into the night. When she woke next morning, she found the ship had sailed.

The *C. D. Howe* hit field-ice in the Strait of Belle Isle between Newfoundland and the coast of Labrador. During lunch that day, the ship slid to a grinding halt. "Well, that's it," Dr. Sabean announced, clattering a spoon into his empty bowl of dessert. Dorothy sat back in her chair, listening with absorbed interest.

"I heard in Montreal there was a late ice-cover this year," Lyle Faulkner said casually.

"Yeah," agreed the doctor with a grin. "I guess that's it."

What's it? Would they all have to get out and walk? Apparently no one at the table seemed concerned. Heather went to the prow to check on an Eskimo boy who had a bellyache. Father VandeVelde smoked silently and stroked his beard. Dr. Hildes poured more coffee. Glenn, the helicopter pilot, started a conversation with Dr. Sabean about a possible bridge game that evening.

Dorothy liked the tall, unassuming Dr. Sabean. As a hospital nurse she was not used to informal contact with doctors, but this man was different from the remote personages in white coats who had swept through her wards. She discovereed that the patrol chief had worked as a radio technician on the DEW Line, before going south to study for his medical degree. He admitted he was fascinated with the Arctic, and she was envious of his knowledge of the North. After his current stint on the medical patrol, he would go to the Anglican mission hospital at Pangnirtung, a settlement on the east coast of Baffin Island. The physician grinned affectionately when he talked about the outlandish-sounding place. Pangnirtung. Dorothy stored another name into her head. Pangnirtung. Frobisher. Pelly Bay.

Another day, she had helped Heather, Dr. Sabean, and Fred Lee begin uncrating the equipment for the ship's surgery and examination rooms – everything had been packed and stored after the previous year's patrol – sterilization equipment and X-ray machines, tables, lamps, instruments.

"I wonder," she asked Dr. Sabean, "whether there's a book around here I can read."

"About what?" he asked absently. "You want something to read?" He rummaged through a crate. "What on earth have we got in here?"

Dorothy carefully stacked a dozen boxes of surgical gloves. "I'd like to read a book about nursing in the Arctic," she said. "Are there any manuals or guides? What kinds of things should I know about?"

The doctor was unpacking sections of an operating table. "Well, you're going to have antibiotics and other drugs at the station, you know. You'll have a lot of pneumonia and bronchitis, and you'll treat that with antibiotics."

Dorothy absorbed this information. *Bacterial pneumonia.* Shaking chills. Chest pains. Rust-colored sputum. Headache, sweating, and rapid respiration. In hospital, she had once put a stethoscope to a pneumonia patient's chest to hear the sounds of diseased lung wall rubbing against pleura. The sick man turned his head to spit into the waxed cardboard box she had placed near his head. She had checked his temperature. It was 104 degrees. "How much pneumonia will there be?" she asked Dr. Sabean.

The doctor sighed as he looked into another crate. "You know, there should be a full carton of screws in here. So what happened to them?" He looked up at her, blinking as he considered her question. "Oh, there's always pneumonia, Dorothy."

Now they were stuck in the ice. With lunch finished, she went out on deck, alone. The ice stretched endlessly ahead, white and unbroken. A small pile of garbage from the galley had already accumulated at the side of the ship. Behind the *Howe,* the ice-pans floated freely in the astonishingly blue sea. Some of the floes, she saw, held their own pools of melted water, each as colourful as the sea itself. She had never imagined it would be like this. It was summer and she had scarcely expected to see ice in the summer.

She faced the sun, luxuriating in its warmth and breathing the clear, cold air. After the constant throb of engines in the Gulf of St. Lawrence, the silence was eerie. She could hear the barking speech of the Eskimos as they went about their tasks on the lower deck. *Inuit.* That was what Dr. Sabean called the Eskimo. The people. "There are the white people, the black people, the yellow people," the physician had grinned. "Then there are The People. The Inuit."

There was a low growl and a shudder as the ship's engines came to life again. She clung to a railing in excited expectation. After all, since the *Howe* was an icebreaker, she supposed it was about to slice cleanly through the frozen sea. The ship backed, stopped to a clatter of bells, then plowed full speed ahead.

"Tally-ho!" someone shouted. The massive prow whacked at the ice, rode up for several feet before smashing through to clear water. "Hear we go again!" She looked up to see Glenn standing near his lashed-down helicopter on the poop deck. The *Howe* backed, stopped, then sped again to tilt at the thick ice-pack.

Below decks, she heard the smash of chinaware. There was a whine as the screws reversed, another shudder, another thud of steel against ice. The *Howe* heaved like an injured sea-monster, floundering in the cracked debris of the pack.

"Oh my God," she laughed up at the pilot. "How long does this go on?"

He waved at the white horizon. "Until we get through that lot."

There was fog along the Labrador coast, and Dorothy was asleep in the lingering Arctic twilight when the ship passed Cape Hope's Advance on the south shore of Hudson Strait. The next morning she stood on deck with Father VandeVelde and forced herself to ask the priest about her spiritual welfare in the Arctic. She had attended the mass he celebrated that Sunday with the help of two grave-faced Inuit altar boys. But it was impossible to confess to a man with whom she would be dining and socializing during the trip.

"Pay attention to your catechism my child," she heard Father O'Conner of St. John's parish saying over the wide gap of years. "Go to mass, come to confession regularly, and make an act of contrition." With a small flush of dislike, she remembered the musty smell of the dark confessional.

The Belgian priest shoved his hands into the pockets of his cassock. "If it is impossible to go to mass or to confess, it is impossible," he decided. "I think God will accept that. But if there is any opportunity you must, of course, try." He fingered his gold pectoral cross. "Lake Harbour is Anglican," he said, and he laughed. "They got there first."

Dorothy nodded. "Then it will be impossible."

"I suppose so." He stared out to sea as though he were trying to glimpse something that was not there. "The Anglicans have done some fine work in the Arctic. They will be your colleagues."

She felt the same kind of giddy relief that used to wash over her in church when she had done her penance. She clattered cheerfully down to the sick bay to ask Dr. Sabean when the patrol would be handling its first batch of Eskimo examinations. He looked up from his clipboard and said he figured it would probably be Sugluk on the northern coast of Labrador. "Small place," he grunted. "Pang's much bigger. And Lake Harbour's prettier."

"Is it?" she asked eagerly. "What's it really like there?"

"Really pretty," The doctor scratched his balding head. "Have you seen any auralgan drops around here, Dorothy?"

She hesitated for a moment, wishing she could continue the conversation about Lake Harbour. But Dr. Sabean was absorbed in his drug list again. Heather Matthews darted into the cabin, looking for a fresh supply of aspirin and dispensing news. The *Howe* would stop briefly at the settlement of Wakeham Bay to dump supplies, then put into Sugluk for medicals. Oh, and another thing. The parka Dorothy had ordered from the Eskimos was finally finished. Nice job, too. Hudson's Bay duffle cloth, trimmed with rabbit, and coloured embroidery. It was in her cabin.

Dorothy pulled the parka over her head, shoved impatiently at her hair, then raced to the deck with her camera. Good Lord, she knew she was acting like a tourist rather than a nurse headed for a responsible northern posting. But she couldn't resist posing in the spotless new parka against the dramatic background of sea and ice-pans. Click. Thanks, Glenn. Another click. This is a picture of Dorothy Knight, RN, on the ice-breaker, *C. D. Howe*, and I'm wearing an Eskimo parka. Wide grin, photogenic ice and, oh God, that's enough. She stalked to her cabin and threw the camera on her bunk. Sugluk. She wanted the *Howe* to reach Sugluk. Her hands itched to be at work. And she wanted so much to meet the Arctic.

Sugluk was a disaster. She waited impatiently at the ship's gangway, ready to jump into the steel landing barge as soon as it was ready to leave for the shore. But when the craft grated into the stony beach, she stood, staring unhappily at the drab settlement.

"I have a friend here," Father VandeVelde told her. The priest was the only passenger to go ashore beside herself. The first load of Eskimos were expected that afternoon, and the patrol was gearing itself for the exhausting routine.

The priest stretched his arms lazily in the warm air. "Not very exciting, is it?" he smiled. Dorothy was grimly silent. There were four, no, five houses in Sugluk, plus a few other nondescript buildings. There were one or two skimpy patches of grass. An untidy cluster of canvas tents straggled down to the beach and dozens of Eskimos sat or stood together, pointing now and then at the *Howe* anchored down the inlet near Sugluk Island. The ship's chopper, with Glenn at the controls, clattered overhead, and she wondered if rumours she had heard on the ship that the helicopter was sometimes used to round up runaway patients were true.

Then she swallowed. *Grandeur*, she thought. How had she

always pictured the North? Unspoiled grandeur. She had been prepared for the lack of trees in the Arctic. But this place was a mud flat! Her throat ached with the same dull disappointment she had felt when she quit school one fall to return to a fruit farm where she had worked in the summer. *Nothing is the way I thought it would be.* The farm had been cold and lonely, and the work was harder than she had remembered. She had gone home in a week.

"I'm going off to see my friend," said Father VandeVelde. "He is a priest from Belgium, also." He chuckled. "He does not have very much to do, I'm afraid. The Anglicans beat us here as well."

Dorothy walked towards the tents, wishing she could look inside. Eskimo women dressed in long *amoutis* sat at the opening of their canvas shelters, sewing at their little machines or feeding their babies. None acknowledged her. A small boy ran from behind a tent and stood staring at her. Then he giggled and disappeared. Suddenly, she felt conspicuous in her wool skirt, the new parka, and a pair of high-heeled shoes that wobbled uncomfortably in the gravel and loose stones. Apparently, though, the Inuit were not surprised at anything a *kabloonah* said, did, or wore. Their eyes slid over and through her.

She stopped to look at black strips of meat and animal entrails drying on a cruciform-shaped rack. Did the Eskimos enjoy eating this ugly-looking food, or was it all they had? She wished she knew the language so she could ask. She even wished she could taste the meat. She turned towards the tents, hoping again that someone would speak or smile. The Inuit continued to ignore her.

It took just a few minutes to explore Sugluk. Father Vande-Velde was chatting to his friend in the doorway of one of the houses. The men were speaking in French but they switched politely to English when she approached.

"There's not much to see," she said, trying not to show her dismay. "I'd better get back to the ship. I've promised to help when the Eskimos come on board."

The Sugluk priest studied her kindly. He was a tall,

aesthetic-looking man, who seemed as though he belonged before the altar of a cathedral rather than a wooden house in Sugluk. "You're going to Lake Harbour, I hear."

"Yes, do you know it!"

He nodded. "They say it's the prettiest settlement in the eastern Arctic. You're fortunate. But it's very lonely."

Dorothy was surprised. "Lonelier than here?"

"Just as lonely as here. Radio communications are a problem in the North. There's the aurora borealis and the sun spots. Reception can be very bad. And then there are the high mountains around Lake Harbour. Do you like to read?"

They walked the short distance to the waiting barge, talking about books. She climbed gratefully on board while the two priests exchanged good-byes, then glanced across the beach to the standing group of Eskimos. Surely they must be experiencing some emotions about visiting the *Howe*. Were they interested? Bored? Scared?

"I suppose," she had asked Dr. Sabean on the ship, "the health of the Eskimos has improved a great deal since the Arctic patrol began?"

"Thirty years," the doctor nodded. "If you can call it a patrol thirty years ago. The thing is to get the tuberculosis under control. There's all kinds of it in the Arctic, Dorothy – pulmonary, miliary, spinal. The Inuit simply don't have the immunity. And then there are the housing and ventilation patterns. Overcrowding isn't really a problem, but there's close contact in tents and snow houses. Oh, we're making a dent. But more than ten per cent of every Eskimo community is still under treatment in southern sanatoriums. I'd say we've got more Inuit down there than the number living today in Frobisher."

She had never nursed a tubercular patient, but she had learned about symptoms during those three gruelling years of training in Sarnia. Difficulty in breathing. Lassitude. Loss of weight and appetite. Night sweats. Some chest pain. Coughing.

And general health among the Inuit? "Well, there's a lot to do." Dr. Sabean was growing restless. "You have to remember that the whites brought disease to the Arctic in the first place.

We've been buzzing around here since the seventeenth century, you know. There's diphtheria, whooping cough, polio, you name it. It's up to us to clean it up as best we can." *Or catch it back from the Eskimos.* Dorothy thought irreverently.

She sat on the landing barge, remembering the talk with Dr. Sabean and frowning again at her own ignorance of these things. If the white man had brought disease to the North, what had the Inuit died from in their untouched world? Old age? Hunting accidents? What about diet? Did the Eskimos really eat a lot of blubber, or was that a popular myth?

Back on the ship, she hung her parka in the cabin before reporting to sick bay. Dr. Sabean, Heather, and other members of the medical patrol were already dressed in white coats, rechecking their equipment. There was a reassuring atmosphere of clinical order in the cabin, the subdued buzz of voices and the familiar scent of antiseptic. She bit her lip, remembering Sugluk and realizing that once she left the *Howe* she would leave this order behind. When she asked what she could do, Heather passed her a starched coat and told her she could shuttle.

The older nurse sat at her desk. "Get the patients ready for examination. See that they get from one station to the next. X-ray, dentist, things like that."

The Eskimos began climbing on board from the barge, fiteen or twenty at a time, within the next hour. It seemed useless to say "this way" in English, so she simply smiled encouragingly, pointed, and showed them to the table where Mary Paneegoosho was sitting with her registration papers. The Inuit men and women listened silently to what Mary had to say, produced numbered metal tags, and waited for the interpreter to check them against the official lists. When this was done, Mary marked their palms with an *R*.

Like branding cattle, Dorothy thought. But someone in Ottawa must have decided this was the most efficient way of handling the work of the patrol. She pushed the thought out of her mind.

The public health nurse was next on the shuttle. The men removed their shirts and stood waiting patiently for Dorothy to point the way. It was a more difficult job for the women. Many were carrying naked babies in the hoods of their *amoutis,* and they struggled to hold the infants while they pulled the long parkas over their heads and tried to open the fronts of their dresses or blouses.

After Dorothy guided a group of men and boys to the nursing station, she went to one young mother. "Let me have the baby," she said. The woman shook her head, not understanding, so Dorothy stretched out her hands and took the child. Before she cradled it in her arms she saw there was a blue patch at the base of its spine. Later, she would learn this was a distinctive mark of the Eskimo that would disappear in one or two years. The young woman's eyes crinkled slightly as she dealt quickly with her buttons.

After that, Dorothy helped three young boys with their parkas and shirts, then another mother. The baby began to urinate as she held it, and the woman clucked a distressed *"agai"* as she went to a corner where she had left a small pot. Pots, it seemed, were carried by all Inuit mothers. Obviously, Dorothy decided, the native women knew what she learned during her paediatric nursing experience in Detroit – that infants react with a small, startled spasm whenever they are about to evacuate or urinate. She saw a woman handle the toilet situation with a quick swing of her arm from *amouti* to pot. Even without the protection of diapers, no hoods were soiled.

The shuttle continued without a break. At one point Dorothy felt faint and rushed to the deck to breathe some fresh air. The Inuit were wearing sealskin boots and the footwear reeked like decaying fish in the warmth of the cabin. Her weakness annoyed her. Messy or malodorous work in hospital had never affected her, and she warned herself she would have to get used to all kinds of alien smells in the Arctic. She walked quickly back to the sick bay.

At the nursing station, Heather sat with an Eskimo interpreter from the settlement. As the shuttle thinned out, Dorothy stood behind the nurse, listening curiously to questions and answers and realizing how much more public health training she could have used in her general nursing course. These were some of the things she should be aware of in her new job. How often did the Eskimo wash himself? What sicknesses had there been in the camp during the past year? Was the mother giving her children cod liver oil and vitamin supplements? Were there any new babies needing to be immunized against diphtheria, whooping cough and tetanus? Was there any infant in the family who did not have the scar from a BCG – Bacillus Calmette-Guerin – anti-TB vaccination?

The Inuit answered Heather promptly and without expression. One aged man actually giggled a little and showed the nurse a set of ivory dentures he had carved for himself. Another rolled up his pants and proudly exhibited a homemade wooden leg. "Wonderful!" the nurse approved. "*Ee, ahaloonah!*" echoed the interpreter. Palms were extended and marked with an *N* for nurse and *I* for immunization.

Dorothy gestured, palms upwards, and the Eskimos imitated the gesture so she could check where they had been and where they must go next. *D* for dentist. *E* for physical examination. *X* for X-rays. The Inuit stared at the accumulation of little blue marks, then dropped their hands to their sides. When it was over, they knew they could look at the ship's engine room, be treated to hardtack and tea, and be shown a program of National Film Board shorts and cartoons. And then there was the ship's canteen. Already, dozens of Eskimos were dipping into bulging paper bags and tearing the wrappers from candy bars and chewing gum. *D for dentist,* thought Dorothy. She wondered bleakly how many new cases of TB would be detected that day and how many families would have to face the agony of knowing that one of their members must go south for treatment.

"*Ayonamut,*" she had heard Dr. Sabean say one morning in sick bay. "It means 'it can't be helped.' You'll hear it quite often in the Arctic. It explains a lot about Inuit philosophy. The only time it seems to fail them is when we have to take them from their families and send them south."

The patrol went on throughout the sunlit evening and the twilight of night. Stewards came to the sick bay with meals on trays and pots of tea and coffee. She knew the team would keep working until all of the Eskimos had been seen and X-rays developed. The shipping season was short in the Arctic; captains did not care to hang around ports for too long. Dr. Sabean came out of surgery, mopping his perspiring face. He accepted some tea and a sandwich and grinned wearily at her.

"Why don't you go to bed? Your work starts when you get to Lake Harbour."

She grinned back at him. Despite her fatigue, the patrol was turning out to be a new and intriguing experience. She had always wondered what it would be like to be on non-stop duty during some major disaster. But she caught the doctor's red-rimmed eyes again and she went.

The trip to Lake Harbour from Montreal normally took ten days, but Captain Fournier had mentioned a delay even before they stopped for medicals at Sugluk. "This was a rotten year for ice," he told her in his matter-of-fact way. He would try to get her ashore by helicopter after putting in at one or two other settlements. But then, the unloading of Lake Harbour supplies and the medical patrol would have to wait until later in the month.

The sombre-faced captain had looked faintly astonished when Dorothy nodded smilingly at his news. He stared down at her. "But you must be wanting to get there?"

"Oh, yes. But it's okay."

She decided not to explain that as long as she was on the ship, there was always the possibility of learning something more about what to expect when she was finally left alone to handle her job. The captain paused as though he wanted to talk. She was about to ask him about other ports the *Howe* would be visiting when he turned and walked moodily back to his quarters.

She was curious about the settlements, so she had gone to the ship's library to find a map of the Northwest Territories. The names of eastern Arctic ports looked back at her from the page. Cape Dorset. Port Harrison. Churchill. Eskimo Point. She slammed the atlas shut and stared at the other books on the shelves, not really knowing what she wanted to find. Nurse's training had not equipped her for independent research. Even her teachers had been ignorant of research methods. Students did things by rote and from approved texts.

She picked out a few titles. Dickens. Hemingway. O'Hara. A French-English dictionary. There were grubby paperbacks of popular novels and mysteries. Mary Roberts Rinehart. Agatha Christie. She slumped into a chair, thinking back to her days in training and at the hospitals. *Let's see. Diptheria, an acute, contagious bacterial disease characterized by the formation . . . the formation of a fibrinous pseudomembrane . . . upon the mucosa.*

"Okay," she had said to Heather on a rare occasion when she could talk to the nurse alone. "So the kids get their DPT shots when they come on board the *Howe*. But what about follow-up injections?" The tall nurse was poised to rush back to work again. There was always the clean-up and sterilization chores to be done after the ship left a port. "We're the follow-up," she said. "The nurses at the posts." Dorothy sighed. Public health nurses, of course, were trained to know about these things. In hospital, she had never even given a DPT injection.

As the days passed, though, she added to her store of information about the Arctic, filing it away in her head or making notes in the privacy of her cabin. In the old days, Eskimos died mostly of accidents. But they also committed suicide if they were old or were executed if they were a hazard to the community. Fred Lee told her that infanticide and voluntary death among the aged were now disappearing since the federal government began paying family allowances and old age pensions. And also because of income from trading skins at the Hudson's Bay stores.

Problems? She chipped away at the questions whenever members of the patrol were free of the endless medicals or preparation for another stop-over. Well, there was toothache. God, she had never pulled a tooth in her life! There was impetigo because of poor hygiene. Keratitis, or corneal ulcerations. No one was sure of the cause, and there were medical quarrels about treatment. There were influenza epidemics after ship-time. There were always epidemics, usually followed by pneumonia. And watch out for dysentery as well.

"One of the really frustrating problems in the Arctic is getting around, of course," Dr. Sabean said one evening after the patrol had stopped at Cape Dorset. "Between seasons is the worst. The snow is no good for *komatiks* – the sleds, that is – and the Eskimos can't use boats because of the sea-ice. So how do you get a patient to the post from the outer camps? Or make it there yourself? Tragic. I've seen a lot of the Inuit die because of that."

But how about other kinds of transport? She leaned forward, clasping her hands on her knees. "How about automobiles? Jeeps?"

Dr. Sabean laughed and shook his head. "Ever hear of roads? There are none across the tundra. No way. No way at all."

That night, she lay awake in her bunk, worrying about a possible time when a patient might die because the snow was too thin or the ice too thick. The vision of streetcars running on dependable schedule along Queen Street in Toronto seemed almost hateful. She had loathed the mornings when she had been forced to stumble through the snowdrifts on Waverley Road to the car stop. Now, she had been told that survival in the Arctic often depended on a good blizzard.

She had thought that the more she learned, the more confident she would become. Instead, she grew more apprehensive. "I think I'm worried," she whispered aloud to herself one morning as she dressed. That was the day after the patrol had stopped at Ivujivik, a small settlement across Hudson Strait from Dorset. The sea had been more than usually choppy, and as she stood at the ship's rail, she watched the barges battling the heavy swell to bring their cargos of Eskimos to the *Howe*.

At other ports, it was always difficult for the Inuit with their babies and small children to transfer from the landing craft to the ship's gangway. That day, it was impossible. Captain Fournier sent two crew members to the bottom of the ladder, but the barge tossed and lurched, always out of reach. One young Eskimo made the dangerous transfer but almost lost his balance. The *Howe's* sailors grabbed at his loose parka and hauled him to safety. The rest of the native passengers stared stolidly and without comment. Another man rose to his feet, contemplating whether to demonstrate his agility, but sat down again. The crew members stood clinging to the sea-drenched gangway and shouting up at the bridge. Dorothy could see Captain Fournier hunched over the rail, frowning down at the unruly waves.

He turned to glare at the ship's crane, mounted at the stern, then bawled some orders. Sailors began assembling a rope sling, and a wooden flooring was brought from the hold. The crane whined across the deck and the hook lowered. *My God,* Dorothy thought. *They're not going to get them on board in that thing!*

The platform was open, with no protective netting. There was only a strip of wooden railing, about waist-high for an adult. But what about the children? The sling went over the side, then down to the crowded barge. Even then, it was not easy for the Eskimos to stand on the flooring. All wore sealskin boots, which by now were soaked and slippery. Three or four adults bunched together on the platform and several children stood clutching their parents' skirts or pant-legs. Then the crew hoisted the sling up from the barge and on to the deck.

"Do you always do it this way?" she asked a sailor after watching two trips. "What if the flooring tipped?"

"Can't wait for better weather," the man told her. "We'd be here all week at that rate."

She had offered to help shuttle the Eskimos through the various stations, but the hoisting operation fascinated and horrified her. Whenever there was some time, she hurried on deck to see if the sea had calmed. But the crane was kept busy throughout the day. She searched the faces of the Eskimos as they scrambled from the sling to the safety of the deck. As usual, they were expressionless.

At one point, she thought she would ask Dr. Sabean if he could spare a moment to see what was happening, but the physician waved distractedly as she approached, then hurried into the surgery. Heather looked up at her briefly then went back to her work. Dorothy returned to the pitching deck. "Look," she asked another crew member. "Why don't you lash some nets around that thing? A kid could fall through, you know."

The sailor grinned. "They never do."

"Never?"

"Not since I've been sailing around the Arctic. They hang on okay. Don't worry about the Eskimos. They're a smart lot."

But she continued to worry, even though no child did slip off the primitive crane sling that day or the next at Ivujivik. She also had to admit to herself that she was becoming bored with the sameness of the medical patrol and more apprehensive about Lake Harbour. At Port Harrison, a somewhat larger settlement just south of Ivujivik, the ship anchored for three days. She went ashore on a barge loaded with supplies.

It was a cloudless July day, and Port Harrison actually looked interesting. There were hills behind the settlement, splashed with colour, and she could see neat gravel walks between the houses. She picked out a comfortable skirt and a soft blouse to wear under her parka. After Sugluk, she had realized that high heels were impossible in the Arctic, so she pulled on a pair of red leather boots she had bought in Toronto.

The beach at Port Harrison was rough and uninviting. Beaches at home were used for picnics, but she shuddered at the thought of such outings at a place like this. Her boots crunched along the shore as she made her way to higher ground. There were no Inuit standing near the shore, she noticed with interest. No whites, either. She turned to comment on this to the two crew members who were unloading the barge, but at that moment, she was attacked by a black cloud of mosquitoes. The insects settled on her face, invaded her eyes and nostrils, buzzed angrily at her ears. She opened her mouth to scream and gagged on dozens of them. She flapped her arms. Her legs, she saw with horror, were swarming with small bodies.

"Use your net!" she heard one of the sailors yell. What net? Only then did she notice the men had covered their heads with closely woven mosquito nets and that they were wearing heavy gloves. Dorothy groaned. Why on earth hadn't someone warned her?

She pulled the hood of her parka over her head and as far as possible across her face. "When can we get back?" she shouted.

"Ten minutes," the voice came from the barge. "You'd better keep running if you can't get into a house."

Dorothy began to run. The faster she travelled, the fewer mosquitoes seemed to settle. She reached a house and banged loudly on the door. She wanted desperately to call for help, but she dared not open her mouth. She banged again on the door, but there was no answer. She kept on running. No answer from the next house, either. Had everyone escaped to the ship on the early-morning barges? Down at the beach, she saw the sailors had almost finished the job of unloading. She pulled the hood of her parka tighter around her face and kept on running.

That night she lay on top of her blankets and tried to laugh at the thought of her sprint around Port Harrison. It was hard. Her mosquito bites hurt so much she had gone to the dispensary to fetch a bottle of calamine lotion. Her legs were badly swollen. Her hands were scarlet with bites. She turned on the lights and got up to stare at herself in the cabin mirror. Her cheeks were puffy, and one eye had almost closed from an enormous bite on her eyelid.

"Hit mosquito country, I see," Dr. Sabean commented next morning at breakfast. Her face and legs were streaked with pinkish calamine lotion. "Yes, indeed," he nodded. "Fierce little animals, aren't they? They can kill, you know."

"I hear they can kill polar bears," Glenn said from across the table. "They get into the bear's nostrils and bite away until the animal can't breathe. Right? So he opens his mouth. The mosquitoes zero in, sting his throat and it swells up, just like the nose. So the bear strangles. Polar bears stung to death by mosquitoes! Incredible."

Incredible. "Hey, you've got a load of bites!" Heather had remarked. "Didn't anyone tell you about the mosquitoes in Port Harrison? They're famous. Bet you went without a net."

No one told her anything. She went to her cabin again before the Eskimos came on board for their checkups and swabbed herself resignedly with fresh calomine. Would Lake Harbour be like Port Harrison or Sugluk or Churchill? Churchill had probably been the worst, now she came to think about it. When the *Howe* had crossed Hudson Bay, she had felt a stirring of anticipation – Churchill was a real town, not one of the stark little settlements she had already explored.

The night before arrival, she had fantasized about some of the things she might do when the ship was in port. Eat a good meal in a restaurant, maybe. The food on the *Howe* was beginning to pall for everyone on board. Perhaps there would be some respectable department stores. She'd buy some thick woolen socks in case there were insects in Lake Harbour. And she'd get herself a head-net as well.

Churchill was even more of a let-down than the other Arctic stop-overs. Oh, it was bigger and some of the streets were paved. But there were no department stores, and the houses were quite as drab as those in Sugluk or Ivujivik. Since the town had its own hospital, the members of the medical patrol were free to relax while the *Howe* refuelled. Dorothy and Heather explored the main street together. They could find no restaurant, so they lunched at a depressing cafe that sold rubbery hamburgers. Outside of the window, Dorothy could see the railroad connecting the town with southern Manitoba and the rest of the world. She looked longingly at the tracks. *This is your last chance,* she found herself thinking. *Why don't you quit right now and get on a train?*

Heather was watching, as though she guessed what was crossing her mind. "It's been rough on you, floating around with the patrol like this," she said. "You've got your own job to go to. I hear there's a western playing at the local cinema tonight. Why don't we go with some of the boys?

Dorothy picked at her awful lunch. "Why not? I don't suppose there'll be any movies in Lake Harbour." She looked up at Heather. "Will there?"

The nurse examined the check. "Oh come on. I bet there'll be plenty of things to do."

But what? Dorothy wondered. What?

Captain Fournier made another stab at sailing into Lake Harbour after steaming back across Hudson Bay, but ice conditions were still bad. Bay ice, he explained crisply, was far thicker than ice in the open sea. And besides, once the ship got into inlets or harbours, there was less manoeuvrability. Glenn was ordered to fly Dorothy into the settlement provided it was in the helicopter's range. For a while, it seemed they would go. But after her trunk and skis were hauled from the hold, Fournier came off the bridge and announced the *Howe* could get no closer than thirty-five miles. The helicopter could never make it to Lake Harbour and back again.

Dr. Sabean was cheerful about it all at dinner. "Well, the Lake Harbour Inuit will just have to stick around the place for a while longer, that's all. Pity if you can't connect with the other nurse for a briefing, though."

Dorothy was worried. "But could she leave the place?" she asked the doctor. "I mean, the *Howe* can't get in. So how on earth could she get out?"

Dr. Sabean shrugged. "A plane might have dropped in from Frobisher. One thing you'll learn about this part of the world. If you want to do something, you don't fool around thinking about it. It the nurse wanted a lift out, she'd take it when she got the chance. Maybe the *Howe* won't get in this year, anyway."

"Not get in?" Was she feeling relief or acute disappointment?

"It's happened before. Oh, I guess Fournier will drop you in Frobisher, or maybe Coral Harbour. Might take a few weeks, but an aircraft going in the right direction will turn up some time."

The possibility of languishing in Frobisher Bay or some other settlement, waiting for transport, had never occured to her. She strolled around the deck wondering whether she would ever see Lake Harbour. The information she had milked from the ship's medical personnel had been useful in the beginning. But as the patrol got busier and sources dried up, she pinned her hopes on meeting her predecessor and discussing her duties at the post. For the next couple of days, she asked anxiously about the planes that flew in and out of Arctic settlements.

There were RCMP Otters, she heard. Some Beavers belonging to the Hudson's Bay Company. Other small aircraft bringing geologists, archaeologists, or other individuals having business in the area. There were scarcely any military aircraft around. The DEW Line was too far north. Airfields? There was no airfield in Lake Harbour. There was a helicopter pad near the Hudson's Bay store, and when the ice was out in summer, planes equipped with floats could land on the bay.

It was a week later that the *Howe* steamed again towards the settlement. This time, there seemed no doubt the ship could sail well within flying range. The pack-ice had shifted with the wind and white chunks of it were drifting freely in the strait. Dorothy packed her cabin luggage and repeated her good-byes. Mary Paneegoosho laughed about shopping for mosquito nets the moment she landed, and Lyle Faulkner said he might drop in for lunch when the *Howe* returned on patrol. Heather reminded her that Frobisher was only ninety miles east as the crow flew. If the crow ever flew, that was.

Dorothy stood on the deck, surrounded by the now-familiar group. She had abandoned the idea of wearing special clothes for her arrival in Lake Harbour and had pulled on slacks, her white parka and a pair of nurse's shoes. When she was tying the laces, she suddenly felt a wave of homesickness for the ordered ward in Detroit. And, again that apprehension about the coming year of isolation among strangers and her ability to do the job.

Since her trunk was too big to cram into the helicopter's cabin, two crew members strapped the luggage and her skis to the rubber landing pontoons. Dr. Sabean was missing. She mentioned this to Heather. "Yes," the nurse nodded, "an Eskimo boy is sick." Heather guessed the doctor would be back on deck before Dorothy took off. They talked again about a visit to Frobisher before the year was over, but neither really believed it would be possible. Glenn had joined the nurses to say it was about time to go when Dr. Sabean appeared from the direction of the Eskimo quarters.

"Well, I'm off at last," Dorothy said. Her cheeks were flushed and the nagging apprehension had been replaced by excitement. The doctor frowned down at her. "I'm sorry, Dorothy. A kid's got measles. This ship's under quarantine until we can assess the situation."

Everyone began to laugh. Dorothy tried to grin along with them, but instead, she wandered to the ship's rail. In the far distance, she could glimpse high, purple hills. She thought she could see white specks that could be buildings, but perhaps they were merely patches of snow in the rock crevices. The sky was very clear and once again she noted the intense colour of the sea, the contrast of the ice floes, and the blue of their self-contained pools of water. A few weeks ago, the sight had stunned her with its beauty. Now, she merely felt frustrated and disappointed.

3

Glenn swung the helicopter over the low hills, then up the fjord to Lake Harbour. It was the first week of August, 1957. Almost two months getting here, Dorothy thought incredulously. In two months, you could sail around the world. Then she laughed to herself. At least she had been given a free trip around the Arctic. She sat forward in the passenger's seat, shoving her glasses impatiently against the bridge of her nose and staring ahead towards the site of the settlement. The pilot grinned.

"Want a tour before we land? It's not big, but it's pretty."

Yes, it was pretty. Not like the dull mud-flats of Sugluk. Nothing like Port Harrison or Churchill. The hills were lavish with green lichens and purple saxifrage, and below, she could see the reddish lump of rock she later learned to know as the Heel. Beyond, craggy against the vivid sky, there were the mountains of the Meta Incognita Peninsula. She had been awed when she had found the name on the map. The unknown land. Untouched, unexplored, and alone.

"There she is!" Glenn shouted in her ear above the flap of the rotor blades. She craned to see. Just two buildings and a flagstaff?

"The cops," the pilot explained. "That's the RCMP detachment. The main settlement's over there on the left."

The helicopter banked steeply. They were flying lower now, over ice-free water dotted with small boats. Ahead, there were more hills and the letters HBC picked out in white boulders against the sandy side of the cliff.

"Here Before Christ," Glenn was yelling. "The Hudson's Bay Company. Actually, the Anglicans got to Lake Harbour even before the Hudson's Bay. Back in the first part of the century, I believe."

Red roofs. Green roofs. More flagpoles. White spots that came into focus as tents. Gravel paths bordered with the whitewashed rocks to help show the way in the long nights.

"That's the church," Glenn was pointing. "St. Paul's Anglican Mission. And that's Mike and Marg Gardener's house. Mike's the missionary and Marg teaches school in the summer when the Eskimos are in from the camps. That's your place and the hospital."

Her heart thumped. The hospital appeared to be a Quonset hut with a red cross painted on its side. The house was set at the end of a gravel path, overlooking the bay. She saw with a surge of relief that it was neatly built and painted a spotless white. "Ever hear of Dr. Dewey Soper?" Glenn asked. "A Department of the Interior bird man. He was the fellow who figured out where the Canada geese went in the summer. I hear he built your house back in 1930."

Gardener. The RCMP. Didn't Miss McDonald say there were others in the community? And what was it Dr. Sabean had said when they had wished each other good luck and good-bye for at least the fifteenth time? "Just try not to go stir-crazy!"

She glanced again at the jagged barrier of mountains and down at the isolated little settlement. "Is there anyone else?" she asked.

"What?" Glenn was heading for flat space that seemed to be the helicopter pad.

"Is there anyone else in the place?"

"Don Baird," replied Glenn. "The Hudson's Bay man. That's his place right here. You've got Don and you've got Gerry Heapy and Terry Jenkin at the detachment. You've got a few Eskimos who work here all year around. The others are out at the camps in winter. Then you've got Mike and Marg, of course."

Try not to go stir-crazy! The helicopter hovered over the pad, then settled for a landing. She stared curiously out of the bubble window, but all she could see was the sand and gravel kicked up by the blades. "Okay, you're home," she heard Glenn say. "Ever think you'd make it?"

The dust cleared, and when the door opened, she saw faces. Eskimo faces, mostly. Then a white face. "Don!" yelled Glenn. "Here's your new nurse. And the mail. Take delivery, feller. I've got to get back to the *Howe*."

Don Baird was about her own age, good-looking with a small mustache, chunkily built and friendly. He was wearing jeans and a light parka, and she liked the feel of his arm as he reached up to help her to the ground. "Dorothy Knight," he said, looking down at her.

"Yes," she smiled. "How did you know?"

"Everyone knows the name of the new nurse," the Hudson's Bay manager answered. He shook his head. "Bessie was sorry, but she couldn't wait. We had no idea when you'd arrive."

"Bessie?"

"Bessie Parsons, the nurse who was here before you. An Otter came in a week ago, and she and her husband and two kids got a hitch to Frobisher."

Oh, Holy Mother of God. No overlapping. She really was on her own. She struggled not to show her dismay and disappointment. Baird turned and beckoned to an Eskimo who was standing with a group of Inuit. "This is Ishawakta." The Eskimo, Dorothy saw, was handsome, muscular and probably in his mid-twenties. He grinned a slow, sideways grin that showed he was more confident in white company than most of the other Inuit she had met. "Ishawakta is your interpreter," said Baird. "I supposed you could call him a general maintenance man. Take the *aniatitsiyuk's* luggage to her house, Ishawakta."

Ishawakta grinned again and nodded. "*Ee. Aniatitsiyuk.*" He went immediately to the helicopter to help Glenn unstrap the trunk and the skis from the pontoons.

"The Inuit will probably decide on a special name for you, once they figure one out," Baird said. "But right now, you're the nurse. The *aniatitsiyuk.*" He looked down at her with concerned brown eyes. Funny how much he suddenly reminded her of her brother Jim. "Too bad about Bessie. But you can't wait around too long in the Arctic."

Too bad. She wondered if the phrase was the *kabloonah* equivalent of the Inuits' philosophical *ayonamut.* How could it be helped if ice had blocked the way to Lake Harbour? How could it be helped that if you waited around too long in the Arctic, you might be stuck for another year?

"Ice problems, eh?" Baird was saying to Glenn. "The *Rupertsland's* around, you know. I hope it makes it into the bay. My future wife's on board."

"Hilda?" grinned Glenn.

"Yeah. We made up our minds on my last leave in Newfoundland. How about the medical patrol? And the supplies?"

"Maybe in a week." The pilot stubbed out his cigarette and pulled on his flying gloves. "We were lucky getting as close as we did today. Don't forget to have your requisitions ready when we get back, Dorothy."

She had been told about requisitions on the ship. Orders for future medical and food supplies had to go out with either the *Howe* or the Hudson's Bay ship, *Rupertsland.* But surely Bessie Parsons had done the job before leaving for Frobisher. How could she know what supplies would be needed at an Arctic station before she had even begun to live in her house? Her house. She looked across the compound at the neat building that would be her home, wishing that someone would suggest she go there now.

"Don –" She ventured, then stopped. A woman was hurrying down the path from the Anglican mission. Marg Gardener, Dorothy decided. The only other white woman in Lake Harbour. She watched curiously as the missionary's wife came closer. She was a large young woman, dressed in plain clothes with a white apron tied around her waist. The apron seemed strangely incongruous in the Arctic setting. Marg Gardener wore no make-up and her face was unsmiling. She spoke with an English accent.

"Can you come to the hospital right away?" Dorothy was startled. The hospital? Now?

"I think it's an emergency," Marg said. "A very sick baby, I'm afraid. A little girl. Could you come and take a look?" She smiled

44

a little. "It's Dorothy Knight, isn't it? I'm sorry. I'm Marg Gardener."

"Yes," said Dorothy. She forgot about Bessie and the annoying requisitions. "How long has the baby been sick?"

"Her mother brought her to me two days ago. I've been stumped, not having Bessie around. It could be just the flu, of course, but I know it might be serious. I'm so glad you're here."

Dorothy nodded. The woman's confidence was reassuring, but there was still that lingering sense of inadequacy. Would she know what to do for the child? She had nursed hundreds of babies at the Detroit Children's Hospital and had observed some rare diseases and conditions. But could she really diagnose and treat a case on her own? She swallowed apprehensively. There had always been a doctor around to decide what to do.

Glenn put his arm briefly across her shoulders to say goodbye, and the helicopter was already flapping down the fjord by the time she and the missionary's wife reached the Quonset hut. Dorothy glanced around the room, but there was no time now to explore. In the space used as a ward, there were four empty hospital beds and a bassinette. Even before she reached the crib she heard the child's high-pitched, almost piercing cry. She caught her breath. She had heard that cry a dozen times at the hospital. She stared down at the baby. It was listless and wasted. It wailed again. "Can you get me a thermometer?" she asked. Marg bustled across the room, then returned with one.

Dorothy examined the child. Hot, dry skin. Stiff neck. Rigid, slightly-arched back. Again she noted the listlessness as she turned the baby gently on its side and inserted the clinical thermometer.

"What do you think?" Marg asked.

"I think –" began Dorothy. She bit her lip, trying to hide her apprehension. What *did* she think? *Nurses don't diagnose,* she remembered Miss Beamish saying in Sarnia. For one thing, it's illegal! Five years after graduation, she could still see the coldly impersonal face of the nursing director as she pounded her awed students with the Rules.

Dorothy checked the thermometer. It read 106 degrees. "I think it's meningitis," she said quietly. The missionary's wife was silent for a long moment. A bee buzzed loudly at the open window.

"What are you going to do?"

Dorothy thought. What could anyone do for a child as dangerously ill as this? Even a doctor in a fully equipped hospital? Doctor! Dr. Sabean, after all, was on the *Howe*. She could talk to him by radio if the ship was still in range. She could describe the symptoms, and perhaps Glenn could come back with the helicopter to collect the patient.

"Where is the baby's mother?" she asked.

"In a tent not far from here. She has other children."

"Do you think she would give permission for the child to be flown to the *Howe*?"

"If I told her it was necessary. I'll go now."

Out in the warm sunlight again, she stared at the house Dr. Soper had built. A small group of Eskimos were standing near the porch doorway, waiting for the new *aniatitsiyuk* to take possession.

"Sure, I think I can still raise the ship," said Don. "What's wrong with the kid?"

She hesitated to say it again, but she did. "I think it's pretty serious. Probably meningitis." She saw the shock in the man's eyes. Perhaps he was wondering whether her judgement was sound enough to summon Glenn back with the aircraft. Hadn't she heard somewhere that it cost a hundred dollars whenever a chopper lifted off the pad?

"Who is it you want to speak to?" the manager asked. He walked into his house and sat at the radio.

"Ask for Dr. Sabean." She mentally rechecked the symptoms, making sure she had missed nothing. There had been that time in Detroit when a doctor had chewed her out for half an hour because she had failed to report every detail. In a few minutes, she was repeating the story to the doctor.

"I see," crackled the familiar voice. "So what do you think, Dorothy?"

This time there was no hesitation. "Meningitis. Do you think Glenn can come back to pick her up?"

46

"Well, we're sailing right now," came the voice. "But I don't see why he can't make an emergency trip." There was a pause while the doctor apparently conferred with Captain Fournier, then he replied. "Sure. Glenn will refuel and get back there as soon as possible. Have the baby ready to travel and don't forget to get its name and registration number. I'll send Heather to help."

Ishawakta was waiting outside the Hudson's Bay post when she completed the call. He grinned at her, and she remembered that her luggage must now be safely in her house. But the anticipation of going there had evaporated. She was relieved the meningitis case would be in Dr. Sabean's hands, but shocked at what she had done. She was sickly aware that the responsibility and the aloneness would continue for a year. People would expect and need her to be right. To do the correct thing. And Dr. Sabean would not be at the other end of the radio signal. "Radio communications are bad in the Arctic," she recalled the priest in Sugluk saying. And in Lake Harbour, there are the mountains.

"Say, that was lucky," Don said, coming out of the post. "Just as well you spotted the problem so quickly." The Hudson's Bay man frowned. "Meningitis, eh? Do you think the kid will be okay?"

She decided not to say what she really thought. Meningitis at that advanced stage was usually fatal, but she had seen some babies recover. "You never know," she replied. Suddenly, she felt terribly weary.

"I'll get the baby ready for the trip. Marg Gardener should be at the hospital with the mother. I'll come when Glenn and the nurse get here. Then I'd like to go home."

What I really want, she was thinking, *is to go home to Toronto. Home to Waverley Road.* But home was now a small wooden house at the end of a gravel path in Lake Harbour and soon she would go through the door.

Ishawakta had placed her luggage and the pair of skis in the exact centre of the livingroom floor. The old trunk and two suitcases she had bought for the Arctic adventure sat like familiar friends in strange surroundings. The young Eskimo moved quietly into the house behind her and when she turned, she saw he was followed by a woman. "Oola," said the interpreter.

"Oola?"

Ishawakta grinned and pointed at the woman. "Oola!" Good Lord. Couldn't the Eskimo explain better than that? He was supposed to be her interpreter. Ishawakta scratched his head in amused puzzlement and the woman giggled, revealing blunt, nicotine-stained teeth.

"Oola," the Eskimo said again. "*Anana*. Mother."

Later, Dorothy discovered the small, leathery-faced Oola was Ishawakta's mother-in-law, but apparently he felt there was no real difference between the two relationships. Or perhaps he simply did not know the correct word. Oola wore a swallow-tailed *amouti* over a blue cotton dress but made no attempt to remove the garment in the warm house. She giggled again, then grabbed the suitcases and took them into another room. Dorothy was about to follow when she heard a clatter of boots on the porch.

"Hoo there!" Dorothy mentally checked off the inhabitants of Lake Harbour she had already met. These two, large young men had to be the Mounties. No red coats, though. "Dorothy Knight, eh?" one was saying. "I'm Gerry Heapy. This is Terry Jenkin. We live across the bay at the detachment."

All of them laughed self-consciously. Dorothy knew she looked a fright. She had carefully fixed her hair on the ship that morning, but the helicopter flight and the rush to get the baby to the *Howe* had ruined the effect. Something was always ruining her hair. She was aware she needed some fresh powder and lipstick, and she blushed. "You can come in," she said, a little formally. "But I'm not even unpacked yet. Haven't even seen the rest of the house. There's a sick child, you see –" *Oh my God*, she thought. *I'm actually babbling.*

Heapy had his eyes on the trunk. "Hey, what you got in the trunk, eh?"

The trunk? The question surprised her. "Clothes," she said. "Records. Some books. Stuff like that."

Jenkin tapped the box with the toe of his boot. "Come on now. What you got in the trunk?"

She giggled. This must be some kind of a local game. "Well, I think I've got some of Charlie Sharr's candies somewhere."

"Some what?" Oh well, she figured the Mountics could never have heard of Sharr's candy from Toronto. Aunt Nell had given her a box as a farewell gift, and she knew it was stowed somewhere.

"How about booze?" asked Heapy.

She laughed some more. "Oh, I didn't think about bringing any liquor." The men were silent. "You mean, you thought I would?"

Jenkin shuffled around a little, staring balefully at the trunk, then into the other room where Oola was fussing with the suitcases. "Not even in the cases?" Jenkin asked.

She was crushed. Why hadn't someone told her it was important to bring liquor to the Arctic? She had never been much interested in drinking except for some wine with dinner. Once again, she felt a surge of resentment towards those who had sent her here without telling her what to expect.

"I guess," she ventured, "you can't buy booze at the Hudson's Bay?"

The two men laughed harshly. Heapy swore under his breath.

She flinched. "What?"

Heapy sighed. "No, you don't buy liquor at the Hudson's Bay. You wait for your own supply to come on the *Rupertsland.* Or you hope people with some sense will bring it in when they come. Like the mail."

She wanted to say she was sorry, but muttered instead about unpacking – maybe if she looked underneath her opera albums there might be a mickey of Scotch slipped in by one of her brothers. But she knew there was no Scotch. She blushed again, feeling a sudden wave of silly guilt.

After the policemen left, grinning their forgiveness, she pulled off her parka and stood, alone, in the livingroom. The house was even smaller than it had looked from the outside, but she was pleased about that. Somehow, its compactness made it all the more appealing. The furniture, she noticed, was ordinary. Even ugly. There was a nondescript red rug on the floor, worn threadbare in patches. There was a plush sofa and a chair of some rusty colour that reminded her of merchandise she had seen in a second-hand store on Queen Street. There was a Coleman oil space heater against one wall and a combination radio and record player on a small side table. She had already spotted an electricity generator in a shed not far from the back door.

She tried the radio immediately, swivelling the dial and longing to hear some music. All she could raise was the deafening sound of static. She switched off the machine and looked into the next room. The bedroom was spartan. It held a double bed, a dresser, a brown veneer wardrobe, and a plain chair. A thin scrap of carpet lay beside the bed.

She glanced quickly inside the wardrobe at the clothes Oola had unpacked. They already seemed hopelessly inappropriate. She had stopped wearing the short muskrat jacket as soon as she had acquired the parka. And would she ever wear that midnight-blue silk party dress with the starched crinoline under-skirt? Or the green gabardine suit? Or the three pairs of high-heeled shoes?

She slammed the wardrobe door and went to inspect the sparsely furnished diningroom with the two cots stacked against one wall. She assumed this was where Bessie Parsons' children had slept. Would the nursing assistant Miss McDonald suggested have had to bunk in here as well?

The kitchen was next door. She liked to cook, but it had never been one of her most overpowering interests. She examined the black, coal-burning stove, the kerosene refrigerator with its empty shelves, the plain kitchen table, and the two chairs. The linoleum was a bilious green, worn brown under the table and around the stove. She walked through the enclosed porch, noting the settlement telephone on the wall and went into the bathroom. There was a chipped enamel tub, a medicine cabinet, a wash basin, and a can. No running water. She stared curiously at the can. That was all it was – simply a metal can equipped with a seat. *So how,* she thought, *do I get rid of what goes into it?*

Still thinking about the intriguing toilet arrangements, she headed for the narrow flight of stairs that lead up from the livingroom. The attic, she found, was a storehouse. There were just a few items on the shelves – canned blueberries, apples, dehydrated vegetables. Some tins of meat and beans. Crackers, detergent, stove-black, and toilet soap. She wrinkled her nose, remembering that more supplies would be arriving on the *Howe* and the *Rupertsland.* She had better search for Bessie Parsons' requisitions to send away. She hoped there would be some food she liked in the crates that would be coming. Plenty of butter. Bacon. Canned chicken. Crunchy dill pickles.

Downstairs again, she stood at the window of her house, marvelling at the view. There was the blue vista of the fjord on one side, the sea glinting in the high, late-afternoon sun. Through the other window she could see the Anglican mission and the Hudson's bay post, backed by the reddish bulk of hills. Some children ran across the compound to the window, plastering their palms and noses against the pane. She smiled and waved at them and they grinned back, watching with unblinking attention.

She thought they would go away after she had gone into the bedroom to fetch some books. But they stayed, staring, as she arranged her copy of Saint Exupery's *Little Prince,* the works of Oscar Wilde and her Daily Missal on a shelf. She stacked her Gray's *Anatomy,* a medical and surgical nursing text, and books for a correspondence course in English she had decided to take during the year. The rapt curiosity of the Inuit unnerved her. She tried the balky radio again, but the children laughed and pressed closer to the window as she wrestled vainly with the dial.

Finally, she went into the curtained bedroom and closed the door. *I feel so terribly alone,* she confessed to herself as she lay on the bed. *They're expecting so much of me.* She threw an arm over her closed eyes. It was like the time she had given the valedictory address at her graduation exercises in Sarnia. *They're expecting so much of me and I feel so terribly alone.* After a while, she got up and walked into the livingroom again. The children were still outside the window. This time, it was comforting to see them there.

That twilit evening, she ate dinner in the kitchen of the

mission house with Mike and Marg Gardener. The hot meal of canned stew and vegetables with slices of freshly baked bread was welcome after the seemingly endless day. But even though she asked eager questions about the station and the duties of the INHS nurse, the missionaries made it clear they had never considered this to be their business.

"We've always had confidence in the nurses," the Reverend Gardener said. "I'm sure you'll get used to things before you know it."

Mike Gardener was a bespectacled, serious young man. He and his wife had met at the Anglican mission in Pangnirtung. They had been in Lake Harbour for three years, and both he and Marg were devoted to their work in the Arctic. The missionary was friendly in a hesitant kind of way. He considered Lake Harbour quiet, God-fearing and not at all beset by the problems of encroaching civilization like, say, Frobisher or Churchill.

When he asked whether she was Anglican, she replied that she had been brought up as a Catholic. The clergyman thoughtfully brushed crumbs from his grey sweater. "I see. I see," he nodded. "Then I suppose you won't be coming to services. Will you?"

She buttered another chunk of the wonderful bread and did not reply. She toyed with the idea of being truthful and telling him she had been looking forward to not having to go to church at all, but decided against it. This was not the night for a philosophical discussion about religion. Instead, she asked the question that had been nagging all day. "Do you know whether Bessie Parsons left any message for me?"

"Message?" Marg Gardener was serving canned peaches and custard in pressed-glass dishes.

"Well, instructions about patients. The names of people needing follow-up immunization injections. Innoculations. Things like that."

"I have no idea." Marg shook her head. "Have you looked around the house or in the office at the hospital?"

"There's nothing in the house," said Dorothy. "But, of course, I haven't really explored the hospital yet."

"Well, there could be some records there. You know about requisitions, of course?"

Dorothy nodded. "I was going to ask. Do you know whether Bessie did them to send out this year?"

"No, she didn't," replied Marg, taking her place at the table. "Bessie thought you'd like to make out your own orders. After all, everyone has their own idea about how to run things. Don't forget to do them in sextuplicate. It's a job we've all got to tackle, you know."

"All of us," nodded Mike, dipping into the custard. "Ship time is busy time." He repeated the words like the title of a popular song. "Ship time is busy time. And don't forget your mail. You have to get that out whenever you have the chance."

Dorothy sighed. "You can't wait around in the Arctic."

"That's right!" laughed the missionary.

Marg laughed along with her husband. "We knew you'd catch on fast."

"The trouble is, I have no idea what to order. Particularly medical supplies. I just got here! So how would I know what to order for an Arctic nursing station?"

The missionaries stared silently back at her. "Well, you're a nurse," Marg said, folding her arms.

Why do people have to say things like that? Dorothy thought. Was the title enough to guarantee a knowledge of everything?

She tried another question. "What kinds of cases did Bessie have to deal with?"

Again the silence. The ticking of the huge clock on the kitchen shelf was very loud. "All kinds of cases," replied Mike. "The usual kinds of cases, I suppose."

Marg got to her feet and began to clear the table. Suddenly, it seemed incredible to Dorothy that these were Arctic missionaries and that she was sitting in their house, poised on the edge of the empty Meta Incognita Peninsula. But what kinds of people had she expected to meet in Lake Harbour? Tough, rugged individuals, she supposed, who talked about hardship and survival and cold. The Gardeners looked like some of her family's friends in Toronto. Don Baird and the two policemen could have stepped straight from the stag line at the Balmy Beach Canoe Club's Saturday night hop. She wondered what had attracted them to the North.

"Where did you train, Dorothy?" Mike was asking. She found it took her mind off requisitions and messages from Bessie to tell her story. Sarnia. The three months psychiatric nursing in London, Ontario. Detroit. The tale of the nurse who had worked with the Indians and taught out of the Eaton's catalogue. The interminable voyage on the *Howe*.

"I would think," Marg said after they had sipped more tea, "that you'll be glad to get to bed. I'll bring you some fresh bread in the morning. I bake twice a week, and there's no reason why I can't do an extra loaf for you."

Mike walked with her down the gravel path to the little house. It was not completely dark, but someone had turned on the porch light and the white building looked comfortable and inviting.

"Thank you for dinner," she said. "It was a help."

"It will be all right, you know," the missionary said quietly. He hesitated, as though he wanted to say something more. Perhaps something profound. But instead he wished her goodnight and turned away.

The Quonset hut hospital, Don Baird told her laughingly next morning, was a kind of mistake in Lake Harbour. Actually, there had been a double error. During the Second World War, the United States Army had sent two huts to Lake Harbour instead of Pearl. The buildings, complete with mosquito-netting windows, had been ceremoniously unloaded from a military ship in 1945 and set up on their present sites. The United States had been so embarrassed about the snafu, they had left the huts where they stood. Later, a Canadian nurse at the station decided to make use of an unwanted building and converted it into one of the rare hospitals in the Arctic. Most northern nurses, Dorothy was informed, used the porches of their houses as dispensaries. The other hut stood, empty, near the graveyard, and was sometimes used for dances.

Dorothy laughed with Don about the Quonset hut story. It

was the kind of zany tale she would store away to tell the family when she got home. Besides, she was quietly pleased it had been a nurse who had had the foresight to do the converting job.

She scarcely remembered what the inside of the hospital had looked like when she was there the day before. But now she hurried across the compound to explore the building and to see whether there were any communications addressed to her attention. She walked through the ward into the little office. There were some blank scratch-pads on the desk top, but she could find no messages, no lists of patients' names. No sign of a welcoming note. A copy of the previous year's requisitions, probably made out by the nurse who had preceded Bessie, was tacked to the wall. She tore it down to study it. Well, at least she could copy the various items and add others as well.

In the meantime, she decided to take a quick look around her new territory. The beds in the ward were familiar, but yesterday she had not noticed the two large oxygen containers in the corner. A door led to a kitchen furnished with a coal stove, a table, and three chairs. She went back to the office which, apparently, was also her surgery.

There was an ancient, metal and leather examination table and a white enamel cabinet containing surgical and dental instruments. The sight of the instruments was intimidating enough, but she also noted with a groan that the dental forceps were right-handed. She was a southpaw. She looked with interest at the medications stored in boxes and glass containers on the shelves. Perhaps these would give her a clue to Bessie Parsons' work in Lake Harbour. There were the usual antibiotics, several sulpha drugs, and bottles of analgesics – aspirin, APC, codeine. There were some eardrops, cod liver oil, cortisone ointment, and a few bottles of ascorbic acid. There were vials of demerol and diuretics.

There was a small, black copy of a medical manual – a source of ready reference for the physician, with emphasis on diagnosis and treatment–which she gratefully grabbed to take back to the house. Her nursing texts, she already knew, would be of little use in this job. She grimaced at some containers of blood plasma and intravenous fluid, hoping she would never have to make the decision to use them.

She stared again at the papers on the desk, found some carbon paper and blank requisition forms in a drawer, and began work. She breathed thanks for the 1956 copy. She read the section headed "personal supplies," noting the kinds of goods she could expect to get when the *Howe* and the *Rupertsland* arrived. Canned fruit. Canned meats. A Christmas cake? She laughed and began copying. Candied peel. Flour. Toothpaste. Canned and dried vegetables. Potatoes. Dried egg and milk powder. Oatmeal. Salt.

She bit the end of her pen, remembering the rules of thrift she had learned in hospital work. *Have you completely finished that jar of ointment, nurse? It's not your money, you know.* Then she grinned and added to the section. Four jars of caviar. Cans of smoked oysters. Olives. Chocolate bars. After all, this was the Arctic, and a year was a long time away from civilization. She hoped the nurse who would take delivery of the supplies when the ships came in 1958 would approve of her taste.

She sat silently, wondering about the hospital supply section. There was the 1956 guide to help, but she worried that other drugs and equipment might be needed. Did a nurse use more aspirin than antibiotics in the Arctic? Was there always enough oxygen? Enough morphine? Were some of these items ever used at all?

She shrugged, glanced at her watch and walked out of the hospital into the brilliant summer sunshine. Again, the beauty of Lake Harbour surprised and delighted her. The temperature was in the balmy sixties and she could glimpse enormous butterflies fluttering near clumps of lupin and heather. Robins hopped boldly along the gravel path, and there were sandpipers foraging down near the beach. Later, she would be able to identify the Arctic tern and the ptarmigan, a bird so much a part of the North that it grew feathers on its feet for winter protection. Then there were the giant gulls, wheeling and screeching in the cloudless sky or etched for a dramatic instant against the mountains of the peninsula. She was relieved that Lake Harbour seemed plagued with few mosquitoes.

A group of Eskimos walked toward her from the tent colony. As usual, they ignored her. These, she supposed, were some of the Inuit who were waiting in the settlement for the patrol. Summer, Don had told her during their chat that morning, was trading time and ship's time for the 200-odd Eskimos of the Lake Harbour area. There was money to be earned for fox, caribou, and bear skins brought to the Hudson's Bay post, and there was extra pay for unloading jobs. They could get married at the mission, collect government benefits, visit their friends. As the season waned, they would pack up and return to the winter camps down the coast. They would be back for Christmas parties, though, or if they needed help.

She had strolled near the tents earlier in the day, wondering if she should make rounds. She decided not. The *Howe* would be back soon for complete medicals, and Don had promised she would be called if there was an emergency. She had stopped to stare at dozens of sled dogs staked out on a heavy chain near a stream. They howled miserably at her, and she was horrified at the sight of their skinny bodies and the piles of filth around the line.

"Well, it's summer," said Don as they had smoked a morning cigarette on the steps of the company post. The dogs were useless as workers at this time of the year and they had to survive as best they could on scraps and occasional handouts. Food was a luxury in the Arctic only to be spared for those who earned it.

She heard the complaints of the dogs now as she headed for her house. Some of the animals, Don had said, were the property of the Department of Health and Welfare. If ever she needed to get around by *komatik* in the winter, Ishawakta was there to handle the team. She blushed at the thought of Ishawakta. That morning while she was still in bed with her hair in curlers, he had padded silently into the house, removed the can from the bathroom, and returned with it a few minutes later. Her bedroom door was open, but there had been no words between them and their eyes never met. This, she supposed, would be daily ritual so she had better get used to it.

Some things, too, were beginning to bother her. Her hair was definitely a problem. She wished it was long enough to wear in uncomplicated braids, like the Eskimo women did. She hated the business of pulling the parka on and off over her head. The Inuit never changed from outdoor to indoor clothing, but she found the parka hot and uncomfortable in the house. She decided to have it equipped with a zipper so she could shuck it more easily. She hoped there were zippers for sale in the store, And why on earth hadn't she thought of bringing a cookbook to the Arctic? Her shelves would soon be jammed with supplies and the only recipe she could remember was one for shepherd's pie.

"How's the mail coming?" Don called from across the compound. The young manager was supervising two laughing Eskimos, who were raking the path gravel. The path looked so smooth and neat, she was sure she could never bear to walk on it.

"Haven't started the mail yet," she called back. "Got to get the requisitions in shape."

"There aren't many definite mail services, you know," Baird warned. "There's the *Howe*, the *Rupertsland*, and the time the RCAF make its Christmas drop. Ship time is busy time."

If I hear that again, I'll scream, she thought. The words echoed in her ears as she went into the house. Ship time is busy time. She saw that Oola was in the kitchen, clattering with the stove. *She must think I'm such a fool*, Dorothy thought, trying the radio again. It produced static as usual. *I don't know how to set the stove. I don't know how to dispose of my own wastes. I don't even know yet how I can be of help to these people.*

She tried to communicate her helplessness, apologetically spreading her hands and shrugging her shoulders while smiling at the stove. Oola stared at her impassively. "I'd like to have a zipper put into my parka," said Dorothy. She was sure Oola understood little English, but there was no harm in trying to tell her something. Oola looked up at her, crinkled her eyes and giggled. Then, because the fire was blazing in the stove, she turned and left the house.

Dorothy sighed. All ready for a magnificent lunch. A hot stove, plenty of pots, some cans on the kitchen shelf. What would she eat? She thought for a moment about the caviar and smoked oysters she had ordered; then, unaccountably, about the steamed lobsters she and Miss McDonald had eaten that night in Toronto. She felt a wave of nostalgia. She found a small enamel saucepan, then ceremoniously opened a tin of baked beans.

4

There was little to do during those first days in Lake Harbour. No patients came to her door and she was not summoned to a house or tent. So she continued with the requisitions, copying the lists of medical supplies she had found in the hospital, adding such items as a left-handed pair of dental forceps – just in case future nurses might need them – some plaster of Paris for casts, two pairs of crutches, and a cane. She had not seen these ancillary aids in the hospital and wondered if Eskimos with leg injuries had been expected to get around with rough sticks. She changed the one cane to two.

The settlement telephone in the house remained silent. She had encountered Don Baird and the Gardeners during walks around the compound, but apparently her neighbours thought she must have little time for socializing. Twice, Marg brought her fresh loaves of bread and stayed for a cup of tea. There had been no telephone calls from the RCMP detachment. But then, the constables must have mail and requisitions to attend to as well. During a pass across the dial of the uncooperative radio, she did hear the thin sound of music, but it quickly faded. She clicked on the record player and brought out her albums. *La Traviata. La Bohème.*

Many of the settlement Eskimos owned transistor radios and electric record players, and the popular rage was country-western music. The fondest dream of the Lake Harbour Inuit was to own a refrigerator, a spyglass, and a peterhead boat. She was curious about the Eskimos who chose to work for the *kabloonahs* rather than live in the camps, and she asked about them whenever she chatted with her neighbours.

She knew that Ishawakta, his wife Leah, and Oola lived in the square frame house that stood not far from her home. She had also met Georgie and his wife Nylee, who both worked for Don at the Hudson's Bay post. Georgie wore a black leather jacket over his checked shirt; his eyes always hidden behind dark glasses. He apparently spoke English better than any other Eskimo in the area. Now she learned that young Sandy, another company employee, was Georgie's brother; that their father, Akavak, was special RCMP constable and undisputed leader of the settlement Inuit.

Only Kooyoo, whose camp was 150 miles away at Amadjuak Lake, boasted as much status around Lake Harbour as the stocky, large-nosed Akavak. "There's white blood in there, somewhere," Don told her. "This was a Scottish whaling station in the last century." Most of the Eskimos with white blood seemed to be working in the trading settlements. Akavak was wealthy by Eskimo standards and had made enough money working as a ship's pilot in the straits to buy his own peterhead and telescope.

She sorted out more names. Akavak was married to the gentle-faced Pitsulala, and another of their offspring, Annie, was housekeeper for Heapy and Jenkin at the detachment. An assortment of native helpers seemed to come and go at the Anglican mission. Then there was old Silasee, the settlement's permanent convict. Silasee had killed his sick wife in Port Harrison a few years before, had been sentenced to life imprisonment and transferred to Lake Harbour. The RCMP had a jailhouse, but Silasee roamed freely, doing odd jobs for the constables or smoking and laughing to himself in the summer sun.

She sat, listening to an aria from *La Bohème. Yes, they call me Mimi, but my name is Lucia . . . my story is a brief one . . .* She went back to a letter she was writing to her family. "I haven't met them all yet, but I'm slowly learning about the Eskimos who stay here all year round. Ishawakta, my handy man, lives in a three-room house, furnished by a sofa scrounged from some previous nurse, a table, chairs, and a bed. When you walk in the door you have to avoid stepping on the dead seal that always seemed to be there, waiting to be chopped up for dinner."

I am contented and happy, and I delight in making roses and lilies . . .

"Believe it or not, I'm listening to *La Bohème* right now. It's funny. I have electricity from a generator so I can play records, read books by proper light, and even try to get something on the terrible radio. But there's no running water in the bathroom, though I do have some in the kitchen for drinking and cooking. By the way, the water here is wonderful."

Wonderful! *Ahaloonah!* The drinking-water pipe, which ran from a small, rock-bottomed lake behind the settlement, had been connected by Ishawakta the day after she arrived. The young Eskimo clearly considered it to be a special occasion and waited expectantly as she took her first sip. "Good!", she said, and meant it. The water was clear, ice-cold, and delicious.

Ishawakta smiled happily. *"Ee. Peoyook!"* Southerners, quite obviously, were always pleased and surprised at their first taste of unspoiled Arctic drinking water.

She put down the glass. This was going to be somewhat embarrassing, but after the can episode the question was easier to ask. "Is it possible for me to have a bath?" It seemed like years since she had showered in her cabin on the *Howe*. A jug of water standing near the bathroom handbasin enabled her to wash her face and hands and brush her teeth. But she longed for a bath, and she had no idea how the water could be heated or the tub filled.

Ishawakta grinned and rubbed the back of his head. Puzzlement again. "Bath?"

"Bath." She pointed to the bathroom and patted at her arms and neck. If only the Department of Health and Welfare had sent her a booklet of useful Eskimo words and phrases.

"Ee. Bath?"

"Ee?" She laughed and nodded encouragingly.

"Ee!" The Eskimo loped up the steps to the attic then returned, carrying two large copper cauldrons. He filled these from the kitchen faucet then hauled them over to the hot stove.

Good Lord, she thought. Again, there was that feeling of helplessness. *I could never lug things like that. Without this man, I can't even take a bath!*

"How much do I pay Oola and Ishawakta?" she had asked Don Baird, deciding beforehand that any sum he named was probably too little.

"The current rate is sixty dollars a month for the man and thirty dollars for the woman," the Hudson's Bay man told her. "You write me an authorization chit every few weeks and I give them credit tokens at the store. It's a lot of money, but they're worth it. Oola will chew your boots, you know."

"Boots?"

"Sealskin, You don't think those things are going to last for too long, do you?" He laughed, looking down at her red leather footwear. "Sealskin is waterproof but it gets as hard as iron, and the women chew the boots so you can get into them. That's worth thirty bucks alone."

Now, Ishawakta was dragging the cauldrons of hot water off the fire and emptying them into the bathtub. At least there was a drain so she could pull the plug when she was through.

"*Ee,*" nodded the Eskimo. "Bath. *Peoyook!*"

"*Peoyook,*" she agreed. "Very good." That was another word to add to her slim Eskimo vocabulary.

He padded out of the door, shutting it behind him. She decided she would use the expensive bar of soap she had packed in her trunk and soak in the water for a while. No need to waste government time. She would read the chapter on respiratory problems in the medical manual. That day, she had realized that hospital training had not prepared her for the treatment of influenza or the common cold. Or even for ordinary first aid. Illnesses were always far more serious when a patient was admitted to hospital. Actually, it might have been better, she thought as she stepped into the tub, for Health and Welfare to have sent someone from the St. John's Ambulance Brigade.

The *Rupertsland* would not be anchoring in Westbourne Bay down the fjord for at least another week. From signals on the cranky radio, it seemed that the *Howe* would not be back in Lake

Harbour until later in August. She suddenly felt restless. She had finished the requisitions, written a dozen letters, and explored the drinking-water lake behind the settlement. One morning she had spent some time in the Hudson's Bay store, rummaging among the graded bales of furs in the attic and examining Eskimo soapstone and ivory carvings. Don told her she could buy a giant walrus tusk made into an elegant cribbage board for fifteen dollars. Some of the soapstone sculptures were priced at thirty dollars. She felt they were shockingly expensive.

Downstairs in the store, she had looked at the items the Inuit bought with their credit tokens. Duffle cloth. Pablum. Sailcloth for tents. Needles and thread. Sanitary napkins. Cigarettes. Candy and chewing gum. Rifles and ammunition.

"Baby food, eh?" she said, pointing at the shelf. Strained carrots. Spinach. Purees of meat and chicken.

"It's a fairly new item," grinned Don. "As a matter of fact, I've been having trouble getting rid of the stuff. The Eskimos think the picture on the outside of a can shows what's inside. Peas, beans, things like that. A lot of them look at the photograph of the chubby kid on the label and figure the *kabloonahs* down south kill their babies and sell them in cans to the Inuit."

It made a mad kind of sense. She joked with Don about it while they had a cigarette together. She liked and respected the Hudson's Bay manager and understood why a young girl from Newfoundland had agreed to leave her friends and family and come to the Arctic to marry him. Don himself admitted he had no intention of ever living in a large city. He had met the North on its own terms and it suited him. A few years back, he and an Eskimo named Ootooke had been lost for thirty-seven days during a winter *komatik* trip between Cape Dorset and Frobisher Bay. Five dogs had been killed to feed the other eight before the men had been found. The story shocked but impressed her.

"Why were you going to Frobisher?" she asked.

Don shrugged. "Dorset was iced in that year. I had to get out the year's requisitions."

They smoked for a while in silence. "I'd like to take a trip along the coast by boat," she said. "Make some rounds. Though

I suppose all the Inuit are right here in Lake Harbour at the moment."

"Not all of them. There are still some at Mingeriak's camp, I hear. That's only a few miles away, and they usually don't bother to set up tents in the settlement until they know the *Howe* is in. I'll tell Ishawakta to get his canoe ready if you like."

She packed carefully for the trip. This would be a chance to check out the kinds of supplies and medication she might need later on visits to Inuit camps. She had found a medical bag in the hospital and stocked it with five-day shots of penicillin, some dental anaesthetic. Aspirin, and sulfonamides. She added some ointments, cod-liver oil, and vitamin supplements, as well as standard first-aid equipment. Because the patrol ship was due, she decided not to take DPT vaccine for booster shots. It was doubtful they would spend the night at the camp, but in any case, she brought a sleeping bag from the attic and added it to her small pile of luggage. Her own, down-filled Arctic Five Star bag, thoughtfully provided by Ottawa, was still in the hold of the *Howe*.

Food was a puzzle. She was uncertain about cooking arrangements in Eskimo camps, so she cut and buttered some of Marg's bread and found a can of luncheon meat, some bouillion cubes, and for dessert, a tin of peaches. She packed the food into a wooden box together with a can-opener, a yellow mug, a plate, a knife, and a spoon.

Ishawakta's canoe was a roomy craft, equipped with an outboard motor. Apparently, the Eskimo figured it was unnecessary to take food or any personal possessions with him, except for a .22 rifle. He stowed away what she had brought without comment, started the motor, and they puttered down the bay. She would have liked to have talked to him; once, she asked him something about the height of the tides that washed so far up the beach towards her house. But the motor drowned her voice. Besides, she already glumly realized that conversation would have to be a combination of pidgin English, pidgin Eskimo, and pantomime.

She passed the time luxuriating in the warmth of the sun and shielding her eyes from the glare to see the round heads of seals bobbing in the choppy water. Ishawakta took occasional shots, but missed. Even though she knew seals were essential to Eskimo survival, she was glad she did not have to share the canoe with a dead, 150-pound animal. She wondered idly whether it was true that seal liver tasted good. "You'll love it," Don had assured her. "Sometimes the Inuit will trade some for canned butter or jam. Don't ever refuse."

The thought of food and the scent of the sea sharpened her appetite. She was thinking about munching a slice of Marg's bread when Ishawakta yelled over the chug of the engine. *"Noonalee!"* He pointed to a small, sheltered inlet.

Mingeriak's camp, Dorothy saw, consisted of three canvas tents pegged out near a gravel beach. The camp dogs were unstaked; they ran, yelped, and howled as the canoe slid closer to the shore. Several Eskimo men stood unsmilingly, their arms crossed across their duffle parkas, waiting for them to land. When the boat finally scraped to a stop, there was no welcome. Ishawakta said something brief, laughed, and began unloading Dorothy's luggage. She heard the familiar word *"Aniatitsiyuk,"* and the Inuit nodded. She stood on the beach, her black bag clutched in her hand, wondering what she should do next.

It was impossible to tell if the Eskimos were really interested in whether or not she did anything at all. She knew it was pointless to say anything like "hello," but she had seen Don talking to the Inuit around the settlement, and he always made a point of shaking hands. She extended hers to one of the Eskimos. It was taken carefully and lightly, then released. The man's dark, slanted eyes crinkled. She shook hands all around, then walked up to the tents, avoiding slippery patches of rotting blubber, bones, and dog excrement. Women were sitting near the openings to their *tupiks*, some sewing, some scraping sealskins with their *ooloos*. Three children ran out of hiding and stood staring at her. She nodded to the women and children and shook hands.

Ishawakta came up behind her. "Lutiapik," he said.

She did not recognize the word.

"Lutiapik," he repeated, laughing a little. He pointed at her.

"Lutiapik. Little. Helps pain." He rubbed his belly. "Looks after."

The Eskimo women giggled. One nodded, measuring off a foot or so from the ground with her hand. She grinned, exposing stained teeth. "*Ee . . .* Lutiapik!" On her first day in Lake Harbour, Don had told Dorothy the Inuit would find their own name for the new *aniatitsiyuk*. She laughed and nodded, deciding she liked the sound of what the Eskimos had christened her.

"Ishawakta," she said, carefully. Well, at least her interpreter knew the word "pain." "Ask if any pain in camp."

The Eskimo nodded, then spoke to the group of men. There was silence for a moment. The Inuit still stood, their arms folded over the fronts of their parkas or shirts. The women continued with their work. One man spoke briefly, then sat on a rock, chewing thoughtfully at what Dorothy supposed was a wad of tobacco. There was a tin can on the ground not far from him, and he suddenly turned his head and spat at it. He missed by at least six inches. One of the older women scrambled to her feet, said something to the man, then moved the can. He immediately spat again, scored a direct hit and laughed.

"That man Adamee," said Ishawakta. "*Towtoongeeto*," He put his hands over his eyes. Blind. The interpreter pointed to the woman who had moved the spittoon. "That Saa. Has pain."

Dorothy spread her hands. "What kind of pain?"

She had no idea whether Ishawakta understood, but he pointed to his head and said: "*Neakoongooyok*."

Headache? She picked her way across the camp site, followed by two interested dogs and a child. Saa looked up at her and Dorothy again extended her hand. The woman took it. Dorothy pointed at her head. What was the word for pain? She pointed again and groaned loudly. The woman nodded and giggled. Dorothy supposed Saa was in her mid-fifties. She wore a cotton dress covered by the traditional *amouti*, brown woolen stockings, and sealskin *kamiks*. Her black hair was neatly divided into two braids. She turned her head, scratched furiously, and said, "*neakoongooyok*."

Impetigo, decided Dorothy. Poor hygiene, close living quarters, and probably a complication of other skin problems. She had never seen the uncomfortable condition in an adult before now. There had been some cases among infants in the Detroit hospital; she also suspected some children she had seen scratching their heads in Lake Harbour were sufferers. Saa's symptoms were typical – scalp sores, some of them yellow-crusted, others oozing. It was an advanced case, needing immediate attention. She called to Ishawakta, pointing at Saa's head. "More pain in camp?"

He seemed to understand. *"Ee,"* he said and pointed to three of the men and some of the children.

Dorothy found a place to sit, lit a cigarette and took the medical manual from her bag. "Impetigo contagiosa: A common, contagious, autoinoculable, acute, pyogenic skin infection. . . ." The treatment for impetigo, she read, involved a thorough washing with soap and warm water, removal of the crusts and an application of aureomycin ointment. Thank heaven she had brought some with her.

"Ishawakta," she said. How could she tell him she needed a lot of hot water? She looked around the camp. A pot was already boiling on a primus stove outside one of the tents. She walked towards it, catching a glimpse inside as she bent to put her medical bag in a safe, clean spot. As usual, the entrance to the Eskimo home was dominated by a dead seal.

"Tupik," Ishawakta said behind her. *"Mingeriak."* He pointed at her and then at himself. "Sleep."

"Sleep?" It was still only mid-afternoon, but she supposed the impetigo treatment would take several hours. She was glad she had brought the sleeping bag. Dormitory arrangements in the tent, she noted, consisted of a single, raised sleeping platform covered with furs and blankets. There were a few metal cannisters on the stony floor, some tobacco tins, and a lantern. On one side, there was a lighted stone lamp with a black iron pot hanging above it.

She pointed to the pot bubbling on the outside stove. "More," she said, and indicated one, two, three, four with her fingers. Ishawakta nodded. *"Ee.* More."

Work on the impetigo cases took the rest of the afternoon. Bandages were wound around the patients' heads to keep the ointment from being rubbed off by parka hoods, and soon the camp began to look as though it had gone through major surgery. By now, though, there was a relaxed air about the entire operation. Children laughed and played tug-of-war. Old Adamee giggled as he pinged brown spittle unerringly into his can. Tea was made, and although no one presumed to invite her to the party, she left the man she was treating and poured herself some of the strong black brew.

Later, two women dragged the dead seal from Mingeriak's *tupik*, turned the animal on its back and slit it from nose to tail. She watched the seal-butchering with interest. The skinning of the animal was amazingly skilful. One woman took the silver-grey pelt to flense with her *ooloo*, another threw the carcass into a tin tub. After the thick seal blubber was cut away from the skin, it was put into the pot she had seen hanging from the lamp in the tent. For heating and lighting, Dorothy remembered someone explaining on the *Howe*. Where ever had she got the idea that Eskimos ate blubber?

The woman cut the flippers from the seal, sliced deeper into the carcass to extract the liver, other organs, and entrails – then through the ribs to disjoint the backbone. There were sounds of "*ee . . . ee*" throughout the camp as the Eskimos padded forward to eat their meal.

Some took raw pieces of meat in their teeth, cutting it into bite-size chunks with their knives. Seal blood ran down Adamee's brown chin. The woman tossed portions of the seal into a pot of boiling water, waited for a moment or two, then fished them out again. The meat had scarcely been warmed. Afterwards, Dorothy saw some of the diners dunking bowls into the bloody water, drinking it like soup. One mother transferred meat she had chewed into the mouth of a small child. Dorothy finished treating the scalp of a young boy, and he ran to the tub, gouged an eye from the seal-head and popped it into his mouth. The sight suddenly sickened her. She stood with her back to the camp, taking deep breaths of fresh sea air.

After the meal, members of the camp sprawled on the rocks, laughing and smoking. Ishawakta was clearly having a good time. She smoked one of her cigarettes, found her wooden box, and opened a can of meat to make a sandwich. The Eskimos showed no interest or curiosity in what she was doing. There was more hot water bubbling on the primus stove; she mixed some bouillon and sat, slowly sipping it. There was a chill in the evening air so she pulled her parka hood closer around her face.

The evening was tedious. There were brief moments of talk, constant smoking, explosions of laughter. The women fed their babies, swinging them under their loose outer garments from hood to breast. Older children grew sleepy and wandered off to the sleeping platforms. Dorothy stubbed yet another cigarette than walked to a place behind Mingeriak's tent which, she had noted earlier, was favoured as a toilet.

By now, most members of the camp were disappearing into the tents. She picked up her sleeping bag and went to where Ishawakta sat with two other men. "Where do I go?" she asked, pointing at the bag. She wondered if she looked as dishevelled as she felt. As far as she could remember, she had not combed her hair or used her powder compact since she arrived.

The Eskimo pointed to the tent. *"Tupik,"* he said. "Me too."

She saw when she entered the big tent that the Inuit had made an extra sleeping platform for her. It was a thick layer of skins set against the wall of the tent at a right-angle to the main communal bed. Saa, her head wrapped in bandages, was already stretched out on the platform, her closest neighbour. Adamee lay next to Saa, and a man she had assumed must be Mingeriak, the camp leader, lay on the other side. Two women snored loudly. She spread out her sleeping bag, wondering if she should remove her clothes. Then she sat on the bag, pulled off her boots and parka, and decided to wriggle out of her sweater and slacks inside the sleeping bag.

She lay, looking around the tent. The light from the stone lamp was friendly, and she caught the sweetish smell of blubber from the pot hanging above it. She took off her glasses, then quickly put them on again. Was that a row of spittoons on the floor? When someone coughed and spat, she knew it was. Ishawakta came through the flap, closed it behind him, removed his clothes, and climbed into the skins beside Mingeriak. Saa turned on her stomach, coughed convulsively, then spat at the tin can nearest her head. There was more coughing and spitting, and once, she heard Adamee's giggle. She struggled to erase the memory of the rodlike tuberculosis bacilli she had seen in texts and on slides. Finally, she drifted into sleep.

There were two Eskimo men, a woman, and a small child sitting near her porch when she returned to Lake Harbour next day. "*Anneayoo*," said one of the men miserably when Ishawakta questioned him.

"Sick," said Ishawakta. "Inuit all sick." He pointed to his head and his stomach.

The child sneezed and sniffled. The woman dried her dripping nose on the sleeve of her *amouti*. Dorothy went into the house to fetch a large bottle of aspirin. As far as she could tell, the Eskimos were suffering from common colds. She counted out tablets into each outstretched palm and pantomimed her instructions. Stay in bed, drink plenty of water or tea, swallow two of the tablets every four hours. Ishawakta helped her indicate the timing on his cheap wristwatch.

It had surprised her that so many Eskimos owned timepieces. Privacy and time seemed to be two aspects of life that had little importance to the Inuit. She suspected the clocks, like the generally balky transistor radios, were regarded as novel *kabloonah* toys. Food was important. Tools for survival were important. But toys were like Arctic flowers – interesting but useless.

Don walked quickly across the compound from the Hudson's Bay store as the Eskimos wandered back in the direction of their tents. "I see you've got some patients," he said. "What is it? Colds?"

"How did you know?"

"I could see them sneezing and snuffling. This could be an epidemic, you know. It doesn't usually stop at four."

It didn't. That night, she was suddenly dragged from sleep by

Ishawakta's voice saying softly: "Lutiapik. Lutiapik. Inuit sick in *tupik*."

She felt a sudden sense of shock that the Eskimo had entered her bedroom, stood by her bed, and watched her come awake. But, she told herself with a gulp, this was probably the way it would be in the Arctic. Ishawakta left the house and waited near the porch as she dressed and collected her medical bag. It was a quarter after midnight, cold and clear. She was glad of the white border-boulders as she and the young Eskimo walked quickly along the path.

There were five new cases of colds. Three patients, she was reasonably certain, had developed influenza. There were complaints of fever, aches and pains, sore throats. The patients stared up at her from their fur-covered sleeping platforms, eyes expressionless as she used her clinical thermometer. She squinted to read temperatures in the soft yellow light of the blubber lamps, struggling to ignore the stench of sealskin and stale tobacco mingled with the odour of sweating bodies. Twice, she almost fell as she stumbled over the body of a dead seal. She dispensed more aspirin and analgesics with codeine and managed to make Ishawakta understand that the patients should stay in bed.

He came for her again before morning. Then, when she arrived at the hospital, there were more Eskimos standing dejectedly at the door. This time, she told them to wait in the ward where there were magazines to look at while she sat for a moment in her office deciding what to do. It was possible that if she left the influenza cases in the tents, they could deteriorate into pneumonia. She shuddered at the thought of having to treat dozens of pneumonia patients without medical direction, but quickly checked her stocks of penicillin and sulfonamides. Because the ships had yet to arrive, supplies were alarmingly low, particularly for an epidemic situation. She opened the office door. She would hospitalize every Eskimo who registered a temperature of more than 100 degrees, even if she had to borrow every spare mattress in the settlement to do it.

Within a couple of days, the Quonset hut ward was jammed with Inuit. Mattresses were spread on the floor, and relatives of the patients sat, or stood around chatting or attending to the physical needs of their ailing wives, husbands, or children. It was a new experience. At the hospitals, it had been Dorothy's job to make sure the sick were comfortable, fetch liquids and bedpans, and follow doctor's orders. Now, she made her endless rounds in the infected tent area and looked in at the hospital to check temperatures and administer medications. The Eskimos unquestioningly took charge of the toilet patrol, as well as feeding both the sick and themselves from the hospital's kitchen stores.

After a careful check of the medical manual's respiratory section, she had diagnosed seven cases of bronchopneumonia. Most serious was an infant who had been put into her arms by a worried mother. There had been no cries, only the sound of quick, laboured breathing. There seemed little doubt that this was a case of laryngotracheobronchitis.

Dorothy shut herself in the surgery with the manual, then began injections of penicillin and oral doses of sulfonamides. She scuttled around the compound for supplies, then constructed an improvised croup tent from a sheet of plastic, a bucket of ice cubes from her refrigerator, and Marg Gardener's electric fan. The child's breathing improved almost immediately, but there was still the danger that the throat-swelling could cause the baby to choke and die. "We'll have to do a tracheotomy, nurse," she remembered a doctor saying in Detroit. "We cut into the throat about here and insert the tube into the windpipe." As she had done that day at the city hospital, she prepared a surgical tray with a sterilized tracheotomy tube, scalpel, and clamps and placed it near the crib.

Ishawakta was hovering near the hospital door and she called to him. "Ishawakta. Get *iliniatitsiyuk*." This, she had learned, was the Eskimo name for Mike, the teacher-preacher.

She waited for the missionary, watching the sick baby. The mother sat on the floor beside the small bed, legs stretched stiffly out before her, her hands busy at some sewing. Other Eskimos in the ward, who had recovered enough to take an interest, were having an unexpected party. Cans of orange and grapefruit juice were being passed around, and the children were sucking noisily through straws. The giggling kitchen helpers were preparing a new batch of pilot biscuits lavishly spread with canned butter and sweet strawberry jam. The hospital reeked of sealskin, bacon fat, warm bodies, and cooking oatmeal. She had tried to discourage smoking, but she could smell tobacco smoke as well.

"Dorothy!" said Mike as he came through the door. He fumbled for his glasses. "Is there anything we can do?"

"Not really," she said. "The Inuit are doing most of the work. But I'd like you to explain to this woman that she must stay with her baby. If she sees the child is having trouble breathing, or if she begins to turn blue, someone must come for me right away."

"That sounds serious."

"I might have to do a tracheotomy." She turned away to check temperatures as Mike began talking to the mother.

That night, she lay exhausted in her bed, worrying about whether she was making the right decisions. Ottawa had not given her any instructions about where, when, or how to seek a doctor's advice. But she had dropped in to ask Don Baird if he could raise the hospital at Pangnirtung or Frobisher Bay by radio. Later, the manager had called on the settlement telephone to say that atmospheric conditions were so bad, he had got nothing but static.

He caught up with her again in the morning to say that reception had not improved but that he would keep trying. When she reached the Quonset hut, though, she felt that the epidemic was waning. Several more patients were up and about, there were no new cases at the door, and the sick baby seemed to be breathing comfortably. The mother looked up at her and grinned. *"Peoyook!"*

Dorothy grinned back at her. She went into the kitchen to find some tea and stood sipping it at the door of the hospital before making her rounds with the thermometer. There was no sun that day; a cold wind blew off the bay. She shivered. Ishawakta was walking towards the hospital; when he saw her at the door, he quickened his pace.

"Lutiapik," said the Eskimo. He pointed down the fjord. *"Anneayoo!"*

She understood. Someone was sick in a camp down the fjord. She took a quick look around the ward, deciding it was safe to leave her patients for an hour or so. Then she grabbed her medical bag, zipped her parka, and walked to the beached canoe with Ishawakta. It began to shower as they chugged along the coast, and again she shivered. The day's weather was a reminder that summers were brief in the Arctic. Fall was a bleak time without the bonus of autumn leaves.

The trip to the camp seemed interminable in the rain. She sat, her arms wrapped around her body as the boat grated in for a landing. Two children sat playing with stones on the beach and a man hurried out of the single *tupik*.

"*Anneayoo!*" he said urgently.

She nodded, shook his hand, and stepped over a tub of bloody seal meat to enter the tent. A young woman lay on the sleeping platform, naked under the blankets and skins. She wheezed painfully as Dorothy put a thermometer under her tongue and took her wrist. The woman's pulse was weak, but her temperature was not excessively high. Probably not pneumonia. But then, Dorothy reminded herself, because of modern chemotherapy, she had never really seen a severe case of untreated pneumonia. The really alarming signs were the blue tinges around the woman's lips, earlobes, and fingertips. Cyanosis. Dorothy tried not to show her concern. This could be a case of congestive heart failure. She began the job of explaining to Ishawakta and the Eskimo man that his wife should go with them to the hospital.

The Eskimo shook his head, bewildered.

It took patience and time, but he eventually understood that his wife was very sick, that she could get good medicine in Lake Harbour, and that it was better for him to stay at the camp with his children. Ishawakta would come later to bring news, and it would then be decided if the entire family should come to the settlement.

The man nodded. He carried the woman, wrapped warmly in furs, to the canoe. The children stood, silently watching as the craft sailed back up the fjord through the driving rain.

Dorothy again checked the woman's temperature when the

patient was bedded down in the crowded ward. It was a point or two above normal. She knew that patients with this kind of condition should be enclosed in an oxygen tent, but there was no tent in the hospital. She found an oxygen mask in the surgery, then went to the corner where the two cylinders of oxygen had been standing, untouched, since her arrival in Lake Harbour. She read one gauge. Full. The second registered empty. She bit her lip, annoyed with herself for not examining the cylinders sooner. But then, how could she have managed to locate a fresh supply? She decided to ask Don again if he could radio the hospital at Pang or the nursing station at Frobisher.

The woman responded well to the oxygen, but as soon as Dorothy removed the mask, she again turned blue and began fighting for breath. Because of the possibility of pneumonia, there was no doubt the woman should be given a massive injection of antibiotics. A shot administered intravenously would be the most effective, but that was a physician's job and could be dangerous. She would do it only as a last resort.

Instead, she prepared 300,000 units of penicillin and injected it into the patient's buttock. She went to her shelves for some sulfonamide tablets. The sight of her badly depleted stock of antibiotics unnerved her. She asked one of the Eskimo women to keep an eye on the new patient and hurried to the Hudson's Bay post. Again, as in the past few days, it amazed her that Health and Welfare assumed the employee of a private trading company would automatically accept responsibility for contacting the outside world on the department's behalf.

"Don," she said as the young manager greeted her at the door. "You've got to try again for Pang or Frobisher. I need advice. And oxygen and drugs."

"You need a drink," he said. "You're drenched." He poured a Scotch and brought a towel so she could dry her limp hair. Then he listened as she told him about the dwindling drug supplies and the new patient.

"Okay," he said. "We can only try."

He fiddled gamely with the radio for an hour. She went back to the hospital to check the sick woman. When she returned he was still at it. He got up and stamped impatiently around the room, tried again and Pangnirtung came shakily through. Yes, came the voice, the doctor was available and could talk to the nurse in Lake Harbour. There was a short wait, then Don passed the microphone to Dorothy. She described the patient's symptoms. Cyanosis. Laboured breathing. Normal temperature.

The doctor sounded calm. Why sure. It sounded like congestive heart failure, all right. He suggested digitalis. Did she have some at the station? She replied that she thought she had a supply. But could she call back for another consultation?

"Sure," the voice wavered back. "Oh, and incidentally, I would think . . ." The words were lost in static. She did not know it then, but it would be the last time she would ever receive advice from an Arctic doctor by radio.

The digitalis did nothing to improve the condition of the Eskimo patient. Her breathing became more difficult, her pulse was growing weaker, and she was sinking into deep lassitude. Her chest hollowed with the extreme effort as she struggled for air. Dorothy checked the gauge of the dwindling oxygen cylinder then ran again to the Hudson's Bay post. Perhaps the doctor in Pangnirtung was still around. Don sighed. Yes, but would the radio decide to be cooperative?

She went into the kitchen to fix sandwiches and tea for them both as he wrestled again with the radio dials. Static. After a while, he thumped his fist against the table.

"Look," he said. "Why don't you leave me to it? I'll call you later if anything happens." He had another suggestion, though. If he had no luck reaching Pang or Frobisher, he would send out a May Day call on his ham radio set. Anyone who picked it up would be asked to alert the Frobisher Bay station. Frobisher, in turn, would be asked to send oxygen and drugs if an aircraft was heading in the direction of Lake Harbour. Or at least the station could try to raise the settlement by radio. "Okay?" he grinned encouragingly.

"Okay," she said, and tried to grin back at him.

That night, there were no emergency calls, and she slept until late in the morning. Don called to her as she hurried down the path to the hospital. He had sent the May Day call, but there were no signals from Frobisher as yet. He'd send a runner if a message came through.

The Eskimo woman was no better, and there was just a quarter tank of oxygen left. She saw the patient's husband had come from their camp during the night. He stood against a wall, his face impassive. Dorothy met his eyes and smiled, but there was no response. Children began to scream excitedly when the kitchen brigade clattered into the ward with morning tea and pilot biscuits. She wanted to quieten them, but she knew the Eskimos would not understand. Children were always allowed to do exactly as they pleased among the Inuit. She made her rounds of the other patients, stopping to see that the child in the croup tent was still breathing well. Then she accepted a mug of tea and went to read her manual in the little office.

A big United States Air Force banana helicopter landed noisily and with no prior warning in front of the Hudson's Bay store two days later. It had been an agonizing wait for some kind of message, with Don sleeping near the crackling radio and Ishawakta poised to let Dorothy know the moment a call from Frobisher or any other source of medical advice came through. She had given the sick woman more injections of antibiotics and had rationed the remaining oxygen. That morning, she seriously doubted whether the patient would live for another twenty-four hours.

She joined the group of interested Eskimos gathered around the pad and waited for the aircraft door to open. It was showery and cold and she pounded her gloved hands together.

"That's quite a response to a May Day," Don laughed at her elbow. "Looks like they've flown in a hospital staff and a pharmacy."

She had to agree. There seemed to be four men and a young woman in the helicopter, and she could glimpse oxygen equipment and a stretcher piled with neatly folded blankets. The first man out of the aircraft was carrying a medical bag.

"Dr. Howerd," he said as he shook hands with Don and herself. "Your May Day message was picked up by a ham operator in Halifax, then phoned to Ottawa. Health and Welfare relayed it to Frobisher. I just happened to be in from the DEW Line, so I was asked to come. Sorry about the delay. We ran into snowstorms in the mountains and couldn't get through until now. What's up?"

She told Dr. Howerd what was up while Don greeted the pilot, co-pilot, and helicopter mechanic. The woman, who was hastily introduced as "the nurse," trailed along behind as they walked to the hospital.

There was a fascinated silence as the newcomers entered the Quonset hut. Children raced to hide, patients lay rigidly still, the usually-talkative kitchen workers retreated behind their teapots. Dorothy led the doctor to the dying woman's bed.

"Cyanosis, eh? And you're all out of oxygen?" He examined the patient. "Well, I can understand the diagnosis of heart failure, but personally, I think it's pneumonia. Possibly secondary to tuberculosis. You've been doing the right thing, though. We'll take her back to Frobisher right away. Rose will help you get her ready."

Rose, she learned, was a French-Canadian biology student who had trained as a nurse and was doing summer relief work for Health and Welfare at the Frobisher Bay INHS station. The young woman chattered brightly about the terrible weather in the mountains and how nice it was to get out of Frobisher for a while. But how could Dorothy ever stand working in a remote place like Lake Harbour? What did one do for entertainment? The Eskimo convalescents stared intently as the stretcher was brought from the helicopter by Don and Gerry Heapy and the woman transferred to it from the bed.

Ishawakta padded forward. "Lutiapik. Pauloosee want go."

"Pauloosee?" She was helping with the straps that would keep her patient secure on the stretcher.

"*Ooeenga.*" He turned to Don and began speaking in Eskimo.

"Pauloosee is the woman's husband," Don told her. "He wants to go with her on the helicopter. Other women are taking care of the children."

Dorothy looked up. The Eskimo man was still standing

against the wall of the Quonset hut. She wondered if he had moved during the past couple of days. "I think it should be all right," she told Don. "We'll ask Dr. Howerd."

Dr. Howerd said Pauloosee was welcome to come to Frobisher with his wife, but that they better get going as soon as possible. Bob, the RCAF officer who had been detailed to pilot the American aircraft, agreed with him. The weather was treacherous, the country between Lake Harbour and Frobisher Bay was a nightmare of jagged peaks, and he wanted to use the remaining daylight hours for the trip. An emergency supply of antibiotics and two full cylinders of oxygen were handed to Dorothy out of the helicopter, then the door slammed. She saw through the windows that the Eskimo woman was already receiving oxygen. Pauloosee sat, hunched on the floor at his wife's feet.

The aircraft banked and wheeled over the fjord. The Inuit lost interest in the entire affair and wandered down to the beach or back to their tents. Don dropped the information that he had been counting the days since the last brief radio bulletin from the *Rupertsland* and figured the ship would be anchoring within forty-eight hours. *Ship time is busy time,* she thought again. But how much busier could she get? Gerry Heapy strolled over to the Hudson's Bay post and announced it was time they all had a party. The helicopter co-pilot had been decent enough to leave a bottle of Scotch. Would she and Don come over to the detachment that night for a drink?

She was surprised at how much the invitation cheered her up. She knew she had been tense and anxious during the epidemic, but now, as she talked to Gerry, she began to smile. She felt almost in a holiday mood by the time she returned to the hospital. The last of the influenza patients were wolfing down bacon, biscuits, and fried seal liver. The pneumonia cases were better, and the sick baby was breathing so comfortably she removed the croup tent. The Inuit laughed and nodded and she checked temperatures and dispensed medicine; one elderly man ceremoniously shook her hand.

She celebrated her relief by going home, opening a can of chicken, and adding the essence to a tin of soup. She ate the mixture with chunks of Marg's bread, spread lavishly with butter and finished the meal with canned raspberries. Then she picked out a dress to wear to the detachment party, but grimaced at the odd combination of red wool and the sealskin *kamiks* Oola had delivered a few days before. She decided to take a pair of high-heeled shoes in a paper bag.

Next morning when she woke, she remembered she had left the shoes under a chair in the RCMP constables' kitchen. She yawned, stretched, and grinned. The party had been fun.

Don had talked romantically of Hilda's imminent arrival and the fact that Mike Gardener had agreed to marry them as soon as she was off the ship.

"You don't wait around in the Arctic," Dorothy had said solemnly, balancing her glass of weak whiskey. There had been a burst of appreciative laughter. Terry had almost choked. Funny, but she had not realized she was making such a hilarious joke. She thought about the two young constables, deciding they were the kind of men she would have liked to have dated in Toronto or Detroit. Particularly Gerry. She wondered lazily how he would look in his scarlet jacket at Don's wedding.

"You know, of course, I want you to be best man," Don had told Heapy at the party.

"Not much choice, is there?"

"I tossed a credit token. You won. Besides, you've got seniority. I want Terry to give the bride away."

"And what do I do?" Dorothy asked. Actually, she thought the whole idea of a formal wedding in a place like Lake Harbour was somewhat overdone, but it was difficult not to feel involved.

"Want to be bridesmaid?"

"No!"

Don laughed, his brown eyes shining. "I didn't think so. You can help Marg at the reception. She's sure to weep all through the ceremony."

Gerry had poured another drink, and he promised to forget that she had not arrived with booze if she would come to the detachment often and play honeymoon bridge. She had no idea how to play the game, but promised she would come as often as she could. Then he talked nostalgically about his hometown in Saskatchewan and the people he had known there. And he sang an out-of-tune chorus of "You Are My Sunshine."

She smiled again about the party at the detachment. But it was stupid, even dangerous to think too much about Gerry Heapy. She closed her eyes for a moment, thinking about what she should do that day. She wondered whether she might get the pneumonia cases moving around. The ward badly needed a thorough cleaning, and she wanted to organize space to accommodate the supplies coming in on the Hudson's Bay ship. Ishawakta came into the house to fetch her toilet can, and she could hear Oola rattling at the stove.

The next sound she heard was that of the banana helicopter chopping back down the fjord and settling with a whine on the pad. She peered out of the livingroom window. What happened? Navigation problems? Engine failure? How was the Eskimo patient? She buttoned on a pair of slacks, zipped snugly into her parka and joined the Inuit swarming curiously across the compound. Georgie grinned at her from behind his dark glasses; Don came out of the post and waved. There was a light drizzle, but the air was clean and sweet. For the first time since she had been in Lake Harbour, she felt a sense of community.

5

The *M. V. Rupertsland* anchored in Westbourne Bay two days after the return of the helicopter. By then, everyone in the settlement knew that the aircraft had been caught in a blizzard and forced to land for a night in the mountains. The helicopter had landed near a lake, so there was no shortage of water. But since there were just three emergency food packs, the seven passengers might have starved if the weather had not improved.

"But I was way off course," Dorothy heard Bob, the pilot, telling Gerry. "I must have circled, looking around for a spot to land. We'd never have got here if it hadn't been for Pauloosee." The Eskimo, it seemed, had sat in the cockpit and guided the aircraft back to Lake Harbour. Landmarks that helped him find his way to traplines and hunting areas on the ground were just as easy to pick out from the air.

By the time the ship arrived, it was apparent that worsening weather in the highlands meant the helicopter party might be stranded for days. Dr. Howerd had been giving Pauloosee's wife intravenous injections of antibiotics, and her lung infection was under control. The patient was returned, looking better, to the Quonset hut, and there was a conference among the six white residents of the settlement.

Everyone agreed that Dorothy's house would make the most suitable emergency hotel. Besides, she had to agree, she was responsible for the big aircraft being there in the first place. There was little extra room at the Gardeners or the RCMP detachment, and Don Baird was expecting Hilda to join him momentarily at the Hudson's Bay post. Dorothy rounded up mattresses, and Ishawakta put them in the attic for her four male guests. The only hospitable thing to do was to invite the effervescent Rose to share the one nursing-station bed.

Storms were still blackening the eastern sky when the first barge arrived from the *Rupertsland* at high tide, loaded with crates, barrels of fuel, and a woman. Hilda was not yet twenty. She was excited, clearly in love, and determined to get married in the white gown that was still in her trunk on the ship. She stood on the beach shaking hands with her new neighbours, her cheeks flushed and her brown hair flying in the wind. But there was a complication in the plans. The wedding had been timed for eight o'clock that night, but the bride's luggage was under forty tons of cargo in the hold.

Don conferred with Gerry Heapy. It was hastily decided to work at unloading supplies for the trading post, mission, RCMP, and nursing station that night. The goods would need to be checked against requisitions and cleared from the beach before high water washed them down the fjord. The wedding was rescheduled for low tide, next morning at ten o'clock.

Don explained the problem of cargo and thirty-foot tides to a bewildered and disappointed Hilda before he sent her off with Marg Gardener to the mission house. The beach was already a clutter of boxes, bundles, drums, and crates, and more were arriving all the time. Dorothy stumbled among them, searching for the Health and Welfare identification label. A bitter wind was gusting, and once the requisition copies from the hospital fluttered out of her hands. Gerry hauled a crate on its side and summoned a group of Eskimos to slide slats under it and take it to a safe spot in the compound. Mike Gardener seemed to be well organized. Don was working in a kind of frenzy.

It was growing dark, and she looked around for Ishawakta. She had not seem him for hours. The three members of the helicopter crew were sitting on the rocks, smoking and staring at the confusion on the beach. They waved cheerfully at her, but she was too preoccupied to respond.

"Have you seen Ishawakta?" she asked, grabbing Don's arm. "How on earth do I get my stuff out of here?"

Don looked up at her, his hair flopping in his eyes. "Georgie's over there," he said. "Tell him I said to get you a crew."

Georgie was helpful. Yes, he replied in his practiced English, there were men who could carry her supplies. But she would have to tell them where to take the boxes. To the house or to the hospital. There would be a number on her hospital list which would check against the number on the crate. He tucked his dark glasses into the top pocket of his leather jacket. Right?

She nodded, squinting in the fading light. She found three boxes with numbers corresponding to her list, then four belonging to the house. When two Eskimos appeared with slats over their shoulders, she pointed and shouted "hospital!" above the screech of the gale. They nodded, slid slats under a box, and hurried off in the direction of the house. Two more helpers took house supplies to the hospital. Wearily she decided there was no point in trying to make them understand. The real priority was to get the goods off the beach, so she grinned grimly, pointed, nodded, and allowed the Inuit to take the crates where they pleased.

She peered at her luminous wristwatch. It was ten o'clock; she could scarcely see the beach. She stuffed the requisitions into the hood of her parka, concentrating on identifying Health and Welfare supplies. There seemed to be no end to the job. At one point, when she thought she had finished, yet another barge ground into the beach with a fresh load. Don, Gerry, and Mike were using flashlights. She knew there must be one somewhere in the house or the hospital, but it was too late to find it now.

"Hospital!" she continued to scream encouragingly. "House!" The Eskimos scurried with their burdens, laughing cheerfully as she waved her arms like a traffic cop on point duty.

"It's the trunk!" she heard Don yell once in the darkness. "Tell Hilda we've found the trunk!"

Her back ached from the crouching; she was hungry and terribly thirsty. She tried to light a cigarette, but the wind snuffed out the match, and she knew her lighter was dry of fuel. "Hospital! Hospital!" She saw that Ishawakta had joined her group of helpers. Now crates seemed to be shuttling the right way. She had figured it would be just like Christmas, getting so many supplies, opening so many boxes. But this was like having an entire store dumped at one's door. She bent to examine another crate. It was for the RCMP. So was the next. She sighed and stared numbly around her. The nightmare, it seemed, was over.

At the house, she picked her way through the mountain of crates and bundles the Eskimos had piled untidily on the porch. The light burning in the kitchen was enough for her to see the jumble of supplies in the livingroom. She heard snores from her guests in the attic. In the kitchen, she tested the stove to see if she could make some coffee, but the coals were dead. She went into the bedroom, struggled out of her clothes, and climbed into bed beside Rose.

"You stay out late," mumbled the nurse. "Wedding in morning."

"Yes," said Dorothy. She had forgotten about the wedding. She turned tiredly over on her side.

She wore her green gabardine suit and borrowed a hat from Marg. It was the first time she had ever attended a service in a Protestant church. She was surprised that the words were similar to those she had heard at Roman Catholic wedding ceremonies. The real difference, of course, was the plain little church itself, the stench of the Eskimo congregation's sealskin boots, and the fact that a bride in traditional white satin and a veil was being given away by a scarlet-jacketed Mountie.

"Jesusee Christusee," she heard the Inuit sing as they stood for a hymn. She was learning that English words adopted by the Eskimos invariably emerged with an *ee* at the end. *Mathewsee, Markasee, Lukasee, Johnasee.*

The helicopter castaways had pressed their clothes and were sitting together in a front pew. Rose must also have borrowed a hat from Marg. Marg herself wept a little through the ceremony, just as Don had predicted. Afterwards, there would be wine and cake in Mike's little library. Then, when the tide was high again, more supply barges were due from the *Rupertsland*.

Beansees, soupee, teamee. . . . This time, she resolved to prepare her survival kit in advance. Cigarettes and windproof lighter. A thermos of coffee. A flashlight. A clipboard for the blowaway requisitions. An advance agreement with an Inuit crew of helpers. Don, she figured, would not be around for the next few hours. She wondered if Gerry or Mike would have time to interpret. Perhaps she would have to deal with the Eskimos on her own.

Once again, she felt the twinge of lonely inadequacy. No wonder Health and Welfare figured it was always easier to send a married nurse into the Arctic.

Dr. Howerd came to the hospital later that morning to take a look at Pauloosee's wife. During the emergency, Dorothy had known the sick woman only by her identification number. But since she had recovered enough to be taken off oxygen, Dorothy learned her name was Evaloo. Pauloosee was still standing vigil in the ward with his two children.

"The pneumonia's under control," said the doctor. "But I still think she's tubercular. When will the *Howe* be in?"

She repeated what Don had told her. Probably in a week.

The physician nodded. "She should be X-rayed and assessed. Then, if she's infected, they can take her directly down south. There's no point in flying her to Frobisher now we've licked the pneumonia. That is," he added with a grimace, "if we ever get out of here ourselves."

It was obvious that even with the distraction of the *Rupertsland,* the wedding, and visits with the settlement whites, the helicopter crew and passengers were becoming more and more restless. Bob and Hugh, the co-pilot, were continually climbing the hill behind the settlement, staring bleakly into the fogbanks to the east. Conversation seemed to revolve almost entirely around the weather and what Ford's new Edsel model was going to look like. Don's radio, as usual, had produced nothing but screeches, and there were mutters about how folks back in Frobisher must be worried sick. Once, Hugh thought he heard an aircraft droning above the low clouds and sprinted for the helicopter's portable radio. He returned to the messy livingroom, grumbling about symptoms of bush fever.

Rose had taken charge of the kitchen and was turning out stews and fruit pies as Oola looked on, giggling. Now, she was chattering excitedly about the tasty goodies she might find if she opened some of the new crates. Glad of discovering a new way of keeping the French-Canadian nurse entertained, Dorothy found a hammer and chisel in the attic and begged her to get busy and cook up a banquet. Then she fled.

The invasion had been diverting in the beginning. But now, even the other whites were beginning to find it difficult to include the strangers into the ordered life of the small community. Dorothy tried to keep away from her disorganized home as much as possible. The second consignment from the ship actually proved to be a relief, and she hurried to supervise the transfer of crates and boxes from the house to the hospital.

Now this was Christmas! Shiny new instruments. A wheelchair. Cartons of liquid drugs packed in dry ice. Three cylinders of oxygen. A fancy new stethoscope. Another pair of right-handed dental forceps. She checked the *Rupertsland* supplies against the 1956 requisition list and saw there still some orders to come. More drugs, surgical instruments, vitamin supplements, DPT vaccine, cod liver oil. The balance of the crates, she supposed, were on the *Howe*.

The thought of the *Howe* reminded her there would be medical help if she needed it when the ship was in port. Right now, it seemed ironic that while there was a doctor in Lake Harbour, there was no call for his services. Evaloo was currently the only patient in hospital, and Ishawakta had not once roused Dorothy during the night since the aircraft had been stranded. One afternoon, Dr. Howerd had gone on an inspection tour of the Eskimo tents, but his only comment was that he had heard an old Inuit woman playing an accordion.

"Music, doc?" asked Rose, her hands deep in a bowl of flour. "You find music? How long since we hear music?"

With an inaudible sigh, the Lake Harbour *kabloonahs* did their best to encourage the suddenly-frenetic round of activity. A dance was organized in the Quonset hut near the burial ground in honour of Rose's birthday. Dorothy wondered why nobody had thought of it before. The Inuit were obviously delighted. Dressed in their best parkas, they poured out of the tent colony to dance the night away. The Eskimos taught the newcomers shuffling Scottish reels. The newcomers taught the Eskimos how to do the conga.

The next evening, Rose told the group in the house that she had heard Mike Gardener had some movies and a projector. Why didn't the missionary put on a show? Bob was elected to call the mission house on the settlement telephone. "And none of those documentaries," said Rose. "See if he's got a Cary Grant." Mike was coaxed out of his library, and everyone sat in the open air, bundled against the chill, to watch Judy Garland in *A Star is Born*.

For a while, the trapped visitors seemed somewhat less bored. But on the sixth day of their stay, Bob and Hugh stamped into the house after a trip to the hill, complaining that they could not stand Lake Harbour for another hour. The four men sat around gloomily. Finally, they started a game of poker. Rose decided to make yet another apple pie. Dorothy left the house and headed for the hospital. She was checking blanket supplies when she heard Bob shouting from across the compound. "We've decided to try for it, Dorothy! Thanks for everything."

She ran towards the helicopter pad. Don and Hilda were there, and Marg was hurrying from the mission, wiping her hands on her apron.

"Thanks for everything, folks!"

"Say hello to Frobisher for us. And don't forget to send us a Christmas card!"

Dr. Howerd turned to Dorothy. "You're doing okay," he said. "Keep your eye on the medical manual."

"Sorry about the apple pie," laughed Rose. "I never did get it in the oven. Ask Oola to finish it for your supper."

The Eskimos came from their tents to stare at the departing *kabloonahs*. A few of the younger Inuit performed a good-bye conga. The engine coughed into life and the big helicopter lifted off the pad in a blizzard of dust, droned across the bay then headed east. It was suddenly very quiet. Dorothy went into the house and looked at Rose's unfinished apple pie. She realized, with a small grin, that she would miss the pies, the chatter, even the dishevelled line-ups for the bathroom in the mornings. Ishawakta was at the door. Through pantomime and pidgin Eskimo she asked if he and Oola would help bring the mattresses out of the attic and clean the house.

They were still at the job when the aircraft flapped back down the fjord and landed on the helicopter pad. Hugh jumped to the ground and stood, kicking irritably at the red gravel. The weather had socked in and the flight back to Lake Harbour had drained the fuel tanks.

The next day was Sunday, and tension in the nursing station was unbearable. Dr. Howerd and Rose seemed moderately cheerful, but the helicopter crew had begun to shout at each other. Bob and Hugh went across to the Hudson's Bay post to ask Don if he would send out a May Day. They returned, complaining loudly about the weather, atmospheric conditions, and their dirty laundry. Dorothy retreated unhappily to the hospital and ate her lunch in the deserted surgery. She walked in the compound during the afternoon, but it was chilly so she finally forced herself to go back to the house.

There were few smiles at dinner. She and Rose did the dishes while the men started a card game. Then she tried reading in the bedroom. But the grumbling she could hear from the living-room was distracting. She switched out the light and was settling down to sleep, when there was a knock on the door.

"Hi!" she heard Don's voice. "I managed to contact Nottingham Island. They've promised to relay a message to Baffin Base. If the weather is okay, a helicopter should get here with some gas pretty soon."

Someone yelled "yahoo!" and there was a unanimous and noisy decision to break out some booze. She knew she should join in the celebration, but she got out of bed quietly and closed the door. When the rescue helicopter arrived from Baffin Base next morning, no one joked about Christmas cards and the Inuit even forgot to do the conga.

Lake Harbour settled into a kind of stunned tranquillity after the departure of the helicopters. There were nervous glances at the sky for a few hours after they left, but by late afternoon, it was assumed the aircraft had made Frobisher safely. Dorothy supervised another clean-up of the house, Oola stoked the stove, and Ishawakta fetched the copper cauldrons so she could have a bath. She luxuriated in the privacy of her empty home. Even the radio cooperated and she listened to an hour of reedy dance music from some unidentified station.

The euphoria lingered into the next day. She saw that her patient was comfortable, zipped her parka, then walked into the hills behind the settlement. Quite obviously, the Arctic summer was over. There was a thin sheet of ice over the drinking-water lake; flowers in the rock crevices were dark and wilted. That morning, there had been hoar-frost on the limp grass around the compound, though the hardy moss and lichens were still crisp and green.

She wondered if it was time to ask Don about having some winter clothing made by the Eskimos. As she came down from the hill, she saw the Hudson's Bay manager come out of his house. He waved his arm and shouted something. "Can't hear you!" she called back, sprinting along the path.

"*Howe's* coming in!" Don repeated. He pulled the hood of his parka over his head. "About time, too. The Eskimos want to get their boats back to winter camps before the ice comes."

"Do I have to do anything?" she asked.

"About getting them to the *Howe?* No. Heapy and Jenkin will see to that. Most of the Inuit know the ropes by now, anyway. They'll probably take their own boats or wait for the barges. You've got a patient, haven't you?"

Evaloo. The woman would have to be X-rayed and the film examined for signs of tuberculosis. If Dr. Howerd's diagnosis was correct, she would be sent south, away from Pauloosee and the children. "Yes," she said. "Evaloo. I'll bundle her up and go on board with her. I suppose we'll have to go through the supply drill again?"

"It'll be mostly your stuff," grinned Don, reminding her again of her brother. "But we'll all help this time."

There were half a dozen Eskimos waiting at the hospital. She stared, half-recognizing them. "Lutiapik!" giggled one of the women.

"Saa!" she laughed. "How's the impetigo?"

The woman could not understand, of course, but she grinned and pointed to her head, the other Eskimos doing the same. The impetigo had improved. She examined each scalp, nodded approvingly, and smiled *"peoyook."* The Eskimos sat patiently while she applied more aureomycin ointment and laughed when she wound on the protective bandages. Perhaps they considered them to be a special mark of distinction. One of the women left the Quonset hut, returning a little later with the children Dorothy had treated at Mingeriak's camp. She worked on their scalps as the adult Eskimos talked with Evaloo and Pauloosee. There were gasps of *"ee . . . ee!"* and she supposed the Inuit had told the story of the helicopter flight and their adventurous trip back to Lake Harbour.

She bit her lip. So far, the couple had no idea there was any possibility they might be separated. She wondered if there was some way of warning them without causing too much alarm. She decided there wasn't. Later, she found Ishawakta and made him understand that he must tell Pauloosee that she would go with them in the barge to the *Howe.* Pauloosee nodded cheerfully after Ishawakta talked to him, and so did Evaloo. She walked home, knowing the euphoria of the morning had vanished.

The crowded scene on the *Howe* was familiar. Sealskin stink, shirtless men, women wrestling with their *amoutis.* Mary Paneegoosho looked up during a pause in the line of waiting Inuit and asked whether she had settled into Lake Harbour yet. Settled in? Good Lord, she confessed to the interpreter, she felt she had been there for years. She helped Evaloo with her clothes then took her personally to Heather Matthews.

"Dorothy!" grinned the public health nurse. She looked pale and tired. "You settled in yet?"

"Sure," said Dorothy. "I'd like you to meet Evaloo. She's been pretty sick with pneumonia, and we're going to take a look at her X-rays."

Heather nodded. "I see. Have you had some pneumonia in Lake Harbour?"

"Yes," said Dorothy. "We've had some pneumonia."

Afterwards, she ate a solitary lunch of ham sandwiches and coffee in the ship's dining salon, before returning to the sick bay area. Evaloo, Pauloosee, and their two children were sitting on benches waiting to be told what to do next. When they saw her, they smiled and held up the palms of their hands. *R* for registration. *X* for X-ray. She motioned them to wait, then went to find Fred Lee.

"Dorothy!" smiled the technician. "You settled in yet?"

"Sure," she said. "I was wondering about X-rays for a couple of my friends. I've got their registration numbers."

Fred checked his list. "They've gone to Dr. Sabean. So you're settling in, eh? So what's it like in Lake Harbour? Many mosquitoes?"

"Fred," she said. "I'll talk to you later."

Dr. Sabean was standing outside the door of his surgery waiting for the new batch of Inuit that would reach him in a few minutes. She hoped desperately that he would not ask whether she was settling in.

He smiled, and he seemed thinner. "Dorothy. How are you? Sorry we took so long to come back. We were tied up in other places." He shoved his hands in his pockets. "A pity about the meningitis case. The baby died a few days after we got her on board."

"It was definitely meningitis?"

"Tuberculous meningitis. There was nothing much we could do, but at least we had the chance to try. Would you make sure the mother is told? Why are you on board, incidentally?"

"I'm interested in an X-ray," she said. "The woman's name is Evaloo. This is her registration number."

Dr. Sabean went into the surgery to collect his clipboard. "Pulmonary tuberculosis," he said. "She'll have to go south."

Dorothy swallowed hard. "How about the husband and the two children? These are the numbers."

"The X-rays look okay. But the woman will have to go."

"Isn't there any other way?"

"What, for example?"

"Well, treatment at home. Has anybody tried?"

"Arctic living conditions aren't suitable," said Dr. Sabean. "Besides, the first priority is to wipe out the disease. Ottawa feels the best way of doing that quickly is to ship the Eskimos south."

She watched unhappily as an interpreter talked to Pauloosee and Evaloo. The woman's face was blank when she heard the news, but the man walked to the end of the ship's corridor, stood quietly for a few moments, then returned. He avoided looking at Dorothy, but she could see his eyes were expressionless. He said something to his wife, took his children by the hand, and went to the waiting barge. The interpreter turned to go, but Dorothy stopped him.

"What did Pauloosee say?" she asked.

"He say he come back with wife's *ooloo*," said the Eskimo. "Women always take *ooloo*."

Evaloo continued to sit patiently on the bench, her hands clasped lightly in the lap of her *amouti*.

After Don, Gerry, and four Eskimos helped her get the Health and Welfare supplies from the beach to the hospital, she drank a cup of tea with the Bairds and went home to bed. For once, it was difficult getting to sleep. The *Howe* would weigh anchor at six o'clock in the morning; thoughts of Evaloo and Pauloosee nagged at her. She had scarcely dozed off when Ishawakta's voice roused her. "Lutiapik! Lutiapik!" *God, she was too tired! Why did the alarm have to go off just now?* "Lutiapik! Woman *anneayoo*. In *tupik*."

"Yes," she said and sat up abruptly in the dark.

The tent was one that had been pitched in the settlement within the past couple of days. She stepped over the dead seal at the entrance and edged her way inside. There were three men and two women on the sleeping platform and in the dim light of the blubber lamp she could see white bandages. One of the women was sitting, her head held over a metal tub. She was coughing convulsively.

"Saa!" said Dorothy.

The woman looked up at her, fear in her eyes. She coughed again and bright red blood gushed from her mouth.

Dorothy turned to Ishawakta, pointing in the direction of the fjord. "Saa go to *Howe*?"

Ishawakta shook his head. "Saa not go."

"Never?"

Ishawakta was silent.

Saa coughed again and moaned. It was a massive haemorrhage from the lungs, and the woman must have realized by now that she would probably die. Dorothy looked at Saa's companions on the sleeping platform. Blind Adamee lay motionless. The other Eskimos seemed to be awake, but they were quiet and still.

"Tell Saa I will be back," she said to Ishawakta, hoping he would understand. "I go to Hudson's Bay."

She banged on Don's door until he answered, yawning in his dressing gown. "Hi! What's wrong."

"It's six-thirty," she said. "The *Howe* sailed a half hour ago. But I want the helicopter to come back."

"Again?" grinned Don. "What have you got this time?"

"Lung haemorrhage," she said. "The woman will die if she doesn't go. At least we can give her a chance, Besides, she's probably infected everyone in her camp who's gone out with TB in the past few years."

"Who is it?"

"Saa from Mingeriak's."

"Saa?" Don laughed.

"I know. 'Saa not go to *Howe*.' Look, I hate to see such an old lady go south, Don. But this woman has reached the point of no return. And she's a danger to everyone around her."

The *Howe* was still in radio contact. There was no detailed consultation with Dr. Sabean. She simply described what was happening in the tent, and the physician said he would send Glenn and Heather back with the helicopter. "Son of a gun," the doctor said before he signed off. "Not go to *Howe*, eh?"

Back in the tent, Saa got obediently to her feet, her eyes fixed on the blood she had coughed into the tub. She rummaged weakly under the sleeping platform, found a small sealskin bag and put her *ooloo* into it. Then she walked with Dorothy into the cold black morning. No one in the tent moved or uttered a word. The woman coughed once again before they reached the pad, sank to her knees, and bled into the withered grass by the side of the path. Dorothy caught at her arm.

She continued to hold it until the helicopter landed, blinking its lights. Then, as the woman was helped into the aircraft, all she could see were the bandages she had wound around Saa's head.

6

Influenza began raging again not long after the departure of the *C. D. Howe*, and this time, there was also diarrhoea. The new epidemic delayed the Eskimos' September exodus to winter camps. Some had already begun packing their pots, pans, and bedding into boats, but the work was abandoned as body temperatures soared, the patients complained of aches and pains, or squatted miserably beside their *tupiks*.

Dorothy dispensed encouragement, antibiotics, and bismuth. Predictably, there were more cases of pneumonia. Mattresses were again spread around the floor of the ward to accommodate the sick and their ministering relatives. The night calls to the tent area began all over again, but now there were gales and sleet storms to fight in the darkness. One black evening, she got lost on her trip home from the Quonset hut and found herself dangerously close to the dog line. She had learned she need not be afraid of the animals provided she stayed on her feet. A stumble into the line, though, might result in some lacerating bites. The excited howls of the dogs warned her to turn on her heel and grope her way back in the opposite direction.

She regretfully refused invitations from Don and Hilda Baird to eat dinner and play canasta. She had already made friends with the cheerful, self-assured young woman from Newfoundland, and they had promised themselves fishing excursions into the hills once the latest bout of ship fever was over. Now, though, there were shots to administer, temperatures to check, new admittances to squeeze into the swarm of snoring, coughing, moaning humanity on the hospital floor.

There seemed to be so many other things to do.Whenever possible, she tackled impetigo cases, clipped heads crawling with lice, and tried not to protest when Eskimo children ate the sweetish *kooma* as the Inuit had done for centuries.

Once, she decided to give a shockingly dirty young girl a bath in her house. The child was suffering from the itching torture of impetigo and scabies, so Dorothy asked Hilda if she would help while she bathed the girl and treated the sores and inflamed skin.

"Do you think it's her first dip?" Hilda asked as Ishawakta filled the tub.

"I wouldn't be surprised," said Dorothy. The girl sat quietly, draped in a towel. But when the women led her to the bath, she began to sob. *"Agai! Agai!"*

"Oh come on, honey," said Hilda encouragingly. "I've brought my best soap!"

"Agai!"

Dorothy lifted the child into the water. The screams grew louder as the girl twisted in her arms, fighting to get away. *"Agai!"*

"God!" said Hilda. "She's terrified!"

Dorothy snatched the child out of the bath and wrapped the towel around her shaking body. Then she sat in the livingroom, the sobbing girl cradled in her lap. *What am I trying to do?* she asked herself glumly. *I can't put bathtubs into every Eskimo dwelling in the Arctic.* She would take the girl back to the hospital and tell her mother to wash her with a cloth from a familiar pot. She had no idea when regular bathing would become a habit among the Inuit, but she would never subject a child to the terrors of the tub again.

The pneumonia cases began to convalesce, but for some reason, the Eskimos continued to delay their departure. She noticed the tide-water was freezing down near the beach; there seemed to be fewer birds around the settlement. Sleet turned to snow flurries. One morning, she found the toothpaste in her tube had frozen solid. After making her chilly rounds of the tents and walking home from the hospital, she huddled close to the livingroom space heater before unzipping her parka.

"How about canasta tonight?" Hilda called on the settlement telephone as she was about to head again for the Quonset hut.

"Maybe not until the Inuit leave," she answered. "I never seem to catch up. . . ."

That morning, Ishawakta was waiting at the hospital with a woman carrying a young child. The girl's scalp had been torn, probably by a wolf or a dog.

"Peoyook," grinned her interpreter, pointing at the wounds.

"Peoyook," nodded the woman, grinning broadly.

The child wailed as Dorothy examined its head. The long and deep lacerations had been carefully sewn together with caribou sinew.

"Lutiapik," said Ishawakta. "Woman good aniatitsiyuk. Peoyook." He stifled a laugh.

She had to agree that the stitches were marvelously neat, but the wounds had been infected by the unsterile animal sinew. She nodded "peoyook," several times then pointed to her instruments and drug supplies, trying to indicate that she would also like to show her skill as an aniatitsiyuk. The mother nodded approvingly, then held her daughter as Dorothy cleaned the scalp, removed as many of the tuktu sutures as possible, and replaced them with surgical thread.

That was also the day she noticed there was something very wrong with a five-year-old girl who was playing with other children in the ward.

"Come," she said to the child, holding out her hand and smiling. The girl was unwilling to go, but a patient laughed, said something in Eskimo, and the child followed Dorothy slowly into the surgery. What was the strange swelling at the back of the child's neck? Horrified, she saw that something was moving under the skin. But what?

She turned to the Skin and Connective Tissue section in the medical manual, but could find nothing that could help her diagnose the problem. She examined the child again. She knew the animals or insects under the skin would have to be small, and it was obvious they had not located themselves in muscle tissue. She was hesitant about making an incision, but under the circumstances it seemed justified.

She called to an Eskimo woman to help hold the child, injected local anaesthetic, then carefully slit into the skin. *"Ee. Peongeto!"* gasped the woman. Bad.

Dorothy stared at the girl's neck. A nest of maggots. Later she learned the child suffered from myiasis – a condition caused by larvae burrowing into an open wound. There were always maggots around dog lines, and the girl probably carried some under a fingernail, then scratched at a sore. She had no guidelines to follow as she treated the case, but it seemed to be a sensible procedure to remove the nest of worms, syringe the swollen area until it was clean and apply an anti-bacterial ointment. Then she covered the wound with a dressing. She shuddered. The child ran laughingly back to her game.

"I'm still catching up," she assured the enquiring Hilda next morning. Three pneumonia patients were ready to leave the hospital, but children with "sick" ears were being brought for her to see. She realized, apprehensively, that they were cases of otitis media.

"You're an R.N. with five years' experience," she recalled Miss McDonald assuring her. "You're in good health. You're clearly interested in a northern posting." She had seen children with infection of the middle ear in Detroit so she knew it was a condition caused by bacteria escaping from the throat through the eustachian tube to the ear. The infection spread rapidly in close living quarters. But in hospital, no nurse had ever been expected to do anything more responsible than to stand by and hand the doctor swabs and ear-drops.

Now, she cleaned away the yellow discharge, probing gently into ears as the mothers struggled to control their screaming offspring. She gritted her teeth, aware that if a child broke free, the swab could tear through the tympanic membrane. "Sure, it's extremely painful," she had heard one intern say as he performed the operation. "But as much of the pus as possible should be removed from the inner ear. The antibiotic drops should come in contact with the infected area." At the time, she had marvelled at how doctors could inflict such pain on children without flinching. Now she knew. They flinched inside. Besides, they knew that untreated otitis media could lead to meningitis or loss of hearing.

"*Peongeto*," hissed an Eskimo mother as her small son writhed in agony and terror when she tried to probe with her cotton swab. Outside in the ward, she knew there were two more cases of otitis media for her to see, as well as another possible pneumonia victim. She smiled grimly to herself, remembering the days when she had wished she could spend at least one hour on the job without doing anything as ordinary as carrying a bedpan.

Oola was not in the kitchen when she went to the house at midday and Ishawakta was tending the coal stove. "Oola at *ilneeshooktoo*," the Eskimo said. He thought hard to find the right English words. "Child coming in *tupik*. Pitsulala there, too."

She had been alerted to the fact that Oola and Pitsulala were the settlement's two official midwives, but so far she had not been asked for obstetrical help. She was relieved. She worried about faulty hygiene, of course, but felt it was wise to leave the Inuit to deal with childbirth as they had always done. *The most sensible way of handling the kind of ignorance you've brought to the Arctic, Dorothy,* she told herself firmly, *is to impose it on others as little as possible.* She shivered at the possibility of having to tackle anything as serious as a retained placenta or a uterine hemorrhage, even if she could rely on Don's radio to get medical advice.

"It is Davidee's wife, Tagalik," said Ishawakta. She had heard that Davidee was a well-known ivory carver in the area. "Davidee want *ilnee*. Son?" Ishawakta laughed. "My wife have *ilnee*. Soon."

She laughed along with the Eskimo. This was the second time Ishawakta had painstakingly explained that his wife, Leah, was pregnant. It was obvious he was excited at the prospect of becoming a father.

"Ishawakta," she said, pointing and using newly learned scraps of Eskimo, "ask Oola if Lutiapik can come to see Tagalik have baby." She had been hoping for an opportunity to be present at an Eskimo birth and now, perhaps, it might be possible.

He came for her at the hospital late in the afternoon after she had treated yet another middle-ear infection. She was still shaken by the experience, standing helplessly in the ward as the mother tried to comfort the weeping child.

"Lutiapik," said Ishawakta. "Oola say you come now."

Davidee's tent was pitched some distance from the others, and the walk was long and cold. There was a sharp snow shower, and she pulled the hood of her parka closer around her face and held a gloved hand over her nose. Ishawakta, she saw, seemed unaffected by the chill. His head was uncovered; he wore nothing on his hands. She thought about the apparent indifference of the Inuit to the cold. She had often seen babies lying naked in the tents and had longed to tuck them warmly under the covers.

Dr. Sabean had discussed Eskimo babies once on board the *Howe*. Infant mortality was unusually high among the Inuit but the majority of deaths had little to do with problems at birth. "You'll find lots of respiratory cases," the doctor had said. "The poor kids die of pneumonia. Or from burns and scalds once they can move around."

There were several Eskimos gathered near Davidee's camp. They scarcely glanced at her as she and Ishawakta climbed the small, rocky incline to the *tupik*. Davidee himself was standing, smoking a cigarette, and talking occasionally to three other Eskimos. Several children laughed and ran in and out of the canvas tent. Inside, the *tupik* was foggy with tobacco smoke. There were two elderly women sitting on the sleeping platform who rocked back and forth, cigarettes clamped between their teeth, chanting "*ee . . . ee . . . ee.*"

Tagalik was a young woman. She was kneeling on a sealskin near the sleeping platform, her red cotton dress hitched around her waist, and her elbows supported by a wooden crate. Pitsulala and Oola sat, chain-smoking, on either side of the expectant mother, and another woman was busy keeping tea mugs filled.

Nobody appeared to notice as Dorothy cleared a box of several tobacco tins and empty pots and sat, quietly watching. Two small boys exploded into the tent and stared for a moment as Tagalik moaned through a contraction. She leaned forward over the crate, then rocked back on her heels into a squat. Oola and Pitsulala moved their cigarettes to the corner of their mouths and kneaded firmly on Tagalik's upper abdomen. *Like squeezing a tube of toothpaste,* Dorothy thought.

Tagalik buried her head briefly in her arms, then took a sip of black tea. There was another contraction, and the midwives kneaded and pushed at the woman's swollen belly. "A'a!" groaned Tagalik. "A'a!" The two children played tag around the tentpole then darted outside.

The labour went on for another hour. Tagalik's face was shiny with sweat, and she mopped it wearily with the corner of a blanket. The midwives sat back on their heels, lit more cigarettes, and accepted tea. "A'a!" moaned Tagalik, clutching at the blanket. Oola and Pitsulala pushed again and one of them grunted, *"enoovok!"* He is born. The child was a boy. Oola bent to cut through the umbilical cord, then took the wailing baby and wrapped it in a white rabbit skin. Pitsulala parcelled the placenta and blood in the sealskin and held it while Tagalik rolled on the floor onto her side.

"*Ee . . . ee,*" chanted the women on the platform, still rocking. The tea attendant rushed out of the tupik and came back with Davidee and Ishawakta. Both men were grinning broadly.

"*Peoyook,*" said Davidee. He held out his hands for his son and Oola handed over the furry bundle. "*Ilnee,*" he laughed. "Nootoosha."

Ishawakta went to Dorothy. "Davidee's son. His name Nootoosha. *Peoyook.*" He thought, then shook his head over the problem of finding words to tell her something more. Later, she learned from Don that Nootoosha had been a fine hunter in the Lake Harbour area who had been killed the previous winter. The Inuit believed the spirits of great men lived on in their names.

Tagalik was now sitting comfortably, smiling a little, and sipping tea. She lit a cigarette. Davidee said nothing to his wife. He returned his son to the giggling Oola, took the sealskin parcel from Pitsulala, and went outside.

There was a blizzard a few nights later, and Dorothy lay awake in her bed listening nervously to the loud whoosh of wind down the chimney of the oil-fed space heater. She had no idea how the heater worked, and she worried the draft would blow the flame at the base of the heater into the livingroom. Next morning, the world was white and still. Eskimo children were tobogganing on sealskins and she ran to watch them. Hilda was there, too, and the women borrowed skins from the children and slid the hill together.

Hilda laughed, brushing snow from her ski pants. "You caught up yet, Dorothy?"

It seemed that she had. The ward was now empty of bed patients, and fewer Eskimos were waiting at the hospital door in the mornings. There was also evidence that the Inuit were at last preparing to leave for their winter camps. Several tents were down. She watched the women piling their possessions at the openings of the remaining *tupiks,* and was surprised at how sad she was to see them go. In a way, the departure was symbolic. The ships had gone. The flowers had gone. The sun was leaving. The Inuit were packing. She realized that soon, she would no longer be able to glimpse the lights from their tents in the darkness. The prospect of the Arctic isolation to come was chilling.

Hilda was saying she had arranged with Georgie to have some caribou-skin winter boots made when they heard a rattle of shots and the sound of men yelling near the beach. Don came running out of the Hudson's Bay post, carrying a rifle.

He pointed across the bay. "Beluga whale! At least a half dozen of them, I think. Killers chase them in."

The Inuit hurried excitedly from their tents, dumping whatever they were carrying, and ran to the shore. The compound suddenly seemed to be filled with laughing children. The sled dogs on the line howled and tugged impatiently at their chains.

"I suppose you could call it a gift from the gods," someone said at her shoulder. It was Gerry Heapy. "It's tough for the Inuit to go out and catch whales. Now, here they are like sitting ducks on their front doorstep."

It was difficult to see through the excited crowd, but it seemed that Ishawakta and Georgie were doing most of the shooting. The whales thrashed in their death agonies staining the bay water with blood. Georgie shouted and pointed, and a dozen Inuit raced for their boats, carrying ropes and metal gaffs. Five white bodies lay motionless in the water.

Dorothy stared silently at the scene. She had not seen a mass killing of animals before. She felt sickened, but the mood of the Inuit was infectious. She followed Hilda and Don to the mission house where a group of grinning Eskimos was hauling a whale into shore. Ishawakta was giving instructions, waving his .22 and laughing. Then he went to his boat, put away the rifle, and brought out a long hunting knife.

"He's not going to butcher the thing here!" she found herself saying aloud.

"Where else?" asked Don. "It's an instant picnic!"

Other Eskimos came running with knives and *ooloos*. They stood expectantly around the whale, giggling and making short, barking comments as Ishawakta sliced into the carcass.

"*Muktuk*," she heard the young Eskimo say as he handed some whaleskin to his wife, Leah. She accepted the morsel. Her eyes widened as she chewed at it. Ishawakta cut more and brought it to Dorothy. "Lutiapik," he said. "*Muktuk.*"

"It's a delicacy," Don told her. "You'll love it." The *muktuk* tasted like a rubber eraser.

By now, the Eskimos apparently felt it was time to cut their own portions of the animal. Women sat on the cold ground with their children, gripping pieces of the red meat in their teeth and slicing bite-size chunks with their *ooloos*. The whale carcass grew bloodier and bloodier. Ishawakta waded through the mess of slippery flesh, cutting pieces and handing them to those who asked for a fresh supply. Don cut a large slice with his knife, divided it and handed some to Hilda.

"Have some," Don said to Dorothy, spearing a dripping portion. She took it in her bare hands. The flesh, she noticed, was still warm. She bit into it and slowly chewed. It tasted better than the *muktuk*. The blood ran down her chin and she grinned. She was remembering her faint disgust when she had seen blind Adamee's bloody hands and face that evening at Mingeriak's camp just a few weeks ago.

Not long after the unexpected whale feast, the Eskimos moved out of Lake Harbour. The meat that was not eaten was packed into the boats and canoes and the entrails tossed to the hungry dogs on the line. The bones were simply shoved into the bay. Dorothy wondered whether any of the remains would be washed up on the islands where camp Eskimos had abandoned their dogs to forage for themselves during the summer. She stood near the porch of her house, watching the boatloads of laughing Inuit putter or sail down the fjord.

A day or so later, she wandered through the deserted area where the tents had been, recalling the nights she had gone there with her medical bag. She kicked at some bones and a forgotten tin spittoon, feeling an acute sense of loss. She was glad the Eskimos would be back in the settlement at Christmas.

One of the young dogs born on the Health and Welfare line that spring ran to greet her. She had named the handsome white animal King and, to Oola's crinkly-eyed amusement, had fed him well from the house stores. She knew she had the authority to keep King out of the *komatik* traces that winter but told herself it would set a bad precedent. Dogs, she already understood, were a part of the Arctic's delicate mosaic of survival. Besides, what would happen to an untrained dog after she left Lake Harbour? King would have to be broken early to the traces like all the others.

The animal leaped and yelped at her heels as she walked across the compound. There was a sudden snow flurry, and she shivered, annoyed that it was becoming too cold for hikes. That morning, the bay had been covered with a thin sheet of ice. The Eskimos must have known it was about to freeze. Hilda was waving from the Hudson's Bay post, and Dorothy walked down the path to join her.

"The *policikut* are having a party at the detachment tonight," her neighbour told her. They went into the kitchen where Hilda was making bread. Dorothy sat on a chair to watch. She had tried making her own bread, but the loaves had turned out to be as hard as bullets. "You want to go?" Hilda asked.

"Someone's birthday?"

"Who cares?" She kneaded into the bread. *Perhaps I don't have enough muscle,* Dorothy thought.

"Gerry tried to telephone you, but you were out. He asked me to tell you about it. I guess we'll leave here about seven. Don says we'll have to walk around the bay because of the ice."

"What do we wear?" She had long known that the clothes she had brought to the Arctic were a disaster. Her stockings were in shreds, and there were no nylons for sale at the Hudson's Bay store. Her red leather boots had long been discarded. She wondered how long her woolen sweaters and the dufflle-cloth parka would be effective against the penetrating wind. She supposed she would have to ask about a caribou-skin outfit. But what should she wear to a special party?

"I've got a couple of fancy dresses," Hilda said. "I'll wear sealskin boots for the hike and carry my heels in a bag."

'Well, I've never worn my blue silk with the crinoline," Dorothy said.

"Terrific," grinned Hilda. "Oh, and by the way. Do you know how to make beer?"

"Beer?"

"Gerry's looking around for a recipe. He and Terry want to make some in their washing machine. No? Oh well, I guess they'll just have to improvise."

She hated every foot of the two-mile walk around the bay to the RCMP detachment. The snow was soft and treacherous. Even with Don's powerful flashlight to show the way, the women continually stumbled over hidden rocks and crevices. Once, Dorothy dropped the bag with her shoes in a drift, and they rummaged around in the cold to find them. Besides the inevitable parka, she had pulled a heavy sweater and a cardigan over her dress. But the cold was numbing and her stockinged legs were frozen. Her Eskimo sealskin boots, she realized, were the most sensible items of clothing she owned.

Don tried to lighten the trip with some choruses from Newfoundland songs. When that failed, he assured the women that when the bay froze solid in a few weeks, they could walk across the ice to the detachment. They would have to wait until there was good, packed snow, of course. He told the tale of some Eskimos who had tried to walk down the bay one October when the ice had been blown clear of snow and was as slick was glass.

"A gale whooshed up," Don said, thumping his arms around his chest for warmth. "Four of the guys lashed themselves together but two others decided they could handle the problem. The last their buddies saw of them they were sailing down the fjord towards the open strait. They were never seen again as far as I know."

Hilda stumbled again and fell. "You got any more like that?" she groaned as they helped her to her feet.

Dorothy laughed. She could see the welcoming lights of the detachment, and besides, the aurora borealis was rippling in a great, curved sheet across the northern sky. She had yet to take the beauty of the aurora for granted. She stared, fascinated at the dancing waves of white light, tipped with blue and flamingo. Don and Hilda had glimpsed the RCMP lights as well; they were hurrying, their boots crunching and squeaking in the early winter snow.

"Canasta is for amateurs," said Gerry Heapy. Someone had cut his hair and he was wearing a tie. "I like bridge."

"Look," said Don. "Why don't we compromise? If we come to the detachment, we play bridge. If you come to the post or to Dorothy's house, we play canasta."

"What if we go to Mike's?" Hilda asked.

"We don't play anything," Gerry grumbled. "The Gardeners don't play cards."

"Well," said Don, reaching for the bottle of Scotch. "Here we go again for another jolly winter. There were some new paperbacks on the *Rupertsland*. I'm happy to announce we'll have something to read when we're tired of listening to static or the 'Northern Messenger'."

The "Northern Messenger" was a weekly radio service from Winnipeg beamed to isolated communities in the Arctic. Southerners could write to the station with communications for their friends or relatives, and the messages were read in alphabetical order. The transmission, if it came through, was late at night. It was agreed there would be a settlement check to make sure someone was always on duty to pick up the messages. Luckily, the surnames of the Lake Harbour whites started with letters that fell early in the alphabet. Bedtime could come right after the reading of the K's. Dorothy wrote her family about the Winnipeg service in a letter that had gone out on the *Howe*.

"It could be the only way I'll know what you're all doing down there during the winter," she had written a little wistfully. "There's the RCAF drop of parcels and mail at Christmas, of course. But the plane doesn't land, so we can't send mail from here. Then we can try to radio for a Hudson's Bay Beaver or a police Otter to come into the bay on skis if we have an emergency. I hope we don't. But at least it would mean mail."

Terry was dancing a tango with the kitchen mop. "We want to make some beer," he said, "in the washing machine."

"How about your laundry?" giggled Hilda. The young woman looked attractive in her green party dress; once again Dorothy was amazed at how effortlessly she had adapted to her new life in the Arctic. Perhaps Newfoundlanders were a special, pioneer breed. Don had once mentioned, in fact, that the Hudson's Bay Company recruited a sizeable percentage of its managers from Newfoundland.

Gerry said something under his breath, then sighed. "I had the foresight," he said, "to order some malt extract. It came on the *Rupertsland*. We're all set."

"Oh come on, fellers," laughed Don. "You need more than malt extract to make beer."

"Malt extract," said Gerry. "Sugar, water, baker's yeast, salt, and rolled oats."

"Ugh!" groaned Don. "How about hops?"

"Hops?"

"You need hops for beer. I'm pretty sure of that."

"I think you need hops," said Dorothy, from the depths of a chair.

"We're doing it without hops," said Gerry. "I guess you haven't got a washing machine, have you Dorothy?"

"No. Oola does the laundry in the bathtub."

"Then how about your bathtub?"

"How about it?" She was getting bored with the conversation about homemade beer. She was a little tipsy and was thinking of that long, awful walk back home around the bay. She supposed there would always be a walk home for someone after evening visits. No taxis. No streetcars. No room at the inn.

"It's late," she said, shucking her ridiculous high heels. The crinoline had been uncomfortable, and she suddenly hated the outfit she had so carefully packed for Arctic festivities. Tomorrow, she would try braiding her lengthening hair, tying it with rubber bands as Oola and Pitsulala did. She sadly noted that the big toe of her left foot had come through a hole in her stocking.

When the ice broke up in the wind and floated out of the bay, just about every man in Lake Harbour boarded the RCMP and Hudson's Bay peterheads to join the settlement's annual walrus hunt at Nottingham Island. Walrus was food for the sled dogs during the winter; it was stored in 100 pound chunks in an evil-smelling shed near the shore. Dorothy longed to go on the trip, but Gerry said it would take a week. She doubted that Health and Welfare would approve of her being away from the station for such a frivolous reason and for so long. She decided to stay at home with Marg and Hilda. Terry Jenkin was still on duty at the detachment, and Ishawakta had asked Mosesee, an old Eskimo who drifted in and out of the settlement, to help Oola with the household chores.

Marg came to her door the morning the two peterheads headed down the bay and accepted a cup of tea. "I thought you should know," said the missionary's wife. "I'm pregnant."

It was an unexpected announcement, and Dorothy showed her surprise. "Are you feeling all right?"

"I haven't been too well," admitted Marg. "But in any case, Mike thinks I should go out as soon as possible. I'll stay with some friends in Montreal."

"How will you go?" She felt a sudden pang of envy.

"Gerry Heapy's going to radio for the RCMP Otter. But it will be a few weeks before the plane can land on the bay." She laughed. "I hear there are a couple of aircraft that misjudged the ice and ended up at the bottom of the fjord. I'd say I'll be going about the middle of November."

"I'll miss you," said Dorothy. She meant it, even though she seemed to see less of the Gardeners than the other settlement whites.

Marg nodded. "I know what it was like for me when Bessie Parsons left. But you'll have Hilda to keep you company."

They talked about how Marg felt about bringing a child to live in Lake Harbour. The missionary's wife seemed placidly unconcerned. "The child will learn," she said. "Like we have learned. And it's better than the city. I'll bring you some fresh bread tomorrow."

Hilda delivered some cookies to the house that afternoon. "And incidentally," she said, as they sat down for some tea, "I'm pregnant."

"What?"

"I'm a bit surprised, I admit. I told Don last night. It's a company rule, though, that pregnant wives have to go south."

Dorothy swallowed some tea. She was beginning to loathe tea. She resolved to switch to coffee immediately. "Funny you told me about this today," she said. "Marg is pregnant, too."

"You're kidding!"

"Not at all. She's going out some time in November. Just as soon as the bay freezes hard enough for an Otter to ski in. When do you think you'll go?"

"Well, I don't see any reason why I can't stick around until Christmas."

Hilda was earthily matter-of-fact about her pregnancy and the fact that her baby would be brought back to the remoteness of Lake Harbour. Apparently the possibility of illness and the danger of radio blackouts in medical emergencies never occurred to her. *I wonder,* the thought flickered through Dorothy's mind, *if I could do the same thing. If I married Gerry and had a baby, that is.*

"The kid will have a ball up here," Hilda chatted on, munching at her own cookies. "Maybe I'll have two. Even three."

Dorothy felt lonely that evening. She brought out the correspondence course in English she had hoped would help pass the time usefully in the Arctic. She wished now that she had chosen something more straightforward, like physics. But she spread the books on the kitchen table and tried to concentrate. It was a relief when the settlement telephone clanged with the two rings that indicated the call was for her.

"Dorothy," she heard Terry Jenkin's voice over the wire. "We've had a bit of an accident at the detachment. Silasee was stacking some drums and hurt his finger."

"How badly?"

"Oh, pretty bad. As a matter of fact, the top's hanging off. It isn't bleeding much any more, though."

"Just a minute." She thought about it for a moment. It was difficult to assess the extent of the damage from Terry's report. But she thought she might be able to sew the finger together again.

"Terry?"

"Yeah?"

"Which finger is it?"

"Right index."

"Okay. Get a board and strap the hand to it," she said. "Make sure the finger is kept in place, then find a plastic bag and put it over the whole thing. We don't want to lose that bit of finger."

"You going to fix it on again?"

"We'll see. Can you use your boat?"

"Sure. There's no ice tonight. We'll buzz right over."

"Meet me at the hospital."

She shrugged into her parka and hurried to the Quonset hut. By the time Terry and a dazed-looking Silasee arrived, she was removing sterilized instruments from the hospital autoclave and unpacking a sterile gown, a mask, and surgical gloves. She noticed with annoyance that there was only heavy catgut and a large surgical needle in supplies. Apart from the time she had treated the Eskimo child's torn scalp, she had sutured a wound only once before. But she knew that for the delicate work she was about to do, she needed the finest needle and silk thread. She asked Terry to remove Silasee's shirt and get him on the examination table. Then she set up an armboard and looked closely at the finger.

The cut was just below the nail; there was a mere scrap of skin holding the tip to the rest of the finger. The simplest thing to do would be to take it off completely, stitch the stump, then give the Eskimo a five-day shot of penicillin. She thought about it, then decided. "Let's try putting it back on."

Terry was pale. "You want me to stay?"

"Of course. I want you to give the anaesthetic."

"Look," he said. "I've never done anything like this before. You sure I won't be in the way?"

"Terry," said Dorothy, "I can't give anaesthetic and stitch at the same time. Would you please sit on that kick-stool and drop the anaesthetic into this mask? I'll tell you how to regulate the stuff as we go along."

She washed Silasee's arm and hand with warm, soapy water, sluiced it with alcohol then painted it with antiseptic. The Eskimo lay quietly. She smiled encouragingly at him and nodded. "*Peoyook!*" He flinched a little in surprise when she put drops of castor oil into his eyes to protect them from the ether. Then she brought a small can of anaesthetic from her supply cupboard.

"This is yours," she told Terry, opening it. "Now I'll get into a gown and gloves. Okay?"

"Okay," said Terry. He watched her nervously. "When do I start dropping?"

She snapped on the gloves. "Now."

She bent her head to concentrate on the finger. The heavy needle and catgut were awkward, even damaging. She wanted to confine the wound to a small area, but the oversize needle demanded plenty of work space. Then the nail got maddeningly in the way. When Silasee stirred, she told Terry to start administering more anaesthetic.

"You okay?" she said.

There was silence, then a thud. She looked up and saw he had gone. She crouched to look under the table. Terry was lying, unconscious, on the floor.

"Oh my God," she groaned. Then she stepped quickly over

the officer's body to reach the drug cabinet. She would have to give Silasee a shot of morphine. She was pulling on a fresh pair of surgical gloves when Terry's head appeared over the edge of the table.

"I'm sorry," he mumbled. "I couldn't help it. It must have been the anaesthetic."

"Sure," nodded Dorothy. "Why don't you get some air?"

"How about Silasee?"

"Silasee's fine." She was glad she had almost finished the awkward stitching. The young constable stood at the Quonset hut door, retching miserably. He came inside again and sat on a bed in the ward as she splinted and bandaged the Eskimo's finger and gave him a shot of antibiotics.

"You think it will work?"

"I'm not sure," she admitted. "We'll know in a few weeks."

Silasee was sitting up now, his legs dangling over the side of the table. He stared curiously at his hand, noting the length of the damaged finger. *"Peoyook!"* he said. *"Enooleeva!"* All cured. His face creased into a happy smile. He looked through the door at Terry sitting on the hospital bed. *"Anneayoo?"*

"Yeah," Terry grinned. "Sick." Then they all broke into help-less laughter.

When Don came back from the walrus hunt, she asked him about having a caribou-skin outfit made in case she needed to move out of the settlement in winter. Caribou, she had been assured, was the warmest skin to wear in the Arctic. The hair of the northern deer was hollow and the air inside acted as superb insulation. She had already looked at a suit that hung limply in the small storage shed behind her house and decided it was too big and too ugly for her to wear. She confessed this to Don and he laughed. "The suit's probably haunted, anyway. It belonged to a nurse who was here about eight years ago. She was killed."

"Oh come on."

"It's true. I don't know all the details, but it happened right at the end of her tour of duty. She was reaching up to get her trunk and it fell on her head. The body was found by Mingeriak. The whole thing scared the living daylights out of him. He probably

114

thought the *kabloonahs* might figure he had something to do with it. Anyway, the *aniatitsiyuk's* body was packed in ice and moss and taken out on the next ship. The suit should have been junked a long time ago. I'll tell Oola to see about your clothes."

She was still thinking about the unknown nurse when the tiny Eskimo woman arrived next morning with Don behind her. God, the nurse had survived the Arctic for an entire year; then had died from an accident that could have happened right in Toronto. She recalled with amusement that her family was actually worrying she would freeze to death or be mauled by a polar bear.

"It could easily happen," Don said when she told him about her family's fears, "but let's get you a winter suit." He talked to Oola in Eskimo, and the woman stood, staring gravely. Then she collapsed into giggles and produced a piece of string to measure Dorothy's arms and legs. A small knot was tied to mark the correct length, then Oola stood waiting for further instructions. Don explained the suit would consist of pants, thigh-length boots and two parkas. The inner parka would be made with the hair turned inwards. The hair would be on the outside of the outer garment.

"How about extras? Pockets, trimming and that kind of stuff?"

Pockets were a brilliant idea. Worried about how to carry liquid drugs in sub-zero temperatures, she had figured she might pack them in a pocket next to her body. Oola was told to provide a pocket. Hood trimming? She thought about it. Blue fox? Wolverine? Something terribly exotic and expensive?

"Who pays for all of this?" she asked.

"Health and Welfare. You give me a chit and Oola gets credit at the store."

"What's the cheapest kind of trimming?"

Don shrugged. "Rabbit, I guess."

Good Lord, when would she get out of the old habit of fretting about thrift? "I'll take rabbit."

Just before Halloween, the sack of potatoes that had come on the *Rupertsland* began to stink on the porch. When she dug into them, she found they had frozen and rotted. No one had told her that potatoes rotted in the extreme cold. She felt sick. She had rationed potatoes because she knew the sack would have to last until next year's supplies were delivered. Now, that was the end of french fries and mash unless she begged some potatoes from a neighbour. When Ishawakta came to the house, she told him to take the malodorous sack over to the dog line.

She sat at the livingroom window sipping coffee and munching at a hard pilot biscuit spread with butter. The outdoor thermometer registered fifteen degrees below zero. At ten o'clock in the morning, it was finally light enough to see across the compound. The bay ice was thickening, but it was treacherous in the strait. Snow was still too soft for *komatik* travelling. No wonder October was known as the loneliest month in the Arctic. She wondered what on earth she could do to keep herself busy that day. Last night, she sorted out her canned goods in the attic, meticulously arranging the tins of vegetables in alphabetical order. The radio still refused to work, and she was tired of her record albums. There had been no patients since Silasee's accident.

Social life had been at a minimum, but she was beginning to learn about spacing telephone calls and visits to her few white neighbours, anyway. It would be better to save this week's evening with the Bairds until Thursday, then ask the Gardeners if they would come to dinner on Saturday. That way, there would be something to talk about if she called Hilda on the telephone that afternoon. Because of the dangerous ice conditions, the police had isolated themselves on their side of the bay. She would call the detachment tomorrow for news.

She went into the kitchen for another cup of coffee. When she returned, she saw that snow was falling again. A wind howled up the fjord, and the houses of Lake Harbour disappeared in the sudden white-out. Twice now, she had found herself lost in the blinding snow as she walked between the Quonset hut and the house. Instinctively, she had huddled on the path with her scarf wrapped around her mouth and nose, waiting for the gale to subside.

Now, she stared glumly at the window. There was nothing,

really, to see. It was as though a sheet had been hung over the pane. She would have liked to go back to bed, but somehow, it felt wrong to be paid for a day's work and not do a thing. Perhaps it would be useful to arrange her other supplies in alphabetical order, like the canned vegetables. Arrowroot biscuits. Bacon. Butter. She was thinking about going to the attic to do the job when Ishawakta came through the door, beating the snow from his parka. He grinned at her before going to check the heater. God, how she wished they could understand each other better.

"Lutiapik," he said, straightening his back after a few moments. "Pootoogook at house. Walk far."

A patient? Why had he waited to tell her? *"Anneayoo?"*

Ishawakta shook his head. *"Agai.* Wife *anneayoo.* At camp."

"I want to see him," she said, and pointed. She dressed in her slacks and parka and Ishawakta led her through the blowing snow to his house. Pootoogook was sitting patiently in a chair. He was probably in his mid-twenties, so she guessed his wife must also be young. When he looked up at her, she tried once again to read expression in the eyes of an Eskimo, but failed.

She turned to Ishawakta. She wanted to know when Pootoogook's wife had become sick, but it was a complicated question and neither of them knew the right words. The only way of getting the information was to ask Mike or Don to help. She glanced out of the window. The wind had eased but it was still snowing hard. "Ishawakta," she said, "get *iliniatitsiyuk.*" The mission was closer than the Hudson's Bay post.

She sat silently, waiting for Mike to arrive. Leah came from the bedroom, her body swollen with Ishawakta's child. The woman sat on another chair, sewing a pair of duffle-cloth socks. She ignored both Dorothy and Pootoogook. Once, the Eskimo man passed his hand tiredly over his head. But he said nothing.

Mike came puffing through the door with Ishawakta. He pulled off his parka and hung it on a rack, then adjusted his glasses. "That's bad snow out there," he said. "Ishawakta was a bit vague about all of this. What do you want to know?"

"The man's name is Pootoogook, Mike," she said. "His wife is sick, back at the camp. I'd like to know about her symptoms and when she became ill."

Mike nodded. He spoke in slow Eskimo and the man nodded and replied.

The missionary sighed and folded his arms. "Well, his wife had a baby about two weeks ago. Then, she became very sick. Very hot, pains in her stomach. Pootoogook says she seems to be half-asleep."

Fever, she thought. *Semi-conscious.* She wondered about discharge from the vagina and realized that Mike would not like asking the question. "Ask," she said, "whether there's anything coming away from the place where the baby came from."

Mike cleared his throat. There were some short sentences then he nodded. "Apparently so. And the man says it smells very bad."

Puerperal sepsis. She had seen it in hospital. A shot of penicillin would cure it overnight. Without the antibiotic the woman would almost certainly die.

"Mike," she said, "it's puerperal sepsis. I've got to get to the camp."

"How? What about the snow and ice conditions? The *komatiks* are useless."

"Can't we walk?"

Mike shook his head. "Take a look at the snow. You'd never make it."

There was silence in the little room. The wind suddenly rattled the windows. Leah's head bent over her sewing. Pootoogook said a few words, then Ishawakta answered.

"What did they say, Mike?"

"Pootoogook said the walk from his camp was very bad. He said there is too much snow to go back now. It's too deep for walking, so he will stay here in the settlement until the storm is over. Ishawakta simply said yes."

Dorothy looked at Pootoogook. The man turned his head and stared back at her. Now there was a flicker of expression in his eyes. *Ayonamut.* It can't be helped.

7

Don and Hilda tried to comfort her about Pootoogook's wife, but she brooded over the tragedy. "I could have *tried* to walk," she argued. "Pootoogook should have tried."

"Dorothy," said Don, his dark eyes serious, "I don't know how that Eskimo made it to Lake Harbour in the first place. And there's no way anyone is going anywhere now until the sea-ice is safe. Or until the snow is packed well enough for the dogs and *komatiks* to travel. No, don't worry about the baby. Women in the camp will take care of it."

She distracted herself by struggling into her stiff new caribou-skin suit and standing like an uncomfortable penguin in front of her bedroom mirror. One day, she brought out her skis and tried some runs down the hill behind her house, but it was far too cold for skiing. She shoved the equipment into a corner of her storage shed. It would be the only time she would use the skis in the Arctic.

She wrote letters to send out with Marg and dutifully composed her monthly report to Health and Welfare, telling about Silasee's finger. She asked Mike if he had heard news of Pootoogook but there was none. She reported what she knew of the story, anyway. She rearranged her groceries in the attic, threw bits of driftwood for King to fetch. She read until her eyes ached. She went to watch the Inuit cut the shallow drinking-water lake into frozen blocks and fled with King when the Eskimos shouted loudly and waved them away. Afterwards,

119

she realized they had been worried the animal would urinate on their precious winter's water supply.

She tagged along behind Don and Mike when they announced they were going to make a freezer where everyone in the settlement could cache fresh meat. She thought it was a brilliant idea. She was already beginning to hoard food traded by the Eskimos for oranges and butter; her cranky refrigerator was stuffed with fish, seal liver, and skinned ptarmigan. The freezer was dug with picks through the permafrost at the side of a hill, then food was transferred from the kerosene refrigerators to the cache. She laughed, remembering the old joke about selling freezers to the Eskimos. Never in her life had she been so aware of the difference between fresh and canned food.

She handed over her sack of fish and meat to Don and watched him store it away in the dark hole. Marg came running from the mission kitchen with an armload of parcels, and Hilda contributed some meat and poultry that had come on the *Rupertsland.* A wooden door was fixed over the opening to keep out the dogs. The men spread packing straw from the Hudson's Bay store around the hole for insulation. Just a few months before, she had been shopping for perfume and sweaters in Montreal. Now, she would give a month's salary for a fresh loin of pork.

She tried shooting ptarmigan with a rifle borrowed from the store, but even though the birds obligingly sat just a few feet away, she missed by yards. She heard howls of laughter from across the compound and saw that Georgie and Ishawakta had been watching her. Well, at least she knew one way of amusing the Eskimos. She tried taking pictures of her house and her laundry, hung by Oola to freeze stiffly on the line, but her fingers froze to the metal of the camera. When she put on her thick mittens, she fumbled ineptly with the shutter release.

Don picked up some news on the radio that a Russian space satellite called Sputnik was circling the earth, but Dorothy was more excited about the "Northern Messenger" broadcast from Winnipeg. Afterwards, as she got into bed, she was amazed at how fascinated she had been in the monotonous litany of birthday greetings, wedding announcements, and cryptic messages from the South. When the K's finally came around, she had held her breath, as though she were about to be told something terribly momentous. The fading voice assured her that everyone in the Knight family was well.

She longed for a patient, but no one came to her door. The gales, snow, and white-outs made it difficult and dangerous for her to travel the short distance between the house and the Quonset hut, so she moved medical supplies to her home and reluctantly closed the hospital. She decided that if a patient needed hospitalization, she would use her small diningroom as a temporary ward.

On the way home from Marg's farewell party at the mission, she got caught in a white-out with winds gusting to 100 miles an hour. She played canasta at the Bairds, and the policemen ventured across the bay-ice one night for bridge at the Hudson's Bay post. She made more lumpy bread. She studied the section on immunization in the medical manual and wished again that Ottawa had given her clearer instructions about what to do about follow-ups. She watched Ishawakta dump a block of crystal ice into a five-gallon drum beside her stove, waiting impatiently for it to melt so she could drink some of the water.

She re-arranged her groceries. She waddled outside in her caribou-skin suit and boots and fell down. It took some time to get up again. She lay in bed at night listening to the pistol cracks of the bay ice and the grinding of blocks breaking and shifting along the shore as the tide changed. She stood on the frozen surface of the bay, watching Marg Gardener climb into the RCMP Otter, then waved with all the others until the aircraft disappeared over the white hills.

She greedily read the mail the pilot had brought in. There were letters from Waverley Road and two from nursing friends. Apparently, Queen Elizabeth and Prince Philip had been in Ottawa, and Lester Pearson had been awarded the Nobel Prize for Peace. She was surprised to discover how remote such news seemed to her now. There was no communication from Health and Welfare, not even a nursing journal. No junk mail because she had asked her family not to bother forwarding it. No magazines or newspapers because she had forgotten to subscribe. After reading her letters again, she put them away carefully so she could re-read them another time. A wind roared down the chimney of her space heater, and again she worried about the possibility of fire. She went to the attic to choose something for dinner. "S" for stew. She had no trouble in locating it right away.

Gerry Heapy called to say it was about time for Dorothy and the Bairds to come to the detachment for cards and a sampling of washing-machine beer. The excursion was arranged for a clear, late-November evening. This time, the women left their party dresses at home and wore slacks, parkas and their new caribou-skin boots. Dorothy spent all afternoon curling and combing her hair, even though she knew her parka hood would wreck the effect. She stared into her mirror, dusting her nose with powder and applying the only cosmetic that made any real sense in the Arctic – lipstick. It saved her lips from cracking and chapping in the cold. She had not bothered to use perfume in weeks, but now she found a bottle in a drawer and dabbed some behind her ears.

It was a rough walk through the slabs of ice thrown in untidy heaps against the beach. Dorothy mistrusted the barrier-ice. At this time of the year, it was still loose enough to shift in the tide. But unless it was negotiated, there was that long, chilling walk around the Heel. This way, the trip to the detachment took less than half an hour. They were singing cheerfully as they climbed among the hummocks and lumps of sea-ice on the *policikut* side of the bay. On their arrival, the staked-out RCMP dogs howled, and Silasee came running out of the little jail that was his home.

"*Peanilksa!*" he shouted, grinning and waving his hand.

"He says his finger is better," said Don. "What did you think when you looked at it the last time?"

She had been pleased and proud of her work. The bone had knitted and the flesh had healed cleanly. She stood on the beach, scrubbing the frost from her eyelashes. "I wouldn't be surprised if it turns out to be as good as new!"

"*Ee. Peoyook,*" chuckled Silasee, running ahead of them to open the door of the warm little house.

The homemade beer looked and tasted like laundry water and Dorothy said so, admitting with a laugh that she had never really subjected her tastebuds to anything as odd as laundry water. "Maybe you got the recipe wrong," she said to Gerry. "Are you sure it mentioned rolled oats?"

"Never had a recipe," the big constable replied. He tossed his cards on the kitchen table and poured himself another mug of the cloudy brew. "I just remembered how a friend of mine used to make it in Saskatchewan."

"I still think you need hops," she said, a little tentatively. She hoped she had not offended Gerry with her remark about the laundry water. She took another sip of the beer.

"Well, it's got a kick, anyway," said Don. "I'll have some more, if you don't mind."

"Don," Hilda said firmly after several more drinks were poured, "we should go home."

"Sure. Hey, Gerry. You gonna make some more of this stuff at Christmas?"

"Don't see why not," Gerry answered. He glanced quickly at Dorothy. "Well, maybe we'll just get Annie to do the laundry and pour some of that. Some people don't even know the difference, anyway." She *had* offended him. The thought flickered uneasily through her mind that tension seemed to be building between her and the constable, but she quickly ignored it.

Terry Jenkin drank more beer and began to sing tunelessly. Soon, she thought, the round-faced young constable would be doing that dance with the mop.

"Don," Hilda said again.

They were giggling happily as they found their way down the beach, switched on their flashlights, and started through the barrier ice.

"I guess it did taste a bit like laundry water," said Don as they emerged from the jungle of hummocks and on to the smooth, snow-covered bay. "But it sure had a kick!"

They walked silently for a while. The RCMP thermometer registered thirty degrees below zero, but there was no wind, and the stars were shining like ice chips. The world was white, vast, and empty, and the crisp air was delicately scented with sea-salt.

Except for the sudden cracks of ice under pressure and the crunch of their boots in the snow, there was silence. The barrier on the other side of the bay loomed into view. They scrambled around the first slab of ice, then a second.

"Almost home!" laughed Don. "So how about a – " Then he disappeared.

"Don!" screamed Hilda.

Dorothy stared, horrified. Don's powerful flashlight was on the ice where he had dropped it; she picked it up and shone the beam downwards. There was a deep crevasse at their feet. She could see Don hanging a few feet below the edge, his elbows hooked to an ice shelf. He looked up at her, speechless with fear.

"Don!" Hilda screamed again. "Oh, for God's sake!"

Dorothy crouched beside the ice fissure. Don was beginning to inch upwards, but he was finding it difficult to get a toehold. She groaned. If he could bring his elbows over the edge of the crevasse, she knew he could pull himself out by his shoulders. Hilda was weeping, then screaming again. She fell on her knees beside the hole and started to reach downwards. Dorothy wordlessly grabbed her by the shoulders and forced her back.

"Don!" Hilda screamed again and fought to get away.

Dorothy hesitated for a moment then slapped the hysterical young woman hard across the face.

"Hilda," she said evenly. "He's all right. He hasn't gone through to the water. He's *all right*, Hilda."

Hilda stopped screaming and stood, sniffing a little and shivering. "We've got to help him," she said faintly.

"Look," said Dorothy, "I don't think either of us can. The ice is so slippery, the three of us could go in. He's managing all right. We might make it even worse for him if we try to do anything."

Hilda stood, looking at the crevasse. "Don?"

"Yeah?"

"You okay, Don?"

"Yeah."

"You making it, Don? You want me to stay back?"

"Yeah. Stay back, Hilda."

The two women stood, watching. The flashlights were on the

ice, their beams aimed at the ice fissure. Nothing happened for what seemed to be an endless stretch of time. Then, Don's head and shoulders were over the edge, and with a heave, he pulled his body free. He lay on his stomach, breathing hard.

Then he was up on his feet, hugging Hilda, asking if she was all right and whether the shock would do anything to the baby. Hilda was crying again. Dorothy collected her light. Her teeth were chattering with cold and fright; for an instant, she thought she was going to break into tears as well. She pointed the flashlight at the tangle of hummocks and ice slabs they still had to negotiate before reaching the beach.

"Let's go home," she said, starting to walk. There seemed to be nothing else to say.

A blizzard began blowing next morning. For three days Lake Harbour was besieged by the driving snow. Oola and Ishawakta managed to struggle to the house to keep her stove and heater working, but for the rest of the time she was alone. The settlement telephone never rang, so on the second day of the storm she began to worry and tried calling Mike Gardener and the Bairds. The line was dead. There had been breakdowns before, but this time she panicked a little and thumped at the telephone, hoping to bring it alive.

The radio was useless as usual, but at least a twist of the dial gave her something to do. She re-read her letters, trying to imagine what it would be like in Toronto at that moment. The Christmas windows would be on display in the city and on Waverley Road, the last of the fall leaves would have been burned. She stood, looking at the white-out, listening to the moan of the gale, and gritting her teeth to stop herself from crying out. But why? There was no one to hear her. She wandered aimlessly into the kitchen.

"I'm . . . lonely!" she said aloud. It was incredible. She had never thought the luxury of privacy would deteriorate into anything as dreadful as this. "Oh my God, I'm lonely."

She sat on the edge of a kitchen chair, rocking a little and staring at the ugly, scuffed linoleum. "I don't think I can stand it!

I've got to get out of here!" She examined her hands. Why was she looking so carefully at her hands? "I'll . . . go . . . crazy," she said loudly. "I'll go crazy if I can't get out!"

She forced herself to eat. She forced herself to wash. She forced herself to read. She found no comfort in the prayers from her Daily Missal, so she read the stories about St. Augustine, St. Louis, and St. Giles. When Oola or Ishawakta stumbled through the door from the storm, she followed them as they went about their tasks, chattering eagerly about the weather, the stove, the safety of the heater. In English and pidgin Eskimo she asked eager questions about how everyone was managing in the settlement.

Oola giggled and said *"ee . . . ee"* to everything. Ishawakta managed to make her understand that the snow was bad, but that it would be good for the *komatiks*. As soon as it cleared, he would take the dogs and go hunting inland for caribou.

"Tuktu good *nilkee.* Good meat for trail," he said as he checked the oil in the space heater.

She leaned forward in her chair when he mentioned the trail. How could she tell him she wanted to go with the sled to make rounds of the camps? "Lutiapik go soon on trail?" she asked carefully. "With *komatik*?"

Ishawakta nodded. *"Ee.* Soon." Then he left her alone again.

But the trail was something to think about. After that awful night with Hilda and Don on the barrier-ice, she had avoided thoughts about travelling in the Arctic winter. Now, she sat in the livingroom, imagining herself packing her medical bag and grub box and visiting the snowbound camps of the Inuit. She pondered. Health and Welfare had given her no instructions about leaving the post and making rounds. But then, she had received no orders about anything at all. She laughed to herself about that. No orders. No instructions. "Nurses do not, repeat, do not make independent decisions," she remembered Miss Beamish saying in Sarnia.

"Yes, Miss Beamish," she said aloud. "No, Miss Beamish." She repeated the words cheerfully, over and over again, as she set about preparing her first real meal since the blizzard began.

126

Her white neighbours in Lake Harbour did not refer to the savage November storm or complain that they had suffered claustrophobia similar to hers during the locked-in days and nights. She was curious to know, but there seemed to be no point in discussing something that could not be avoided. When she met Don in the compound the day the sky cleared, his talk was about repairs to the damaged telephone line and the good five feet of packed snow under their feet.

They stood together, their faces framed by the fur of their parka hoods. Breath spiralled in the clear air. "Now we can batten down the hatches," he said.

Now, the Eskimos could cut snowblocks to pile, igloo-fashion, around the buildings for extra winter protection. Now the dogs and *komatiks* could be used for hunting. Now the Inuit could set their traplines so there would be skins to trade at Christmas and during the summer. Ishawakta and Georgie brought the Health and Welfare and Hudson's Bay sleds out of storage, replaced broken cross-bars, and lashed them with flexible, walrus-hide thongs. The men upended the twenty-foot *komatiks* and spread a thick coating of mud over the wooden runners. She had seen the box of peat in a corner of Ishawakta's house, saved carefully since summer. The mud froze quickly in the forty-below air; the two Eskimos tested the surface for toughness, then brought planes to smooth it down.

"You can use porridge instead of mud," said Don. "We always take rolled oats along with us on trips. To eat, of course, but we can use it if the mud knocks off."

"I'll remember that," she said.

"You going somewhere?"

"I thought I'd visit a camp when Ishawakta gets back from his caribou hunt," Dorothy told him.

Don took a long drag of his cigarette. "Well, the Eskimos come into the settlement if they need help, you know. Or to fetch you in an emergency."

"Didn't Bessie Parsons go on rounds?"

"No, she never did. Bill, her husband, was a lay dispenser. He went out every now and then."

They stood, quietly smoking. "I want to go, Don," she said after a minute. "I need to know how to travel in winter if it's ever necessary. And I should be immunizing new babies and giving DPT follow-up shots. Besides, it's something to do."

The Eskimo men were icing the *komatik* runners for smooth sledding. Ishawakta had melted snow on a primus stove. He took some of the water in his mouth and sprayed it over the hard mud, slicking it down with a pad of polar bear skin. He repeated the spraying until the ice gleamed, half an inch thick. Once again, Dorothy noted that neither Ishawakta nor Georgie seemed to need gloves in the intense cold. She wore three bulky sweaters under her parka, as well as duffle-cloth socks, caribou-skin boots, and two pairs of mittens. The Eskimos stood laughing and admiring their work.

"You could get to Utye's without too much trouble," Don was saying. "It's not too far down the coast, and you could stay in camp overnight with the family. You'll enjoy it. Utye's is the Waldorf Astoria of Baffin Island. Very luxurious indeed." He thought again. "Would you be planning to take any longer trips?"

"I suppose so. Any reason why not?"

"Well, you'd have to sleep on the trail in snowhouses some of the time."

"That's okay. I'd like that. I've never slept in a snowhouse."

Don seemed embarrassed. "We could get Noota to go with you and Ishawakta."

"Noota?"

"Old Mosesee's daughter. She never got married and about the only thing she does well is play the accordion. But she'd make a good enough chaperone, I guess."

Dorothy was startled. "Oh come on, Don!"

"No, really. If I remember right, Health and Welfare can get pretty sticky about trips. You're supposed to have a female companion along."

There was a note of harshness in her laugh. "Health and Welfare doesn't seem to get sticky about anything as far as I'm concerned."

Her annoyance about Don's reference to a chaperone

lingered for a time, but then she was amused. The men in the settlement, including Gerry, must have been discussing her unmarried status, how it might affect the way she moved among the Inuit. Funny, the question had never crossed her mind. She smiled a little, remembering the way Ishawakta had stood by her bed during the epidemic and the unselfconscious way he had removed his clothes that night in Mingeriak's camp. To the young Eskimo, she was sure, she was very much the *kabloonah aniatitsiyuk*. The things she had been sent to the Arctic to do were not among the qualities Eskimos admired in women. She couldn't sew. She couldn't chew boots. She couldn't scrape skins. She couldn't even light a coal stove or a primus. To "laugh" with a useless female was probably as ridiculous an idea to the Inuit as making love to a stone *insuksuk* cairn.

She sat in the livingroom, looking at the reflection of the porch light on the deep, packed snow. The incident explained more about the special rules of living in a small community like Lake Harbour. There was a sense of family in the settlement, but she had become aware of the need for individual privacy and the almost puritanical compulsion to do the right thing. It was probably the only way the isolated whites could preserve the slim thread that linked them to the structured life of the outside world.

She wondered about Gerry Heapy's contribution to discussions concerning her moral welfare. Then she told herself she would have to stop thinking about Gerry. He was attractive, but she knew that the kind of flirtation that was normal in Toronto could lead to disastrous complications within the tiny group. Besides, she sighed, there had been little indication that Gerry was interested in her romantically. She got to her feet and wandered, without interest, into the kitchen to see about dinner.

By the time Ishawakta returned from his caribou hunt, she had forgotten Don's conversation about Noota and was already assembling her medical kit and food for the trip to Utye's camp. Don's reminiscences about his own *komatik* experiences in the North had taught her how to prepare a portable stew for the trail. One afternoon, she had put a large pot on the stove and emptied the contents of a dozen cans into it – meat, beans, vegetables, soup, tomatoes. Then she filled some pie plates with the mixture and put them on the front porch to freeze. The concrete stew looked so appetizing, she melted one of the rounds for supper. She knocked the others into a sack and stored them in the shed.

She filled an entire evening checking her medical kit. The supplies had seemed adequate at Mingeriak's camp, but she added liquid DPT vaccine to her list, opthalmic ointments, and fresh supplies of cod liver oil. She found a small enamel pot and strainer, which she could use for sterilizing needles and instruments. Then she put the dental forceps and some anaesthetic into her black bag. Soon, she knew, she would be asked to pull her first tooth.

Ishawakta had shot three caribou near Mingo Lake. As he had when he had killed the white whales, he seemed delighted when Georgie and Akavak came to his house and hacked off pieces of the animals for their own use. There was a great deal of laughing and talking while the men stood around the carcasses slicing off meat and tossing it into sacks or eating it on the spot. Akavak cut out the stomach of one deer which, she had heard, was a delicacy among the Inuit.

"Lutiapik," her young Eskimo helper nodded when she crossed the compound. The other men grinned, chewing hungrily at the raw caribou meat.

"Ishawakta," she said, "we go to Utye's camp? Okay?"

The Eskimo carved at a haunch, then said something to Georgie.

Georgie turned to her, his eyes shielded by his glasses, even though the sun had gone. "Ishawakta says he will take you to Utye's camp after one sleep." He grinned. "The weather is good now."

"Utye's," laughed Akavak, *"Peoyook."*

"Utye's is very good camp," said Georgie. "You like."

She stared at the fresh meat. She wanted badly to ask for a steak to cook, but she knew the Eskimos' food supply did not arrive conveniently on the *Rupertsland* or the *Howe.* Perhaps

Ishawakta might eventually offer some for barter. She walked away, thinking wistfully of the well-stocked meat markets in Toronto. She decided to go to the hill freezer and fetch some fish for her evening meal.

It took her almost an hour to dress for the *komatik* trip to Utye's She felt she should wear a bra, even though common sense told her it was probably unnecessary. Then she pulled on a shirt, three sweaters, a pair of slacks, heavy woollen socks, and a pair made of duffel-cloth. She laughed as she glimpsed herself in the bedroom mirror. She was already beginning to look twice her 98 pound size. Oola had brought her caribou-skin suit and boots from the cold shed, and she began climbing into the stiff suit. *No wonder everyone tries to avoid wearing these things until it's absolutely necessary,* she thought. She envied old Mosesee, whose skins were so old and bald, they were as soft as kid. But then, they were probably little protection against the biting Arctic wind.

She climbed into the skin pants, tying them with a loose thong at the waist. Then there were the oversocks and the tall boots. The inner parka was difficult enough to work over her head, but then she had to wrestle with the outer piece of clothing. Where was the drug pocket? She heaved exploratively at the parka, lost her balance, and fell to the floor. She lay there for a moment like an overturned turtle. This was going to take some time. She sat up, reached awkwardly over her head and grabbed at the fur-trimmed hood until she had hauled herself free. The pocket, she discovered, had been sewn into the front of the inner parka. She packed it with her supply of liquid vaccines then struggled to get into the outer garment all over again.

She panted at the effort, shuddering when she reminded herself she would have to get out of the suit that night and into it again in some Eskimo dwelling the next morning. As an afterthought, she brought a braided woollen belt from the bedroom and pulled it around her waist until she looked like a large parcel. It would take half the winter for her to discover that because air was an insulator she would be warmer with loose clothing. Her sleeping bag, food box, and medical bag were already in the livingroom so she dragged on her double set of mittens and went out into the dark, frigid morning.

Ishawakta, dressed in ordinary pants and a drill parka, had harnessed the nine Health and Welfare dogs into their walrus-hide traces. The animals were flopped in the snow waiting to be fan-hitched to the *komatik*. King, she saw, was among them. The white dog got to its feet when she came out of the house, but she turned the other way. The animal sat down again, his tongue rolling from his mouth.

"*Eekee!*" she said, beating her skin mittens together. It was a newly-acquired word she knew she would use often. Cold.

"*Ee!*" grinned Ishawakta. He stifled a laugh. "*Eekee!*" She wondered whether the lightly clad Eskimo understood what *eekee* meant at all.

He went into the house and came out with her luggage. The *komatik* was being carefully balanced with boxes, gunnysacks, and skins. Everything fitted together like a gigantic set of building blocks. The front box contained lamps and primus stoves, and it was equipped with a metal handle she later learned was for steering. Her grub box was anchored at the back along with sacks of walrus meat for the dogs. The sleeping bags stowed away, Ishawakta covered the load with caribou skins and a polar bear pelt and lashed it down with thongs.

"*Nanook,*" he said. "*Peoyook.*" He pointed, indicating that the place on top of the bear skin was for her.

She stared at the tall *komatik*. "Now? Do we go now?" It was interesting that no one had appeared from the other houses to wish her good-bye. Maybe all of the *kabloonahs* were becoming like the Eskimos. The Inuit never said good-bye.

Ishawakta laughed as she hesitated, "*Kingmil* go . . . whoosh!" He pointed at the sled, then spread his hands. Apparently she could either sit on the *komatik* or run alongside. She looked down at the rough tangle of the barrier-ice and shivered. It was frightening enough to walk through the slabs and hummocks, but could she ride through them, perched on top of a loaded sled? Ishawakta lodged the butt of his long whip beside the front box before picking up the dangling traces. The dogs yelped and scrambled expectantly to their feet.

"I walk through ice," she said, acting out the words. "Meet you on the other side."

She padded down to the beach. Her breath had already frosted both her eyelashes and the rabbit fur around her hood. She was almost through the barrier ice when she heard Ishawakta's shout. *"Hoit! Hoit!"* She slithered quickly around the last obstacles and turned to look.

No wonder *komatiks* were held together with thongs rather than nails. The dogs were sprinting wildly through the corrugated barrier-ice and the sled bumped, thudded, and crashed from hummock to hummock. Ishawakta ran beside the sled, pushing hard to keep it from overturning. The dogs had troubles of their own. When the team slacked off for an instant, two of the animals were dragged, yowling, on their backs when the loose harness caught on the jutting slabs. The walrus hide stretched like elastic. The dogs howled and scrambled to regain a foothold until the traces broke free. Nothing, though, seemed to slow the mad progress of the *komatik*. She stood, listening to the complaints and the crashes, watching the Eskimo shove at the high load until the sled was clear.

Then they were out on the flat fjord and the komatik travelled smooth and fast. "Lutiapik!" yelled Ishawakta. He jumped on board the sled, as she ran in her bulky suit to catch up with him. *"Hoit! Hoit!"* She clutched at the skins and heaved until she was straddling the load.

The sky was cloudless, and there was a sharp wind. She buried her face in the deep bearskin. The runners sang as they slid over the snow-covered fjord. When she looked up, they were alone on earth except for the endless ice and the vast arc of the sky.

The novelty of sledding palled after the first few hours on the trail. When the sun finally appeared, low on the horizon, it was so unexpectedly warm that she found herself dozing. In her dream, she had been strolling somewhere on a summer's day in the Muskoka Lake district. There had been pine needles under her bare feet, and she could hear the soft splash of the lake against the shore. Then, suddenly, she was sprawling on her back in the snow.

She had lost her glasses but she could still see the outlines of the *komatik* skimming ahead of her. "Ishawakta!" she cried out. She fumbled and found her glasses, lumbered clumsily to her feet, and started to run. The wind whipped at her numb face. She wrapped a mitted palm around her nose so she could breathe.

Ishawakta was off the sled, keeping pace with the dogs, but it was difficult to slow the fresh team. He glanced back at her when he could. The animals were defecating as they ran and the Eskimo grabbed at the steering handle to guide the komatik around the droppings. Warm droppings could melt the runner-ice. When she caught up with the sled, she hauled herself onto the load and sat, gasping and grinning apologetically. Ishawakta laughed, but said nothing. He joined her companionably on the sled for a few minutes then got off again to jog.

"Eekee," he said once as he ran. Soon, she knew what he meant. Jogging was the best way to keep from freezing. The sun had waned and the wind was blowing more steadily. Even through the sweaters and caribou skins, she could feel the penetrating cold. She was shocked. She had probably felt as miserably cold as this, standing on the corner of King and Bay Streets in Toronto. The difference was that the awfulness had lasted only until she boarded a heated streetcar. Now, she realized that she had been unbearably cold for some time; that it would go on and on without relief until they arrived at Utye's.

She sighed and slid off the *komatik* to run. She badly wanted a hot drink and a cigarette, but there was no sign that Ishawakta was planning to stop. She could not get at her grub box for cigarettes and a lighter. She clawed back to her perch for another rest and turned her head to avoid the painful sting of the wind. *Oh God,* she said to herself. *Oh God! Oh God!* She was practising how to push her mind into semi-neutral when she heard Ishawakta yelling.

"Mug-up! Mug-up!" The *komatik* slowed. She blinked and rubbed at the frost crusting her eyebrows and lashes. The dog-traces were hopelessly tangled. The animals stood, whining a little as the Eskimo unhitched the harness from the sled. Then the team lay, panting in the snow.

"Mug-up," repeated Ishawakta, looking up at her. She climbed stiffly off the *komatik* and watched, swinging her arms, as he brought the primus stove from the box. He filled a small pot with snow and placed it over the flame. Then he unlashed the skins, unloaded the *komatik,* and turned it over, leaving it supported on boxes. By then, the water was bubbling, so she put a bouillon cube into her mug and made herself a drink. Ishawakta brewed tea and gnawed at a slice of raw caribou. She chewed silently at a pilot biscuit and smoked a cigarette.

"*Peoyook,*" he said, stubbing his cigarette butt. She stood watching as he patiently worked at the knotted harness. It took some time, so she sat resignedly on a skin. She turned her back to the wind and cradled her face in her arms as he re-iced the runners with warm water from the stove. Then he started the job of reloading the sled. She found herself another cigarette. She supposed this would be the routine whenever they stopped to untangle the traces.

"*Peoyook,*" Ishawakta said again. She looked up. After lashing the skin-coverings, he walked to the other side of the *komatik* to relieve himself. She watched as he reappeared and picked up the traces. Dorothy moved fast. It was a struggle to lift the pair of heavy parkas then untie her pants and pull at her slacks and underwear. But by the time the Eskimo shouted "*hraw! hraw!*" and the sled was sliding again, she was trotting smartly alongside.

There was another mug-up in the frigid darkness. An hour or so later, she began to pray. It was the first time she had prayed since her arrival in Lake Harbour, and the words resembled nothing she had read in her Daily Missal.

"Please God, I want to be warm," she whispered into her mitten. "Please God, I want to get there. Please God, can we get to the camp soon?"

The trip was a nightmare of cold, boredom, and fatigue. When she stumbled beside the *komatik,* her body ached with weariness. When she sat on the sled, she gritted her teeth against the implacable cold. There was nothing to see but the eerie glow of the ice and Ishawakta's bulk somewhere ahead in the gloom.

When the dogs began howling, she thought the traces were tangled again and she groaned in protest. But she heard Ishawakta laugh. "Utye's!" Then there were other howls in the distance, and the dogs began to run faster, knowing it soon would be time for them to be fed.

She got off the sled to warm herself. "How long?" she asked Ishawakta. He shook his head, not understanding, so she substituted an Eskimo word she knew. *"Katsheenee?"* How many.

"Soon," he replied. *"Maneela."* Rough ice.

She felt dizzy with disappointment. More barrier-ice. She supposed there would always be barrier-ice before they got into a coastal camp.

She closed her ears to the screams of the dogs as she slithered around the ice hummocks. She had no flashlight. Once, when she thought she saw the dark lip of a crevasse, she dropped to her knees and inched forward, exploring with her hands. It was easy to follow the course of the *komatik*. Its slams and crashes and the loud complaints of the dogs echoed down the frozen fjord.

Utye's camp was a bleak patch of snowy tundra dominated by a structure that looked like a squashed igloo. When she came close, she saw it was really a tent surrounded by blocks of packed snow. There were heavy drifts on the roof and seal-thong harness had been thrown there, out of reach of the hungry sled dogs. At one side of the dwelling there was a raised platform loaded with gunnysacks. *The Waldorf Astoria of Baffin Island,* she thought incredulously.

Two Eskimo men came out of the tent as the *komatik* slowed. She recognized one as a pneumonia patient she had nursed during the August epidemic. The men nodded and smiled. Ishawakta said a few brief words before he unhitched the dogs, pulled off the harness, and threw it on the roof of the tent. She stood, awkwardly uncertain of herself as her Eskimo helper dragged sacks of walrus meat from the *komatik* and tossed chopped chunks of food in a wide circle. The dogs crouched on all fours, their front paws steadying the meat as they chewed.

"Lutiapik," Ishawakta said. He held a stick in his hand and tapped it against her outer parka. Apparently he wanted her to beat the snow from her skins. It made sense. The snow would melt in the warm house, and the clothing would become damp.

She stood at the door of Utye's home, thumping at her parka with a stick. *Good Lord,* she thought, *I'll be black and blue!* She heard Ishawakta laugh, then the Eskimo who had been her patient ran ahead of her into the *tupik,* pulled off his outer parka, and beat at it with his hand. She followed him, blushing a little, and wriggled out of the heavy caribou skin. *Children and kabloonahs,* she thought as she knocked the snow from the parka. It took a little time to learn.

The tent was a surprise. It was warm and softly lit by two lanterns and a blubber lamp. There were wooden walls built inside the canvas, a floor, a table, and two kitchen chairs, painted blue. Three women, a man, and two children were lying on the skin-heaped, spacious sleeping platform at the back of the room. Her former patient proudly occupied a chair.

He nodded and grinned as she stood inside the door holding her parka, pointing to a rack suspended above the oil lamp. It was spread with skin clothing, so she assumed this was where she was expected to hang her own garments during the night. No one moved or spoke as she removed her inner parka and skin pants and found a place for them on the loaded rack. Stripped down to her slacks, sweaters, and socks, she felt relaxed and very hungry. She hesitated for a moment, then sat on the vacant chair. There was a pleased giggle from the sleeping platform. *"Ee,"* someone exclaimed.

The man sitting opposite smiled, nodded and cut himself a generous slice of seal meat from a raw chunk lying on the table. "Lutiapik," he said, and chewed.

Ishawakta shuffled his feet to scrape his *kamiks* clean and came through the door carrying her grub box and the gunnysack of frozen stew. He hurried outside again and returned with the primus stove, her medical kit, and the sleeping bags. She wished she could handle the stove on her own. But she took her largest pot from the box and dropped four of the hard stew rounds into it. It was far too much for her to eat alone. She felt it would be polite to ask her hosts to share it with her.

Ishawakta showed no surprise when he saw the generously loaded pot. He lit the primus, put the pot over the flame, then silently hacked a slice from the seal meat on the table. The man on the other chair wordlessly did the same.

When the stew boiled, she brought a bowl and spoon from her box and ladled the hot food from the pot. She ate hungrily, dug a pilot biscuit out of the box, then ate some more. "Ishawakta," she said. "Which man Utye?"

Ishawakta pointed his knife at his eating companion. "That Utye."

"Ask Utye if he would like some stew," she said, gesturing at Utye and the pot. She pointed at the sleeping platform. "Others too, if they want."

Ishawakta said some words in Eskimo, and there was a low *"ee ... ee"* from the back of the tent. Two women came slowly from the platform wearing green cotton dresses and woollen stockings. They took spoons from the table and shyly dipped them into the steaming pot. Utye did the same, dipping, grinning, then delicately tasting the stew. She could not tell whether the Inuit enjoyed what they ate or whether they were simply pleased she had invited them to take some of her food. A naked child ran across the room and was given a spoonful. The other Eskimo who had met them outside scraped his boots and padded through the door. He took a spoon from one of the women and sampled the hot *kabloonah* stew. Everyone watched as he rolled it around his tongue like someone tasting wine.

"Ee," said a woman.

The man nodded and swallowed. *"Ee. Peoyook."* The Inuit faces broke into delighted smiles.

Everyone lit cigarettes. She opened a can of butter and a large tin of strawberry jam then took more pilot biscuits from her grub box.

Ishawakta laughed. "Inuit like," he said. Then he spoke again in Eskimo, and the men and women moved around the table, digging their fingers into the butter and jam and spreading it lavishly on the tough biscuits. A small boy thrust his fist into the sweet preserve and sucked at it noisily. The red stain of the jam on his face remined her of the happy Eskimos at the bloody whale feast.

The first thing she saw in the half-light of morning was that the outside of her sleeping bag was thick from hoar-frost that had formed from her condensed breath during the night. Utye's tent was cold, and the Inuit with her on the sleeping platform clearly had no intention of leaping quickly out of bed. One of the women turned lazily on her naked stomach, stretched, and lit a primus stove that sat on the floor. Then she put a kettle on the flame and settled back into the furs.

Dorothy groped for her glasses and lay, still and warm, staring at the wooden walls and the contents of the *tupik*. The night before, she had not noticed that Utye had papered his house with pages from a shopping catalogue. For insulation, no doubt. Eskimos were meticulous about organizing their dwellings but they were matter-of-fact about interior decoration. She squinted curiously through the gloom to see how life-styles in the South appeared to the Inuit. There were coloured pictures of swimsuits, bicycles, lawnmowers, summer hammocks.

She laughed to herself. There were two pages glued to the opposite wall showing photographs of girdles and corsets for "lightweight comfort and control." She wondered if the Eskimos had asked themselves why the *kabloonahs* paid so many dollars for such strange garments and for what purpose? Special ceremonies, perhaps? She laughed again, remembering she wore a bra.

The primus helped warm the *tupik*, but she was the last to leave the sleeping platform. None of the Eskimos seemed to notice or care. Black tea was brewed and porridge was made and eaten with a sprinkling of precious sugar. The two children laughed and played tag around the table. One of the women sat at a hand-powered sewing machine, stitching a duffle-cloth parka. Another scraped at a sealskin.

Finally, when Dorothy saw the first streaks of sunshine

through the open door, she wriggled into the shirt and slacks she had kept warm inside her bag, then pulled two sweaters over her head. There was more hot water bubbling on the stove so she washed her face and hands in an enamel bowl brought from the box, tugged a comb through her hair, and made some tea. Her butter supply had been eaten at the impromptu feast, so she breakfasted on a dry pilot biscuit and porridge.

No one apparently expected her to be the *aniatitsiyuk* if she was not in the mood, but she put her medical bag on one of the chairs, and went outside to find a suitable toilet area. At the front of the tent, Ishawakta was smoking a cigarette and enjoying the morning sun. She lit her own *sigalik* and stood, smoking silently beside him. Down beyond the barrier-ice, she could see two shapes on the fjord, bent like chubby question marks.

"*Neche*," said Ishawakta, when she pointed. "*Utye, Johnasee at agloo*." The Inuit were hunting seal at the breathing holes.

She finished her cigarette. "Ishawakta," she said, "ask if there is pain in camp."

Both women had toothaches. An examination showed the offending molars were badly rotted. She told herself to keep calm. She had known she would have to extract teeth at some time or another, and she had rehearsed what she would do. She motioned for one woman to sit on a chair, then injected the patient's gum with local anaesthetic. The woman jumped a little at the sharp pain, but made no sound.

The next stage of the operation was difficult, and she needed help. She brought the other woman from her sewing machine and showed what she wanted her to do. The patient's head, she indicated, would have to be immobilized. Then she stood behind the woman in the chair, circled her head with an arm and steadied her chin.

"*Ee?*" she nodded.

Her Eskimo aide nodded back at her. "*Ee*." Then she imitated what Dorothy had done.

The right-handed forceps were a nuisance. She had to wrap her fingers around the flat thumb handle, and her thumb slipped uncomfortably against the other, rounded side. She opened her mouth wide. The patient in the chair giggled and opened hers.

Okay, she thought, *here goes.* She grabbed the molar with the jaws of the forcepts, pushed downwards towards the gum, squeezed hard and pulled steadily while rocking the tooth out of the socket. She felt the sweat break out on her upper lip. The woman did not seem to be suffering, but she knew local anaesthetic did not always work perfectly. "Come on," she said under her breath. "Oh come on!" The tooth came out. There was no bleeding. When she released the molar, it bounced on the table.

"*Ee,*" grinned her helper. The patient leaned curiously over the table and took the tooth between a finger and thumb. Then she explored the empty socket with her tongue and presented the tooth to one of the children.

Dorothy dispensed aspirin. "Next!" she gestured. The women reversed roles.

Johnasee returned to the camp without a seal and showed her a boil at the back of his neck. She cleaned it with soapy water and alcohol before applying antibiotic ointment and a dressing. She saw the man was also suffering from a mild case of impetigo, so she treated that as well. She brought out her supplies of cod liver oil and vitamin supplements and asked the women if they had enough for their children. It seemed they did. One mother bustled to a box, brought out a bottle of oil and a jar of capsules and dosed the two boys immediately. She thought about how to ask the women if the children had received DPT booster shots on the *Howe,* then simply jabbed at her arm, pointed at the boys and said: "C. D. *Howe?*"

Both women nodded eagerly, replying, "*Ee . . . ee!*"

She wanted to look at the children, anyway, but when she put out her hand, they giggled and backed away.

"*Eejee,*" said one woman, returning to her sewing.

Ishawakta had come through the door and was standing, watching her. "*Eejee,*" he said, pointing at his eye. "That woman Kavanaugh. Boy is Jamesee. *Eejee. Anneayoo.*"

Kavanaugh was apparently not interested in catching the child and bringing him to Dorothy, so she chased him herself and carried him, laughing, to the chair.

"Jamesee," she said, rocking him on her knee.

The boy stared up at her, then rubbed at his eye.

"*Eejee?*" Dorothy asked and the child nodded. She gently widened the boy's eyelids and looked more closely. The cornea was pocked with yellow-grey nodules. She remembered reading something about the condition in the medical manual when she had checked the details of the treatment for conjunctivitis. Could Jamesee be suffering from phlyctenular keratitis? She released the boy from her lap, and he ran to play with the other child. Ishawakta had lit the primus stove to make tea, so she sipped at a cup as she read the section in the manual.

Keratitis was particularly common in children. It was the result of hypersensitive reaction to an allergy – possibly a product of the tuberculosis bacillus. She re-read the symptoms. They corresponded to what she had seen in Jamesee's eyes. Yellow-grey ulcerations. Pain. Itching. The nodules would occur and re-occur if left untreated, and eventually there would be scarring and loss of vision. There seemed to be a difference of medical opinion about treatment. Conservatives tended to recommend yellow oxide of mercury ointment, but the manual mentioned that the application of cortisone had been "highly encouraging."

She bit her lip. She had brought cortisone ointment on the trip, but she had hoped she would not have to make a decision about using it. The powerful drug could have unpredictable side effects, and no nurse in a hospital would ever dare use it or any other drug without a medical order. She sat, holding the open manual on her knees. The tent was quiet except for the clackety-clack of Kavanaugh's sewing machine. Out through the door, she could see the upended Health and Welfare *komatik*, its runners freshly iced for the run back to Lake Harbour.

She reached for her medical bag and found the yellow oxide of mercury. It would be the safest medication to use. Besides, doctors had been recommending it for phlyctenular keratitis for years. She went to catch Jamesee.

There was a small commotion at the door of the *tupik* and Utye backed in, dragging a dead seal. *"Neche,"* he laughed. *"Peoyook!"*

The women in the tent giggled approvingly. The Eskimo's clear brown eyes crinkled, and suddenly she remembered blind Adamee and the childish pinging of spittle as he practised shots at his tin can. Without eyes, she knew there could be starvation in Inuit camps that year and in the years to come. She caught Jamesee and put him on her lap. Then she reached into her medical bag for the cortisone ointment.

8

Don Baird had heard by radio that the RCAF would make its Christmas drop at Lake Harbour on December 12, so Georgie, Ishawakta, and Akavak went out to the bay-ice with oil drums to be used as flares.

The news of the drop generated an infectious excitement within the little settlement. Christmas meant mail and parcels from home. It meant temporary relief from isolation when the Inuit sledded in from camps for visits, games, and the services at the Anglican church. Christmas was an excuse to eat the best of the food supplies and to socialize more than usual. Christmas was an excuse to decorate the plain little house.

Dorothy had heard there were sometimes Christmas trees on the drop, but she decided to make her own from a triangular boot scraper she kept on the porch. With a box of tinsel and Yule decorations from the attic, she spent an afternoon setting up the scraper, hanging it with faded icicles and balls. The tree looked bare without parcels; she hoped there would be some for her in the mail. She wondered what she could give her friends in Lake Harbour and anxiously rummaged through her personal possessions and the attic shelves.

Mike might like a canned Christmas cake. She knew he missed Marg's baking. Don could have the deck of cards she had brought from Toronto and never used. She would give Hilda the bracelet she had admired. She puzzled over gifts for the two constables before deciding to buy cigarettes for them at the store. There was canned butter, jam, and bacon for the Inuit.

144

It was fun writing out her Christmas list. She was humming to herself when the door of her house opened and an Eskimo man came in from the icy darkness. She was surprised. The Inuit invariably stopped first at Ishawakta's home when they came from the camp seeking help. But she got to her feet and politely extended her hand. The man took it. He was handsome, grey haired, and probably more than seventy years of age. "Lutiapik," he said, and his eyes crinkled.

She nodded at her name and smiled.

He pointed at his chest. "Kingwatcheak."

"Ah!" She nodded again. Mike had once told her about Kingwatcheak, the Cape Dorset leader and elder of the Anglican Church, who had been taken by Scottish whalers to Queen Victoria's Jubilee in 1898.

"He still handles his own dog team," the missionary had said. "One day he'll turn up in Lake Harbour to say hello and visit. He always drops in to see everyone."

But was this a social or a professional visit, she wondered. *"Anneayoo?"* she asked the man, patting at her head, then her stomach.

He shook his head. *"Agai."* Then he laughed, walked into the kitchen and sat on a chair. The coal stove was blazing, but he did not remove his duffle-cloth parka. He pushed back the hood and the hoar-frost on the fur trimming quickly melted.

Dorothy was flattered. This was the first time she had received a personal call from an Eskimo, so she decided to make it an occasion. Kingwatcheak watched with interest as she went to a cupboard and brought out her best china tea service. Then she took some sweet cookies from a jar, arranged them on a plate, and poured the tea. Kingwatcheak helped himself to three heaping teaspoons of sugar. He took the cup delicately by the handle and sipped. "Queen Victoria's Jubilee," he said gravely.

"Ee," said Dorothy. *"Peoyook."*

Kingwatcheak sipped again, then munched two cookies. "Punch him in the nose," he said.

She was not sure how to respond to this, but she smiled and poured more tea.

"*Sigalik?*" she asked, offering a pack of cigarettes.

"*Ee,*" he nodded graciously and took one, tapping it on the back of his hand. "*Peoyook.*"

She wanted to ask the Eskimo if he intended staying in the settlement for Christmas, but did not know the right words. She decided to ask anyway, hoping he might understand. "Will you stay here for the Christmas celebrations?" she asked.

He shook his head, either to say no or to indicate he had not understood.

She tried other words. "*Sheelitchea,*" she said. Fine weather. He stared at her with faint amusement for a moment, then he laughed and she laughed along with him.

"*Ookoo!*" she said, pointing at the stove. Hot. He laughed again.

He butted the cigarette in a glass ashtray. "Queen Victoria's Jubilee," he repeated, and got to his feet.

She followed him to the door; again they shook hands. He left without saying good-bye.

Everyone listened all day for the sound of the RCAF boxcar. Ishawakta and Akavak had poured gasoline into the oil-drum flares and took turns, waiting on the sea-ice. It was late afternoon when someone heard the drone of the engines and shouted so loudly and urgently, the dogs began to howl in interested chorus. Dorothy struggled into her parka and ran into the chilly darkness, staring at the sky. The drone grew louder, and then she could see the wink of lights. Akavak lit the flares.

She sprinted excitedly towards the barrier-ice. Georgie had hitched the dogs to the Hudson's Bay *komatik*, and the sled slithered past her in the gloom, bumping and crashing through the hummocks. Don and Hilda were already standing on the flat sea-ice, bundled into parkas and stamping their feet in the bitter cold. She could see Gerry Heapy coming across the fjord with the RCMP *komatik*, while Mike emerged from the barrier-ice with his team as well.

The Inuit laughed and pointed as the aircraft banked and headed up the fjord towards the flares. Two bundles suspended from white parachutes drifted from the belly of the plane followed by a third, then a fourth. After a moment, two spruce trees dropped out of the sky and landed, upright, in the snow. Her eyes blurred a little at the sight of the familiar trees standing so straight and alone on the flat ice. The aircraft gained altitude and vanished over the hills. She wondered where the crew would be that night. In a Montreal restaurant? Walking along a crowded street? At home with their families?

"Let's go," said Don. "This is the closest thing to Santa Claus we'll ever get."

The drop had been made in large wicker baskets which were loaded on the sleds and taken to the mission house for unpacking and sorting. She jogged along behind the *komatiks*, feeling the same kind of anticipation she always felt when her brothers brought parcels home at Christmas. She swallowed hard at the thought of her family in Toronto and found herself a chair in a corner of the mission house kitchen as the men fished the fat mail bags from the hampers.

Gerry, as official government representative, was given custody of the red sacks of registered letters and parcels. She thought he was joking when he announced that everyone would have to come over to the detachment next day to sign for their mail. She started to laugh, but it was no joke. Registered mail was registered mail, even in Lake Harbour. The constable put the red sacks on the porch, then helped his four white neighbours work through the unregistered letters, packages, and periodicals.

Someone, probably at the Air Force base, had stuffed some paperbacks into one of the hampers. Don spread them on the table together with a giant card wishing Lake Harbour a Merry Christmas. The two trees, it was decided after a conference, would be put in the Hudson's Bay store and the mission, because the visiting Inuit would be most likely to see them there.

Mike had some small sacks stored on the porch, and Dorothy asked to borrow one to carry her mail. There were at least a dozen parcels and a small stack of letters addressed to her via Lake Harbour, Northwest Territories, Royal Mail Service, Ottawa. She had riffled through the pile while she waited. Nothing again from Health and Welfare, she noted with disappointment.

Did her employers know she existed? She envied the mountain of mail that had come for the mission, the detachment, and the Hudson's Bay post. Perhaps, if she read one letter a day, hers might last until January. But she shrugged. She knew she would read the letters, one after the other, until they were finished. It was like the Inuit with their food. Mail was such a treat, she would consume it all at once.

When Don and Hilda climbed into their parkas, she decided to leave with them. She told Gerry a little formally that she would come to the detachment next day and sign for her registered mail. He grinned at her. Akavak was at the door, and after a short conference with him, Gerry came back across the room. "It's Kingwatcheak," he said. "He's sick. Akavak has taken him to Ishawakta's house. I hope it isn't too bad."

After examining the old man, it was difficult to tell. He had a slight temperature and was complaining of stomach cramps, but he was cheerful and sipped smilingly at a mug of tea. She was glad she had set up a hospital bed in her diningroom. "Ishawakta," she said, pointing at Kingwatcheak, then towards her home. "I will take Kingwatcheak over there."

The courtly old Eskimo seemed delighted when Ishawakta told him he would be staying at the *aniatitsiyuk's* house until he felt well again.

"*Ee*," he nodded. "*Naak*." And he rubbed at his sore stomach. He followed Dorothy down the gravel path to her home and sat quietly in the livingroom while she heated him a bowl of chicken soup. While he ate from the bowl with the shiniest soup spoon she could find, she checked the bed and put out more blankets. The problem of pyjamas worried her until she remembered she had packed a large flannel nightgown with the supplies transferred from the hospital.

"Kingwatcheak," she said, holding it for him to see.

He laughed, pointing at it and then at himself. "Kingwatcheak?"

She nodded, went into the diningroom, and laid it over the bed. He padded into the converted diningroom, and she left him alone. The parcels looked friendly and reassuring when she stacked them under the boot-scraper tree. She squeezed one or two of them curiously but resisted the temptation to see what her family thought she would like to have in the Arctic. Instead, she opened the first of her letters, reading about Ray and Sylvia and Fred and how the temperature in Toronto had dropped to a frigid low of twenty degrees in November. Aunt Nell was fine and so was mother and everyone was going to miss her a lot at Christmas.

She tore open a letter from a nursing friend, forgetting for a moment about Kingwatcheak. "Things are about the same at the hospital – " Then she heard a low, musical sound from the diningroom. The old man's song was really a chant, and she put down the letter to listen to it. She had no idea what it meant, but she was sure it was about life and loving and hunting, and the harsh beauty of the North. Perhaps, she smiled, it was also about his adventures in London at Queen Victoria's Jubilee. She picked up the letter again.

Two nurses she knew had left. Iris had become a stewardess with an airline; Shirley was working in a New York cancer hospital. She tucked the note back into the envelope, listening to Kingwatcheak's haunting chant. The nostalgia and the aching loneliness she had felt when the green spruce trees landed on the ice had gone. She went into the kitchen to heat her patient some milk before getting ready for bed.

Kingwatcheak hitched up his team a few days before Christmas, patted his well stomach, and departed smilingly for Cape Dorset. His *komatik* had scarcely disappeared from the frozen bay before the Inuit began arriving from the outer camps. Some built snowhouses close to the settlement, but others crowded in with Ishawakta, Georgie, and Akavak. After a talk with Mike, she opened and heated the hospital for any of the Inuit who cared to stay there. The old hut near the cemetery would also provide extra shelter.

Lake Harbour was alive again with the sound of laughter, children's voices, and the constant howl of dogs. The Eskimos jammed into the Hudson's Bay store, trading furs with Don, spending their credits on supplies. The men admired the .22 rifle donated by the company as first prize in the annual dogteam race. Women sat in small, giggling groups, doing almost exactly as they did in their home camps – sewing clothes, making meals, and feeding any child who happened to wander by.

There was an immediate rush of callers at Dorothy's porch door. She saw the first batch of patients in the kitchen, directing the rest to the hospital surgery. She felt comfortable and at home, working in the Quonset hut again. There was the ever-present impetigo to treat, ear infections, boils. She administered DPT shots and boosters to babies. With the help of the Inuit, she pulled several teeth. From Utye's camp, Kavanaugh brought Jamesee to the hospital as Dorothy had asked her to do. Apprehensively, she examined the boy's eyes. The keratitis nodules were no longer visible; there seemed to be no complications from the cortisone. *"Peoyook?"* she asked the Eskimo woman, pointing at her son.

Kavanaugh nodded. *"Ee. Peoyook."*

"Peoyook!" shrilled Jamesee, grinning and blinking rapidly to show the itching and pain had gone. He jumped down from the examination table. *"Koveeashoobik!"* he said. Christmas.

Since the Inuit had always held celebrations in mid-winter, it must have been easy for them to accept the white man's festival when they were converted to Christianity. As far as Dorothy could tell, it seemed to matter very little to an Eskimo whether he ate cookies and bean stew, or slices of raw seal meat during the Yule season. Scottish reels were as much fun as ancient drum dances. Christmas trees were as novel and amusing as other *kabloonah* toys. Religious ceremonies were expected. And games were part of the Inuit tradition.

Hilda called her on the settlement telephone. "We're all having Christmas dinner here at the post," she said. "I'm cooking the *Rupertsland* turkey."

"What can I bring? Oranges? Cake? Nuts?"

"Bring everything. We'll all share."

"How about the washing-machine beer?"

Hilda laughed. "We've been spared. The boys have been saving some Scotch."

The women discussed the feast the settlement whites were planning for the Eskimos. Cauldrons of stew. Sacks of pilot biscuits and cans of butter and jam. Dozens of fresh cookies. Gallons of tea. During a lull in the stream of patients, she brought armfuls of supplies from the attic and dumped them in a corner of the kitchen until she could find time for cooking. Between splinting a fractured finger and bandaging a cut she baked a cake. She dispensed bismuth and aspirin to those who asked, then went back to the house to start on her quota of cookies. That evening, she flopped wearily into a livingroom chair and vowed she would turn in early. But the settlement telephone rang twice, and she rose to answer it.

"Dorothy," Gerry Heapy's voice came over the wire. "The Eskimos have got a dance going in the old hut. You want to come?"

She tried to tell herself it was just Gerry's way of spreading the Christmas spirit around, but it was impossible not to feel as excited as she had when a boy in Toronto had asked her to her first teenage hop. Of course she would go. She found herself laughing into the telephone and asking what on earth one wore to a dance in the old hut with a crowd of Eskimos?

"Well, I sure as heck wouldn't wear a crinoline and high heels if I were you," Gerry told her. "These dances can get pretty strenuous."

She had had no intention of wearing the crinoline, but for some reason she felt disappointed.

"Well, what do you want me to wear? Slacks and nurse's shoes?"

"Good idea. Pick you up in an hour."

She grimaced at the sight of herself in ordinary slacks and sweater, but she took some time with her hair and make-up and used some perfume. The new duffle-cloth parka she had asked Oola to make had been delivered that morning. When Gerry knocked at the door, she zipped herself into it, and they walked through the windless night to the building near the graveyard.

Mosesee's daughter, Noota, was playing an accordion; two Eskimo men were blowing energetically into mouth organs. The music had obviously been inspired by the Scottish whalers who had spent so much time in Lake Harbour. The Inuit men were performing some lively steps, but the women had gathered in a tight inner group and were shuffling in a slowly moving circle. Some had babies asleep in their hoods. Children darted among the dancers clutching playfully at their parkas and *amoutis*. No one seemed to mind.

"Well, let's get a proper reel going," said Gerry. He shouted to the men in Eskimo, and he and Dorothy began dancing hand-over-hand around the room. Noota pumped tirelessly at the accordion. The mouth organs droned on and on. The men and some of the teenage boys decided to join the new dance. But the women still shuffled, their eyes fixed on the wooden floor.

"When do we stop?" Dorothy gasped as she caught up with Gerry during a frenetic turn around the room. The air was stifling and she wished Noota would play something slow. *Dream when you're feeling blue . . .* Gerry was on the other side of the hut again. His good-looking face was shiny with perspiration. *Dream, it's the thing to do . . .*

Hand-over-hand. Two giggling Eskimos, then Gerry. "When do we stop?"

"When you drop," he yelled back over the music and laughter.

For a moment, she thought she might join the circle of shuffling female dancers. "You must be kidding!" she panted. She wondered if Gerry knew how to do a slow foxtrot. "This has been going on for an hour!"

It went on for another two.

Christmas was a non-stop holiday of feasting, carol-singing in the church, and games on the sea-ice. There were competitions in harpoon-throwing and snowhouse-building. There was wrestling and tug-of-war, and the women and children crowded excitedly into the old hut to scramble as Don and Mike upended baskets of candy and oranges.

A young Eskimo from Mingeriak's camp won the running broad jump and received Mike's prize of a new Bible. Young Sandy was a close second in the big *komatik* race that had a dozen crack teams skimming up the fjord to the finish line opposite the mission. No whips were allowed in the race. The drivers knew they must encourage their dogs by voice alone. She stood with Hilda on the ice, listening as the shouts of *"hraw! hraw!"* and *"hoit! hoit!"* came closer and the *komatiks* straggled out of the afternoon gloom. Some were overturned; almost all of the teams were tangled in their hide traces. A man named Lukasee won the .22 rifle and spent the rest of the day shooting a small fortune in cartridges at tin cans. Sandy won a sack of groceries.

She opened her parcels alone on Christmas morning, reading the messages inside and making a neat pile of stockings, boxes of candy, a new sweater, and copies of Nevil Shute's *On the Beach* and James Gould Cozzens' *By Love Possessed.* Both books, she was assured by her brothers, were bestsellers in the South. It was fun, opening the parcels, but the aloneness was depressing and she went back to bed.

Later, she took the candy, together with the cake she had baked and some fruit and nuts, to the *kabloonah* Christmas dinner at the Bairds. The roasted *Rupertsland* turkey was consumed to an appreciative chorus of *"ee . . . ahaloonah!"* and washed down with a bottle of wine hidden somewhere in the post since August. It was warm and friendly in the house, and she forgot her morning loneliness. There were songs and tall stories about the Arctic. To uproarious laughter and applause, Don found some reedy music on the radio. It was yet another Scottish reel. Everyone toasted the absent Marg Gardener in Montreal.

Dorothy was still humming as she brushed her teeth in the frigid bathroom before going to bed. Next day, there would be a whip-cracking contest and a football game. Then there would be the big Boxing Day feast in the old hut. She washed her face with the expensive-smelling soap that Hilda had given her and decided she would read a chapter of the new Shute novel before turning out the lights.

"Lutiapik," she heard Ishawakta say softly from the kitchen. She was startled. She dried her face and went to him. The Eskimo pointed at the porch door. "Seemeega. Come from camp. With son. Iktoluka."

"Iktoluka *anneayoo?*"

Ishawakta shook his head. *"Tokovok."* He dies.

Seemeega was standing by his *komatik* in the black night. She switched on the porch light and saw his dogs were sitting or lying, panting in the snow. Something wrapped in skins was lashed to the top of the *komatik* load. She assumed this was the body of the boy. She waited for the Eskimo to say something to Ishawakta, but he simply stood, gripping the butt of his whip.

She knew it was useless to try questioning the Eskimo, so she walked back into the house and called Gerry on the settlement telephone. The RCMP should be informed of a death, in any case.

"Gerry? A man named Seemeega has come into the settlement with a dead boy. It's his son, Ishawakta says. I thought you should know about it. But could you talk to the man on the phone and let me know what happened?" Gerry sounded sleepy, but he agreed to interpret, so she went to the door and asked Seemeega to come inside. She pointed to the telephone, talked into it to show what it was for, then offered it to the Eskimo. He hesitated. Then he took it, smelled it carefully, held it at arm's length, and put it to his ear.

She watched his eyes widen when he heard Gerry's voice. *"Ee,"* he said, and listened again. After a few moments, he spoke into the receiver. There was another silence, then he gave her the telephone.

"Gerry?"

"It's his son, all right. The boy was hunting seal, then apparently got very hot, with much pain and coughing. He stayed on the sleeping platform for a few days. Then, when he got worse, Seemeega loaded him on the *komatik* to bring him to Lake Harbour. The boy died on the way. He doesn't say why he didn't come in for Christmas."

"How far away was the camp?"

"One sleep, apparently."

"But he left it too late!" said Dorothy. "He should have come earlier with the boy, or sent for me. Doesn't the man know I would have come if he had sent a message?"

There was silence at the other end of the telephone. She

turned to look at Seemeega. The Eskimo's eyes were slits above his high cheekbones. *"Ayonamut!"* he mumbled.

"Oh my God," said Dorothy, suddenly angry. "He says it can't be helped! But it could have been helped. Doesn't he know that? The boy probably only needed some antibiotics."

"Dorothy," Gerry said, "could you leave the body on your porch? I'll come around some time to check it over."

"Sure," she said. "Goodnight, Gerry." And she hung up.

She lay awake for a long time that night, grieving for young Iktoluka, realizing the boy's life had probably ebbed away on the cold sled while she and the other settlement whites had been eating their Christmas dinner. She turned her face unhappily into the pillow wondering again whether she, the Inuit, or even the Department of Health and Welfare really knew why she was there.

The Eskimos packed their *komatiks* two days after Christmas, shook hands around the settlement, and hitched their teams. Soon, the settlement was as quiet and deserted as it had been before the invasion. To add to the let-down, the weather broke and the snow rattled against the side of the house like pellets of gravel. She tried to cheer herself up by finishing the new books and making herself a dinner out of the leftover turkey that Hilda had given her. But she missed the friendly Inuit faces at the door, and she longed to be busy.

She called Gerry again to talk and to ask about the body on the porch. He said he had not been able to cross the bay. "Plenty of time," he said at the other end of the squeaky line. "It's cold enough for the corpse to keep for a while. If you don't mind having it there, that is."

She did, but there seemed nothing she could do about it. Whenever she walked through the porch, Iktoluka's still form was a reminder of that night's anger and frustration. She tried to forget by writing her regular INHS report and long, somewhat rambling letters to her family and friends. She wondered bleakly when the messages would reach their destinations. The next mail to go out would accompany Hilda on the Hudson's Bay

Beaver in a few weeks time. She preferred not to think about Hilda's going. She doubted whether she could be any lonelier than she was now, but she resented the diminishment of the little community. *One little Indian, two little Indians* she began counting compulsively. *And then there were only six.*

When the blizzard petered out next day, she bundled into warm clothes and walked through the squeaky snow to the hospital and back. The dogs were unstaked at this time of the year; King spotted her and raced to jump. She wanted to take him into the kitchen for food, but stopped herself. "King," she said, softly. "King," and turned from him. The animal lowered his head and walked away.

She kept walking beyond the house and began climbing the small hill. It was mid-afternoon; she could see the jagged outlines of the mountains and the white fjord in the glow of the Arctic twilight. There were a few stars in the north, over the peninsula. She could travel for half the length of Baffin Island with nothing but ice-locked lakes and empty tundra until she came to the small settlement of Clyde River. She remembered that tomorrow was New Year's Eve. There would be crowded celebrations in Toronto. There would be toasts in champagne and warm kisses and bittersweet choruses of "Auld Lang Syne."

Nineteen fifty-eight. "Happy New Year, Dorothy," she whispered to herself, pulling her frost-crusted scarf more closely around her cold face. Well, she had always boasted that she did something absolutely different on New Year's Eve. She wondered if anyone had decided yet where the *kabloonahs* would see the old year out. She laughed. There wasn't much choice. There was her house, Mike's, the detachment, or the Baird's.

9

Dorothy decided not to comment when Don brought Noota to her door one black January morning to say the woman had agreed to travel with her as a chaperone on the trail. "She might even take along her accordion," Don grinned, looking more brotherly than ever. Noota stared at Dorothy, smiled a little vaguely, turned, and padded across the compound.

"Ishawakta tells me you're planning a trip," said Don. They went into the kitchen for some coffee, and he hung his parka on a peg.

"Yes. I thought I'd leave in a couple of days."

"But as far as Kooyoo's?"

"Well, I'm not doing anything useful here, Don, and I'd like to make the rounds of winter camps."

"It's 300 miles to Kooyoo's and back," Don said, shaking his head doubtfully. "With stopovers, you can figure on at least ten days away. If the weather holds, that is." He sipped some coffee. "Mike usually travels at this time of the year. He'll probably go part of the way with you. To Napatchee's camp, at least. Then he'll probably strike west to Cape Dorset."

She was happy to hear that the missionary might be along – to help with some of the interpreting as well as for company. Ishawakta's English was improving and she was learning more words in Eskimo, but even so, the job of questioning was tedious for both the patients and her. And she was never sure she was getting accurate information. She wondered if anyone in Health and Welfare had even considered that an orientation course for INHS personnel was as important as a nursing diploma.

After Don left, she sat at a table and made out a list of the food and medical supplies she would need for ten days or more. An extra-large sack of stew rounds. Plenty of "soupee," as the Inuit called her bouillon cubes. Powdered milk, rolled oats, toilet paper. Salt, lard, and flour to make bannock, the simple Inuit bread. She had been pleased with her choice of drugs and other medications for the trip to Utye's camp. This time, she packed extra cortisone ointment, added a mask and two cans of general anaesthetic, hoping she would bring them home unopened.

Ishawakta nodded cheerfully when she asked if he would be ready to leave after two sleeps. He refilled her drinking-water barrel with a fresh block of ice then went off in the direction of the Hudson's Bay storehouse, presumably to chop frozen walrus meat for the dogs. She considered whether she should tell the Eskimo that Noota would be coming with them, but decided that Don had probably done this for her. She supposed she was responsible for the chaperone's food but was unsure about what to take.

"Pack some extra porridge and tea," Don said when she enquired. "And I'll tell Ishawakta to take a double supply of caribou. Oh, and incidentally, Mike will be with you for some of the way. He's taking Judasee from Utye's camp to help on the trip."

She went out of the house into the inky darkness two days later, watching by the porch light as Ishawakta harnessed the dogs to the high, intricately packed *komatik*. Noota was standing stiffly in her winter skins, waiting to be told what to do. Mike came suddenly out of the gloom, wearing a caribou suit and an earflap cap under his parka hood. She envied the cap. She always seemed to be cold around the head.

"We're about ready to go," the missionary said. "We'd better stick fairly close so we can be together at mug-ups and when we camp tonight."

"Where do you think we will camp?" she asked.

"Well, we won't make Napatchee's. It's really up to the Inuit. They'll have to find good snow for igloos." He thumped his arms around his chest. The nursing-station thermometer was registering forty degrees below zero and the wind was fresh. "See you for morning tea."

She stumbled through the barrier-ice, listening again to the awful crash of the sled and the protests of the dogs in their caught traces. She supposed Noota must have followed her through the hummocks, because when she turned, the woman was standing as rigidly as before, her eyes following the tortuous progress of the two *komatiks*. The mission sled emerged first, and she saw Mike running to catch it. Then she glimpsed King's white coat as the Health and Welfare *komatik* swayed drunkenly out of the rough ice.

She jogged beside the sled, grabbing at the skins to haul herself on to the load. The clouds were clearing; the stars were bright enough for her to see Mike's sled just ahead and to the left as they sped down the smooth, snow-powdered surface of the fjord.

She turned her face out of the wind, gasping again at the painful shock of the cold. Soon, there would be thick rime on her mouth-scarf, eyelashes, and hood trimming, just as there had been on the trail to Utye's. There would be the numbing boredom. There would be the exhaustion from running to keep from freezing. Then she remembered her boredom in the house during those early-winter blizzards, and she dug her mittens into the bearskin and laughed aloud. "Dream, when you're feeling blue," she sang, her voice muffled behind her tartan scarf. She slid off the *komatik* to jog. Noota did the same. She turned and saw the Eskimo woman staring at her again, a flicker of puzzled expression in her eyes. "Dream, it's the thing to do." She wondered if Miss Beamish had ever experienced the urge to spend a night in an igloo.

The first mug-up was fun but then the reality of the trip set in. The sea-ice became uneven; the pace slowed. As the day became brighter, the cold grew more unbearable. She nudged Noota as they sat, their legs dangling over the side of the load and pointed to the exposed part of her face and forehead.

"*Eekee,*" she said. The Eskimo woman seemed to understand what she meant, and nodded. Each would inspect the other's face from time to time for white patches of frostbite that would have to be warmed by hand before they got worse. At least it was something to do. She watched the dogteam, marvelling at how the animals continued to run and run, with only an occasional flick of Ishawakta's whip to urge them on. She thought about dogs for as long as possible before switching her attention to the terrain. There was nothing to see but ice, snow, rocks, jagged mountains. She counted rocks until she felt drowsy and drugged.

She longed for another mug-up break, but even when the dog traces had tangled again, Ishawakta apparently wanted to keep going. She jogged for a while. She sat for a while. She named the twelve cranial nerves, remembering the little sentence which gave clues to the initials. *On old Olympus towering top, a Finn and German vaulted a hedge.* She thought about Gerry and spelled his name over and over again. *G.e.r.r.y ... G.e.r.r.y.* She stared fixedly at Noota's flat face. Noota stared unblinkingly back at her. She waved at Mike, but he could not have seen her. Perhaps he was too tired and cold to lift his arm. She almost shouted her relief when the two *komatiks* slowed and they stopped again for tea and pilot biscuits.

"How," she asked Mike, stamping her feet, "can we get out of this beastly cold for a few minutes?"

"Well, a block of snow helps as a wind-shelter," he said, looking at her from red, frost-rimmed eyes. "But there's not much of that on the sea-ice. We'll have to go inland to look for good snow for the igloos tonight."

She inspected the luminous dial of her wristwatch. It was six o'clock. "And when will that be?"

Mike munched hungrily at a biscuit and butter. "Oh, we'll probably go on for another couple of hours yet."

After the runners were re-iced, the sleds packed, and the traces untangled, they travelled until almost nine. Then, Ishawakta and Judasee turned the teams towards the shoreline.

She scrambled off the sled, picking her way through the barrier-ice. The dogs needed constant urging now so it would not be difficult to catch the *komatik* on the other side. She had no idea where they were going, but Mike had said they would build their overnight snowhouses inland. She assumed it was almost time to finish the interminable day. She also assumed from what the missionary had said that morning there would be two igloos. Strict propriety on the trail seemed like a waste of energy, but she shrugged and forgot about it.

She spent the next half hour thinking hard about warmth. *Let me count the ways.* Hot baths. Crackling fireplaces. Heat waves in downtown Toronto. Juicy hot hamburgers with spicy mustard. Good Lord, she was hungry, She tried not to think about food, but visions of steaming roast beef, fresh vegetables, and bowls of fruit kept flickering maddeningly through her mind. Her stomach groaned loudly. She looked again at Noota, but it was difficult now to see the woman's face. She wondered what the Eskimo was thinking as she sat there. Maybe the secret of survival on *komatik* trips was to think about nothing at all.

The dogs slowed and stopped. Ishawakta took a pole from the sled and carried it to a drift of snow at the base of a low hill. Judasee joined him, and the two young men talked briefly as they pushed into the drift with the pole. She got off the *komatik* and stood, clutching her arms around her body. Mike was leaning his face against the skins of the mission sled as though he were praying. It was a good idea. *Oh God,* she thought, *let this be the place we stop.* Ishawakta walked back to the *komatik*.

"*Peongeto,*" he said, avoiding her eyes. He picked up his whip and cracked it over the heads of the team. "*Hoit! Hoit!*" The dogs got reluctantly to their feet. She saw by her wristwatch that it was ten o'clock.

The Eskimos poked exploratively into another drift a half mile or so away and this time, Ishawakta took a saw from the sled. He cut an oblong block out of the snow which seemed to please him. He grinned at Judasee. "*Igluksak,*" he said.

Mike padded across from the mission *komatik*. "Well," he said without smiling. "We've got good snow. Now the work begins."

The two Eskimos traced twin circles and began sawing out snowblocks from the centre. Noota climbed down from the sled, stood watching for a moment, then began helping Ishawakta carry blocks to the outer edge of the circle. Mike was wearily doing the same job for Judasee. Dorothy started to help Noota with the carrying, but the snow was surprisingly heavy and she staggered. Breath fogged the inside of her glasses as she bent her head to work, then froze against the lenses. She stood, blind, helpless, and cold, scraping frantically at the glasses with the thumb of a mitten. But it was still difficult for her to see. She groped her way to the growing wall of blocks and crouched gratefully out of the bitter wind.

Squinting a little, she watched Ishawakta trim each three-foot-wide block until it slanted inwards to shape the rounded roof of the snowhouse. The Eskimo peered at her and grinned. She felt guilty about deserting the workteam. "*Eekee!*" she said, and pointed at her frosted glasses.

He nodded his understanding. "*Ee!*"

Noota, she saw, was smoothing snow between the blocks so there would be no cracks for the wind to penetrate. Dorothy got to her feet. This was something she could do, even if she could only half-see.

"*Peoyook!*" she heard Ishawakta laugh. "*Lutiapik chink!*"

Noota glanced at what she was doing, then went back to hauling snowblocks. Now that the circle had been excavated to the depth of about eighteen inches, Ishawakta was sawing deeper for more blocks to complete the trail shelter. The new digging also left enough snow on one side of the house for a raised sleeping platform. The Eskimo smoothed the inside walls of the igloo with a flat piece of wood and fixed the last of the roofblocks. For a moment, the Inuit stood stooped together in the darkness of the igloo. Then, Ishawakta knelt, pushed at one of the lower blocks and crawled outside. Noota followed. It was almost midnight.

Mike and Judasee were completing their igloo. She supposed she should say something sociable to the missionary, but instead, she huddled out of the wind, watching as Ishawakta unharnessed the dogs, threw the traces on top of the shelter, and fed the animals from the sack of walrus meat. The chunks looked ugly and unappetising, but her mouth watered. Then the Inuit took the skins and sleeping bags inside the snowhouse and unloaded the boxes of lamps and food.

She waited until she could see that the kerosene lantern had been lit, then slithered inside. Ishawakta had knocked pegs in the hard snow, one for the lantern, the others for clothes. Two candles sat on hacked-out ledges. She struggled out of her outer parka and beat the snow from the skin. Two boxes with primuses sitting on top had been placed near the sleeping platform and Ishawakta lit the stoves. Noota filled a pot with clean snow and put it on one flame. Dorothy rummaged hungrily for her gunnysack. She took two rounds of stew, tossed them into a pot, and set it on the other stove. Cooking time was limited inside a trail igloo, Don had warned her. Melted snow on the walls could freeze to ice, and ice was poor insulation against the cold.

But the stew bubbled quickly. By then she had buttered several pilot biscuits, opened a can of jam and a tin of peaches. Ishawakta took a haunch of frozen caribou from his own food sack, quickly cutting thin slices with a hunting knife. He chewed at the raw meat, grinning with pleasure. Noota silently reached with an *ooloo,* hacked a piece of cold caribou for herself, then cut a larger chunk which she put into the boiling water to warm.

"Ishawakta," Dorothy said, her mouth full of hot food. She pointed. "Take some stew if you want. Noota, too."

The Eskimo nodded and spooned some from her pot. He said something to Noota, and she found a spoon and took some stew as well. Then the caribou was warm, and the Inuit fished it from the water and shared the meat. Dorothy felt comfortable and well fed. She ate some of the peaches before giving the rest of the can to Noota. The Eskimo woman giggled a little as she noisily drank the sweet syrup. When more water was boiling, they made tea, lit cigarettes, and put out the stove. There was no talk.

Afterwards, Ishawakta crawled outside again and came back with another snowblock, which he dumped, parallel to the wall of the igloo. "Lutiapik," he pointed. "Bath."

Bath? She sat on her sleeping bag, her stiff skin clothes finally hung on the pegs. "Bath?" she said aloud.

Ishawakta laughed and opened the box in which she had packed soap, paper towels, and other personal items. He found a roll of toilet paper and perched it on the edge of the snow block. *My God,* she thought, *it's my can for the trail!* Without further comment, the Eskimo sealed the igloo, removed his clothes and slid into his sleeping bag. When she and Noota were settled in theirs, he leaned over to turn out the lantern. She lay awake for a few minutes, luxuriating in the comfort and listening to the muted roar of the wind outside. She laughed quietly to herself, realizing that the snow shelter was as warm and as draft-free as a first-class hotel room. She drifted into sleep to the sound of Noota's contented snores.

Ishawakta was reaching out of his sleeping bag to put a pot of snow on the lighted primus stove when she woke next morning. It was dark inside the igloo, and she lay lazily, touching her warm, rolled-up shirt and slacks with her bare toes.

She could see the thick hoar-frost stretching for at least a foot below her chin, and she shuddered at the thought of getting into the cold caribou-skin suit. Noota woke, swivelled on her stomach, and dipped into a food sack for a bag of rolled oats. No one spoke. Come to think of it, there seemed no reason to say good morning. Was it really a good morning? It was difficult to know, although she could still hear the wind howling outside. She was glad there seemed to be no rush to get up and away. She ate some porridge and drank some tea when it was ready. When she pulled on her clothes inside the sleeping bag, there was more hot water on the stove. She reached for some paper towels and washed her face and hands. She tossed her frozen toothpaste back into the box.

She wrestled into the stiff skin suit before crawling outside of the snowhouse. It was after ten o'clock and the sullen sky was brightening. The cold was as cutting as a honed razor, so she turned her back to the wind. Both Ishawakta and Judasee had harnessed the dogs and were carefully balancing the *komatiks* with luggage. Mike sat at the sheltered side of his igloo. The missionary grinned a little as she went to talk with him. He put his mittened hand up to protect his face. Neither of them said good morning.

"How cold do you think it is?" she asked.

"Well, it was forty below when we left Lake Harbour," he answered. "With the wind the way it is, I'd say the chill would make it about eighty below. It's going to be a cool run to Napatchee's."

She nodded. It would be cool. There was nothing she could say. She would have liked to have gone back inside the igloo, but Ishawakta had already packed the sleeping bags and was lashing the skins across the load. Noota stood waiting. The dogs yelped and got to their feet as the drivers gathered up the traces.

Mike lumbered to his knees. The back of his parka was already caked with snow. "Get ready to jump if you want to ride," he said flatly. "It looks as though we're off again."

"*Hoit! Hoit!*" yelled Ishawakta. The dogs threw themselves against the harness, and the *komatik* moved forward. She clawed herself on board. Today, she did not feel like singing.

Not long after that morning's trip through the barrier-ice, the plastic rim of her glasses snapped in the cold. At the first mug-up, she took some tape from her medical bag to stick the rim together again. It was a difficult job, complicated by the fact that the spectacles were in her hands and not on her nose. She removed her mittens to unwind and cut the adhesive; within seconds, her fingers were numb. She groaned as she quickly fixed the glasses, then threw the tape roll and surgical scissors back into her bag. She pulled on her gloves and covered them with the polar bear skin, but it took the rest of the break for feeling to come back into her hands.

They were off again down the coast. She tried to recall some of the names she had seen on a map in the Hudson's Bay store. Big Island. Crooks Inlet. The Spicer Islands. Every landmark looked exactly alike. At one point, she wondered with a mixture of panic and hope if there had been some mistake and they were headed back the way they had come. She could not ask Noota about it. The woman stared silently back at her during the constant frostbite checks and even though Dorothy tried an occasional *"eekee!"*, there was never an answer.

Mike grew gloomier and less coordinated in his jogging sessions as the day wore on. He had little to say at mug-ups. When they found themselves running almost side by side, he scarcely acknowledged she was there. Ishawakta and Judsasee were preoccupied with navigation. There was an occasional *"hoit!"* or a *"hraw!"* but otherwise, the Inuit were silent. Eventually, she was only conscious of cold, exhaustion, and the mesmeric hiss of runners in the snow.

The afternoon was dark when the teams turned again for the coast. Ishawakta was using his whip, but the dogs were tired. One or two stopped in their tracks and were dragged on by the others. They were close to the broken shoreline and she was jogging alongside the slow *komatik* when she heard the sound of dogs in the distance. There was a loud, responsive howl from the teams. Then, suddenly, the animals were sprinting, and she found she was being left behind.

"Ishawakta!" she yelled into the darkness. The *komatik* disappeared. She began to run faster, but the ice was rough and she stumbled and almost fell. Then she heard the familiar clatter of the sleds as they thumped through the barrier-ice. She clawed around the hummocks, following the loud crashes until she caught up with the *komatik* on the other side.

All she could remember of Napatchee's camp that night was a bowl of hot stew, the ache of her limbs, and the warmth of the sleeping bag when she stretched out on the crowded sleeping platform.

She slept for ten hours. When she woke, the family of Inuit in the canvas-walled snowhouse were drinking tea and eating their morning porridge. She turned on her stomach and saw that Ishawakta and Noota were crouched over a lighted primus stove. The camp igloo, she noted gratefully, was much warmer in the morning than the trail shelter had been. She dressed inside her sleeping bag and tugged on her duffle-socks. Ishawakta grinned without speaking when she came from the platform. He handed over her yellow mug filled with sweet tea.

She looked around the spacious snowhouse as she sipped. She recognized several of the Inuit. Two had been victims of the Lake Harbour flu epidemics. Three others had been treated at Christmas for boils and impetigo. Two children ran into the igloo, stopped to stare, then giggled. She smiled back at them. Both children had screamed and struggled when she had treated them for ear infections. She was happy they were not still terrified of her. Oatmeal was ready now, so she filled her bowl and poured evaporated milk over the porridge. Then she gave the rest of the can to the children.

After breakfast, she sat smoking a cigarette and waited for patients. None came forward. The men wandered out into the grey morning, some carrying sealing harpoons. The women began to sew or scrape skins. Perhaps, she thought, remembering her visits to Mingeriak's and Utye's, the Inuit presumed the *aniatitsiyuk* was only the *aniatitsiyuk* when she was at the nursing station.

"Ishawakta," she said, putting out her cigarette, "ask if any pain in camp."

There was more impetigo. There were more ear infections. There was an awkward tooth extraction. There was a baby ready for a booster shot. Two mothers wanted fresh supplies of cod liver oil. Mike ducked into the snowhouse to ask if there were any infants there to be baptized. He said he would be celebrating Holy Communion in the opposite igloo and then he and Judasee would make an early start down the coast towards Cape Dorset.

He cleared his throat. "Oh, and Dorothy – " He hesitated, then started again. "There's a young man in another snowhouse. He wants to see you."

She was counting out some aspirin from a big bottle. "Can't he come in here, Mike?" She looked up at him.

"It would be better," he said slowly, "if you would go to him."

She gave the aspirin to the woman who had asked for it,

pulled on her outer parka, and followed Mike into the cold. She had not noticed when they had arrived the night before, but there were three large snowhouses and two smaller igloos in Napatchee's camp. Mike led her to one of the small shelters and she crawled inside. It was empty, except for a teenage boy who was sitting on the sleeping platform. He eyed her warily.

The missionary nervously adjusted his glasses. "This is Pudloo," he said. "There's something wrong with his, er, scrotum."

"I see," Dorothy said. "Well, I'll have to look at it. Can you ask him to take down his pants, Mike?"

There was no answer and she turned to see why. The missionary had his back to her and his neck was scarlet with embarrassment.

"Mike," she said, hoping she sounded as clinical as possible, "I can't examine the patient unless he takes down his pants."

The missionary kept his face to the wall of the igloo. He said some words to the Eskimo, and the boy slowly unbuttoned his denim trousers. She motioned to show she wanted him to stretch out on the sleeping platform and he did so. She began her examination. The scrotum was badly swollen. She felt carefully around the area. There certainly seemed to be abnormalities. It could be a tumour.

"It could be a tumour," she said aloud. "I can't possibly do anything about it. If Pudloo could get to the station in Frobisher Bay, he could see a doctor or be flown out to Montreal. Could you tell him that?"

There was silence. The boy buttoned his pants. "Mike," she said, "I've finished. Could you tell Pudloo that I think his problem is serious and that he should try to get to Frobisher?" When the missionary turned to speak to the young Eskimo, she left the igloo.

Mike came to say good-bye before he and Judasee left for Cape Dorset. She was washing the head of an aged woman who had come to see her from the opposite snowhouse. It was one of the most severe cases of impetigo that she had seen.

"I've suggested," the missionary said, dropping his mittens, then retrieving them, "that Pudloo come to Lake Harbour in case

168

a plane gets in. Maybe he can go out on the Beaver that's coming for Hilda."

She could see Mike was still acutely embarrassed about the scrotum case so she merely commented that his idea was good, dried her hands, then walked to the door of the snowhouse to watch his *komatik* slide quickly towards the shore. Mike turned and raised his arm once, and she waved back. She supposed she should feel a sense of loss, now that her only white travelling companion had gone. A few months ago, in fact, she might have contemplated the days ahead and grown apprehensive.

She went back to the old woman who was sitting, waiting patiently on her upended grub box. She giggled, and Dorothy smiled back at her and continued the job of washing her head. The only thing really worrying her, she realized with interest, was that there would be so many impetigo cases on the trip, she would run out of aureomycin ointment.

That night, she told Ishawakta she would like to leave Napatchee's camp next morning and head towards Kooyoo's.

"Okay?" The Eskimo, after all, knew better than she did about whether it was safe to travel.

He grinned his approval. "Okay."

"How many sleeps?" she asked, holding up her fingers.

Ishawakta indicated the trip would take three sleeps, then held up another finger. Four. "One camp on trail," he said, struggling to find the words. "Then Kooyoo's."

She sipped at a bedtime mug of bouillon. The Inuit, gorged on that day's good catch of seal, were already drifting to the sleeping platform. The snowhouse was very warm. Blue tobacco smoke clung around the lantern. *Kooyoo's!* The name had a primitive ring. Kooyoo's camp, after all, was the distant boundary of her territory. The turn-around point of nursing rounds. The remote spot was like the furthest bed in the last ward on the hospital floor. She put down her mug.

"Lutiapik," said Ishawakta. He came from the door where he had been speaking with a man. "That man Koopak. Son *anneayoo*. You come?"

She struggled into her outer parka. Koopak led them to the

opposite big snow house. The sleeping platform in the igloo was filled with sleeping Inuit but one young man stirred from where he was lying in the skins and vomited into an enamel basin.

"*Anneayoo!*" grunted Koopak.

"How long has his son been sick?" Dorothy asked, holding up her fingers as she had when she asked about the trip to Kooyoo's. Ishawakta shook his head. It took some time and more pantomime before he understood.

"*Ee,*" he eventually nodded, pleased at his success. He spoke to Koopak then made Dorothy understand that the son's name was Kavavoo and that he had been sick for two sleeps. But not as sick as now. She decided not to try asking why she had not been called earlier. She took her clinical thermometer from the black bag and put it under the young man's tongue. By the yellow light of the seal oil lamp, she saw that it registered 101 degrees. Kavavoo clutched at his stomach.

"*Nangoovook!*" he groaned. Pain in belly.

She stood looking down at the sick Eskimo. Could he be suffering from gastroenteritis? There seemed to be no diarrhoea. Pleurisy? Kidney stones? An intestinal obstruction? She bit her lip, trying to remember what she had learned in training about appendicitis. Mild fever. Nausea and vomiting. The abdominal wall rigid and tight. Direct rebound tenderness over the appendix area.

She patted her stomach, then pointed at the patient. "I must look at Kavavoo here," she told Ishawakta. He understood. He spoke to the young Eskimo and the patient pulled down the bedding skins. His abdomen was rigid. She pressed gently into the right lower quadrant and Kavavoo moaned "a'a" when she removed her fingers. He turned and vomited again. Dorothy sighed and gritted her teeth. It was probably appendicitis.

One night in Lake Harbour she had sweated about what she would do if ever she encountered a "hot" abdomen in the Arctic. The proper thing, of course, would be to have the patient flown out to a hospital – provided the case was conveniently in the settlement and an aircraft could be summoned in time. Surgery? An early operation was always indicated in appendix cases, even when the diagnosis was doubtful. But she shivered to think what might happen if someone as ignorant in surgery as herself tried to perform an appendectomy. Kavavoo continued to groan loudly, but there was no other sound or movement from those on the sleeping platform. Koopak and Ishawakta watched her stolidly.

She dipped into her medical bag and brought out the medical manual. The priority here was to get the infection under control before the appendix perforated and the case became complicated by peritonitis. The only way of doing this was to administer massive doses of antibiotics. She moved to the blubber lamp, lit a match from a box lying on the floor, and studied the section in the manual dealing with appendicitis. When the match burned out, she struck another, squinting to read the small type.

The manual suggested a narcotic for pain. And, for the conservative treatment of appendicitis, two cubic centimeters of aureomycin, administered intravenously. She had never given an intravenous injection, but this was clearly an emergency. She took a syringe, a tourniquet and a vial of aureomycin from the bag and injected the antibiotic into Kavavoo's vein. Then she gave him a shot of morphine.

"I'll sleep here with Kavavoo tonight," she told Ishawakta in words and gestures when the patient seemed to be more comfortable. "Would you bring my sleeping bag?"

The painkiller did its work. She woke twice during the night to give more injections of aureomycin. In the morning, the Inuit were moving around the snowhouse, but Kavavoo was still sleeping. She dressed quietly and went to find Ishawakta and Noota. The Eskimos were making breakfast in the opposite igloo. Ishawakta grinned when she came through the door and handed her a mug of tea. She sat on the upended grub box, thinking about what to do. When Kavavoo woke, she would check his temperature. If it had not gone down, she would give him another two c.c.'s of the drug. But if he had improved, she would administer a five-day shot of penicillin and start him on aureomycin orally. In any case, it would be as well for her to stay at Napatchee's and check the patient for at least another sleep.

"Ishawakta," she said after they had eaten their morning porridge. "See if there is any more pain in camp."

Kavavoo was smiling a little and asking for food by evening. She wrote a note outlining her treatment and made Ishawakta understand that the patient should try to get to a settlement where he could be flown to a doctor. The message would explain what had happened. She had no doubt Kavavoo would keep the note. The Inuit, she had discovered, kept every scrap of paper given to them. When Ishawakta came back into the snowhouse she said she would like to move out next morning. "Okay?"

"Okay," nodded the Eskimo. "We go Kooyoo's."

It was still dark when she and Noota floundered through the barrier-ice and waited for the *komatik*. After two days of rest, the dogs were eager to run; the crashes and pained yowls as the sled slammed against and around the scattered ice slabs seemed louder than ever in the frigid morning air. Once again, there was the exhilaration of sled-travelling, which she knew would disappear as she grew colder, tired, and bored. She was aware there was little she could do about the boredom and the cold. But she wondered whether there was something she could do about the crushing exhaustion.

Both Ishawakta and Noota seemed to be less fatigued than she was at mug-ups and at the end of the day. She asked herself why. Perhaps it was because they were Inuit, or that they were veterans of winter travel. She tugged at her parka hood, wishing it covered more of her forehead. Then she took time to check the differences between the way she and the Eskimos lived on the trail. She was as warmly dressed as they were – even more warmly than Ishawakta, who left his caribou-skin suit on the sled and travelled in a duffle-cloth parka topped with another made of Grenfell cloth. She had as much sleep as the Inuit. And she had as much to eat.

She got off the *komatik* to jog, thinking about food. The Eskimos ate raw caribou at mug-ups, and they scarcely warmed the meat at night. Sometimes they took some of her supplies if they were offered but there was no indication they preferred *kabloonah* food. She wondered if canned stew, porridge, pilot biscuits, and soupee were nutritious enough to keep her from hanging in the saddle. The sled slowed, and Ishawakta unhitched the dogs, unpacked the *komatik*, and lit the primus stove. He put the wooden grub box at her feet then fetched an unskinned haunch of caribou from his own sack. It looked as unappetizing as a carcass hanging in a butcher shop.

She opened her food box and looked at her packages of biscuits and the cardboard cartons of bouillon cubes. "Ishawakta," she said. She swallowed quickly. "I'd like to try a piece of *tuktu*." She pointed at the raw caribou and then at her mouth.

The Eskimo laughed. *"Tuktu?"* He hacked a thin slice from the haunch and handed it to her. She held it in her mittened hands for a long moment, then put it in her mouth. The frozen meat was cold against her tongue. She allowed it to melt, then chewed. She smiled. It was surprisingly good.

"Peoyook!" grinned Ishawakta. Noota came with her *ooloo* and silently cut herself a piece of meat.

"Peoyook," Dorothy agreed and held out her hand for more.

After that, she ate one or two slices of caribou with her pilot biscuits and bouillon at every mug-up. It was difficult, at first, to tell whether she was less tired or whether the experiment was interesting her enough to make her feel more alert. She spent the day trying to remember what she had been taught about protein values and whether cooking did anything to damage the nutritional content of foods. There was the danger of trichinosis, of course, but it seemed reasonable that meat in its natural state would be more nutritious than meat subjected to long periods of heat. She pondered the irony of the white man's well-meaning interference in the Inuit way of life. *D for Dentist. X for X-ray. E for Exhaustion.*

They turned towards the coast again, and she checked her watch. It was only four o'clock, so Ishawakta was clearly not preparing to stop for the night. There was no point in asking the Eskimo where they were going. She had told him she wanted to visit Kooyoo's camp, so she supposed they were heading in that direction. There was the familiar nightmare of the barrier-ice then the sled bumped over low hills marked with black outcroppings of rock and occasional patches of gravel blown bare of snow by the wind. Ishawakta was busier than ever, guiding the *komatik* around obstructions that could knock the precious mud off the runners.

She nudged Noota and the two women stared solemnly at each other's faces.

"*Agai?*" she questioned. Noota shook her head.

God, her face was so numb, she was sure it must be frostbitten. The tartan scarf over her mouth was heavy with rime and an icicle hung from the fur of her hood. She straddled the load, pushing her forehead against the soft bear skin. But it was an uncomfortable way to ride. She got down to run again, but it was more difficult now that they were off the smooth sea-ice. It was dark, and clouds were scudding across the stars. Then the wind gusted and it began to snow.

She stood, frozen with cold and panic. The *komatik* had disappeared in the white-out, and it was impossible to know which way to move. "Ishawakta!" she screamed. "Noota! Over here!" For a terrible moment, there was nothing around her but the roar of the wind and the lash of the hard snow pellets against her forehead. She put out her arms, groping blindly. Then she felt a hand grip her wrist.

"Lutiapik," said Ishawakta in her ear. "*Komatik* here. Sit behind." She took three steps forward, and her shoulder hit the high load. She slid quickly to the ground beside Noota, her knees drawn up to her chin, and her face buried deep in her arms.

The white-out lasted for a half hour, then the dogs shook themselves, Ishawakta yelled "*hoit!*", and they slid off again across the empty tundra. They stopped for one more mug-up before nine o'clock, then Ishawakta began looking for good igloo snow. He seemed to be having trouble. Three successive drifts displeased him, and although he sawed two blocks out of a fourth, he whipped up the team and drove on. Noota watched, her face buried in her parka hood, as the Eskimo poled into yet another drift and returned to the *komatik* shaking his head.

Dorothy groaned. She was definitely not as tired or as hungry as she had been on the first day of the trip, but she longed to get out of the awful wind and into her sleeping bag. The sled stopped again, and the two women stared hopefully into the gloom as Ishawakta poled and thumped thoughtfully at the drift of snow with the soles of his *kamiks*. He pulled his saw from the *komatik* and cut two blocks, then a third. He came back to the sled, grinning. *"Igluksak,"* he announced.

"Now the work begins," said Dorothy. She jumped down from the load. It was eleven o'clock. That night inside the trail igloo she ate frozen caribou along with her stew and part of a raw ptarmigan Ishawakta had brought from Napatchee's.

It was hopeless for a *kabloonah* to try to understand how the Inuit found their way around the seemingly featureless barrens. She sat on the *komatik* noting a distant mountain, a cluster of hills, a tall rock, and wondered how Ishawakta navigated by these few landmarks. There seemed little to guide him to Seemeegak's remote camp in Amadjuak country. But suddenly, she was surprised to hear the distant howl of dogs and to feel the sled gain speed. The stop was a bonus. They had travelled for two cloudy, gale-plagued days. Now, it was just five o'clock on the third afternoon. She swivelled to see ahead, shielding her face from the wind with her mittens. Hummocks, hills, rocks, and snow. It was another ten minutes before the *komatik* slid to a halt near a single large snowhouse.

She and Noota climbed down from the load. Two Eskimo men dressed in bulky caribou skins stood watching them silently. Ishawakta unhurriedly lodged his whip against the front box, unhooked the dogs from the sled, then strolled over to the Inuit to shake hands. There was some talk and short bursts of laughter. The Eskimo returned to the *komatik* and began to unpack. He looked up at her as he knelt to unknot a thong.

"That man Seemeegak," he said without pointing and went on with his work. Dorothy looked across at the Eskimos. They were still standing, as motionless as stone cairns. She had no idea which man was the camp leader, but she walked from the sled and held out her mittened hand to the closest. He held it for a moment, then released it. She shook hands with the other man then went into the igloo.

It was spacious and clean inside. She had already noticed there was less garbage and litter around this camp than at Utye's or Napatchee's, possibly because Seemeegak and his family lived further away from the white trading post than the other Inuit. Now, she saw there was less crowding. Two Eskimo women sat sewing on the wide sleeping platform. Three small children interrupted their game to stare. Together with the men outside, Seemeegak's camp seemed to consist of only seven individuals.

Noota entered the house and said something brief in Eskimo. One of the women nodded and giggled. Dorothy took off her outer parka, beat it with a stick she found lying near the drying rack, and hung it with other clothes over the seal oil lamp. Then she pulled off her inner parka, knocked the snow from her *kamiks* and sat on the platform.

There were other differences about Seemeegak's snowhouse. Unlike other camps she had visited, there were no kerosene lanterns and no primus stove. All of the stone lamps were fuelled by seal oil. There were more skins than blankets on the sleeping platform, and the few white enamel pots were so old they must have been family heirlooms. On one side of the tent there was a wooden box on top of which was a large tin of cigarette tobacco, a box of wooden matches, an *ooloo,* and an enamel basin. A cardboard suitcase sat on the hard-packed snow floor, with three metal mugs arranged on the lid.

Ishawakta came into the igloo with her grub box, medical kit, and sleeping bag. *"Peoyook,"* he said, looking around the house. "Snow come now." He went out again.

She peered through the low door. He was right. Heavy snow was falling and she could barely see the outlines of the *komatik.* The dogs were yelping, and she assumed they were being fed early. One of the Eskimo men came into the house and dumped a large haunch of caribou on the floor. The other beat his parka, hung it on the rack, and sat smoking silently on the platform.

Outside, the storm was worsening. The children were playing again, and Noota had crawled wordlessly into her sleeping bag. There was a loud snore.

"*Peongeto*," said Ishawakta, bringing in gunny sacks and skins. "Big snow come. Maybe many sleeps."

She looked at him, startled, holding up a hand. "How many sleeps?"

He shrugged, counting his fingers. "Two, maybe three." He laughed. "We stay Seemeegak's. *Peoyook*."

Noota snored again. Dorothy hesitated for a moment, then took her parka from the rack and went outside to relieve herself. She kept close to the snowhouse, knowing how easy it was to get lost in a white-out. Inside again, she rolled out her own sleeping bag, wriggled inside and removed her clothes. When she woke, hours later, the Eskimos had eaten their evening meal and were already motionless under their skin bedding. The igloo was dark except for the dim glow of one blubber lamp; she could hear the howl of the blizzard outside. She was hungry, but there was no convenient kitchen refrigerator to raid, and she was not sure where Ishawakta had stowed her box. Besides, it was incredibly cold; she hated to leave the warm bag.

She wondered fleetingly why no one had wakened her, then shrugged. If anyone chose to sleep rather than eat, wash, or relieve themselves, the Inuit apparently felt it was not their business to interfere. If she was really trapped in this place for days, she realized it would be her own responsibility to keep herself fed, comfortable, and sane.

When she woke next, it was morning. The Eskimos were drinking tea and eating porridge. She dressed quickly and went to the primus stove where Ishawakta was heating a pot of snow for tea and washing water. She thought hungrily of the kind of breakfast she would enjoy to eat now. Fresh eggs and sausages. Hot toast, thick with butter. A plate of firm, sliced tomatoes. Percolated coffee. A glass of fresh milk.

"Teamee," grinned Ishawakta, giving her a mug. He walked across the igloo and returned with a large piece of Eskimo bannock. Noota and Dorothy each broke off a lump. She opened a

177

can of butter, spread some on the bannock, then left the can sitting on the suitcase. She hoped Seemeegak's family would take it. Butter, she was sure, was a rare luxury in a camp so far from a settlement. She put extra sugar on her oatmeal, hoping the extravagance would cheer her up. It didn't.

The day deteriorated into an aimless nightmare. Ishawakta asked if there was any pain in the camp but no one came forward with the problems she expected. There was no toothache, earache, or impetigo. She found the family had not gone to the *Howe* and gave the five-year-old boy a DPT booster. There were no boils. One woman asked Ishawakta to tell the *aniatitsiyuk* she would like some aspirin for *neakoongooyok*, simple headache. The other remembered she had had a belly pain many sleeps ago, so Dorothy gave her some bismuth. By midday, there was nothing else she could do. She sat on her grub box staring through the snow porch into the white-out.

She gorged herself indulgently on hot stew, biscuits and jam, and a can of raspberries for lunch, while she studied the chapter on nutritional deficiencies in the manual. She offered some food to Seemeegak and his family. They politely accepted a spoonful of stew and a biscuit spread with jam, but returned to their huge meal of half-raw caribou.

The women continued to sew, the men sat on the skins polishing soapstone carvings with their bare hands or making bird spears. Ishawakta chatted, smoked, and occasionally strolled into the storm. Noota slept and snored.

Dorothy had been using a tin chamber pot in a corner of the igloo, but she had not had a bowel movement since leaving Lake Harbour. The wind had eased, she noticed, and she knelt at the porch watching Ishawakta dig into the snow to rouse the dogs from their nests. There was no real indication that the storm was over or that the Eskimo was thinking of leaving, so she assumed he was merely making sure the animals were not suffocating. Ice covers in the burrows caused from condensing breath could cut off the dogs' air supply. The animals stood, shaking themselves and yelping in the gentle snowfall. She found her outer parka on the drying rack. She would have to beat the skin again when she returned to the house, so she took the stick from the floor together with a roll of toilet paper.

The cold outside was a shock so she hurried to the side of the igloo sheltered from the wind and unbuttoned her slacks. Her buttocks were bare when four dogs appeared around the side of the snowhouse and rushed at her. She struck out with the beating stick and they backed off for a moment, then closed in again. She struggled to finish her business, and pulled desperately at her clothes. The animals growled and snapped at each other as they hungrily devoured her warm feces.

She was shaking with horror when she stood inside the doorway of the igloo, thumping at her parka. No one had moved very much since she had gone outside; no one acknowledged her return. One of the Eskimo men had found some comic books and was sitting on the edge of the sleeping platform leafing through them. She perched on her grub box, lit a cigarette while she calmed herself, and reviewed her choice of activities for the afternoon.

She could sleep. She could read the manual. She could stare into space. She could borrow a comic book. She wished she could talk to the Inuit. She wished she could talk to anybody at all. With a sigh, she went to the sleeping platform and took a tattered book from the little pile. Blondie. L'il Abner. Dick Tracy. She wondered if she had ever thought that comic strips were funny. She stooped her head to look through the porch door and saw the snow was falling thickly again. She threw the book on the sleeping platform, wriggled into her sleeping bag, and undressed. She closed her eyes. This time, she hoped she could stay asleep for the next twenty-four hours.

The blizzard continued for another two days. Each time she dragged herself reluctantly from sleep to eat, wash her face, or squat over a chamber pot she became more determined not to travel on to Kooyoo's. She began by rationalizing that the isolated camp was probably as healthy as Seemeegak's, anyway. Then she admitted to herself that Arctic travel was terrifying and that she was beginning to experience the symptoms of bush fever. She realized it would take all of her mental and physical resources to make the return trip to Lake Harbour.

Ishawakta still seemed to be enjoying his visit to the camp. She marvelled at the way the Inuit men and women patiently whiled away their imprisonment by sewing, fetching caribou meat from their cache, eating, and polishing their carvings. There was frequent sexual intercourse on the sleeping platform, but she closed her ears to the intimate sounds of love-making. The morning the snow stopped and the sky cleared, she sat on the grub box and watched Ishawakta put away the breakfast pots.

"Ishawakta. Snow finished?"

He grinned. *"Ee.* Go Kooyoo's."

She rocked back and forth on the box. "Go Lake Harbour. Okay?"

There was a flicker of surprise in his eyes. "No Kooyoo's?"

"No Kooyoo's. Lake Harbour. Okay?"

"Okay. *Mana.* Go now."

She held up her hand. "How many sleeps?"

Three, maybe four. "Snow finish." He scratched his head to remember another word. "Maybe."

She sat at the door of the igloo, watching him ice the runners of the Health and Welfare *komatik.* The two Inuit men had also upended their sled. Although they had all lived intimately together for so many days, she was still unsure which of the men was Seemeegak.

The men loaded the sled with spears, guns, and a sack of meat, harnessed their dogs, and slid off across the tundra without a farewell glance. Ishawakta began the job of transferring their luggage from the igloo to the *komatik.* Noota yawned and rolled up her sleeping bag. Dorothy stood in the middle of the snowhouse, remembering why she had come to the camp and wondering if there was still something she should do. The Inuit women glanced up from their sewing, grinned, then went back to work again. She began the awkward task of getting into her caribou-skin clothes.

10

She celebrated her return to Lake Harbour by soaking in a hot tub, washing her hair, and cleaning her teeth. The run back from Seemeegak's had taken four sleeps because of a morning blizzard. She filed her nails, dressed in clean clothes, and dashed a little perfume behind her ears. Then she zipped herself into her duffle-cloth parka and brought a ptarmigan from the hill freezer. After Oola had stoked the stove and gone to store her caribou suit in the shed, she covered the skinned bird with strips of bacon and put it in the oven to roast. She stood, looking around the livingroom. Never had the simple little house seemed so luxurious. She put a record on the player and went to the telephone. Iktoluka's body had been removed from the porch. She wondered whether to call Gerry first, or Hilda.

"Hello, Hilda?"

"Hi! We heard you were back. It's about time. We need you for canasta. I'm packing, you know. The Beaver should be here in a week."

"How are things?" Why had she expected her neighbours would be breathlessly interested in her trip?

"Everything's the same. The cops were over a couple of nights ago. Gerry released that body you had on the porch, and the boy's father took it somewhere down the fjord. Mike's still in Dorset. There was something on the 'Northern Messenger' for you and Gerry took it down. We only stayed up for the B's. Hold on. Don wants to say hello."

"Hi! You get to Kooyoo's?"

"No." Would she ever feel regret that she had not visited the farthest camp in her territory? "There was a blizzard. I'll tell you about it later."

"When are you coming for canasta?"

"Not tonight. I'm eating roast ptarmigan and turning in early to sleep in a real bed. And read something besides comic books and the medical manual."

Don laughed. "See you tomorrow perhaps. Give Gerry a call about the 'Messenger'."

She checked the ptarmigan then called the detachment.

"Gerry?"

"Hi! Heard you were back. We need you for bridge." He laughed. "Say Dorothy, why do you tell so many lies?"

"What lies?" Didn't he even want to know what kind of a trip it had been?

"Oh come on. You know what I mean."

"I don't know what you mean. What lies?"

"Well. . . . How old did you say you were?"

"Twenty-eight."

"Not thirty-two?"

"Gerry!" She was suddenly annoyed at the conversation, and she did not want to get annoyed. Not tonight. Not with Gerry. "What lies, Gerry?"

"It's just that something came over the 'Messenger' about your birthday."

"It isn't until May. You know that."

"Maybe your family wanted to get in early."

She wanted to hang up. "Do you have the message?"

"Terr . . . ee . . ." she heard Gerry say away from the receiver. "You got that message we wrote down for Dorothy?"

There was a pause, then the constable came back to the telephone. "Okay. Here it is. 'Thirty-two, not so old yet'."

"Would you repeat that, please?"

"Thirty-two, not so old yet." He laughed.

"Thank you," she said stiffly. She started to hang up, then stopped herself. "Actually, that's very funny," she said.

"Oh? Why."

"I'll tell you later. Goodnight."

She went back into the kitchen, her cheeks flaming. She sat on a chair, gripping her hands together, astonished by her reaction to Gerry's teasing, and telling herself to forget it. *It's just the tension of the past few days,* she thought. Then she began to laugh. It really *was* very funny. Now she wanted to tell everyone in the settlement about it. The message was probably from her sister Sylvia; it involved a house the family was trying to sell at 32 Cranbrooke Avenue. It must have been easy for Gerry, listening to the crackling radio in Lake Harbour, to mistake "Thirty-two not sold yet" for "Thirty-two, not so old yet."

She had been dreaming about soft spring rain. The kind of rain that trickled from the eaves on Waverley Road and nourished the new green growth in the garden. The big cherry tree bloomed in the spring, and Jiggs and all the other dogs and cats the family had befriended were buried under it. She half-woke once during the night, feeling thirsty and wishing she had not had the extra glass of Scotch at Hilda's going-away party. The thermometer had registered forty degrees below when Gerry escorted her to her door at midnight. She had stood for a moment with him in the porch.

"Look, Dorothy. I knew you were twenty-eight all the time!"

She laughed up at him. "I believe you." But did she? Twenty-eight was a bad enough age to be still unmarried. Thirty-two was disaster.

"You're not still mad at me?"

"I never was."

Now she was really awake. It was an impossibility in February, but the sound of running water was real. She thought there might be some turned-on faucets in the house. But then she remembered there were no taps in Lake Harbour. Had she been sleeping for three months, right through until spring? She saw by her luminous clock that it was eight o'clock in the morning. She switched on the lights and belted herself into her robe. Water was pouring off the roof of the house and she could hear the snow sliding and thunking, like the sound of a defrosting refrigerator. She shone her flashlight through the livingroom window at the outside thermometer.

"Oh come on!" she said aloud. The mercury had risen almost eighty degrees during the night, to thirty-eight above.

She sat in the livingroom chair, wishing she could make some coffee, but Oola had not yet arrived to light the coal stove. Thirty-eight above in February? She remembered now that Don had once mentioned there were sometimes mid-winter thaws in the Arctic but she hadn't really taken him seriously. Thaws, it seemed, were worse than 100 m.p.h. gales and severe blizzards. If a *komatik* were on the trail, the sled would bog down in wet snow and be stranded. Igloos in the winter camps would melt, and the Inuit would have to put up tents until they could next find *igluksak*. Meat in stone caches would thaw and perhaps rot. It was stifling in the house. She wished she could open a window.

Oola came silently through the door and began to work at the stove. She knew it was hopeless trying to talk to the woman about the incredible rise in temperature. Ishawakta arrived to collect her toilet can, grinned, and said it was hot. *"Ookoo!"*

"Bad?" she asked.

He nodded. *"Peongeto."*

She finished her breakfast then walked across the squelching compound to the Hudson's Bay post. The sky was brightening now; the mercury had risen to almost fifty degrees. After the biting cold of the past few months, she should have welcomed the balmy air. But there was another thud of sliding snow, and she knew she was scared.

Hilda's open trunk was standing in the middle of the living-room floor. "It's a chinook!" Don said when she came through the door, quickly ridding herself of her parka.

"How long will it last?"

"Probably a couple of days. But the ice underfoot is murder when it freezes up again. No one will be able to travel until we get more good snow. Lucky that Mike got back from Cape Dorset."

Hilda bustled into the room with an armful of clothes, chattering about Florida and the South Seas. There had been some emotional moments at the farewell party, but the young woman from Newfoundland had clearly made up her mind that her departure would be as matter-of-fact as her arrival had been. She dumped shoes into the trunk. "I hope the Beaver doesn't have any trouble."

"It'll be okay," said Don. He seemed to be as cheerful as Hilda. "The sea-ice is six feet thick in the fjord. But it'll be slushy under the runners. Oh, and by the way, I heard from Nottingham Island that there are three Eskimos on board the aircraft. Coming home from the Hamilton San. They're Gerry's responsibility. The Inuit will take them in until they can get back to their camps."

She thought unhappily about the Eskimos at Utye's, Napatchee's, and Seemeegak's and hoped there were no hunters out with sleds. She supposed that if there were they would abandon the *komatiks* and load their meat on to the backs of the dogs. *Meat!* She turned to Don and saw in his eyes that they had both suddenly thought of the same thing.

"Good Lord," he said, getting to his feet. "The freezer!"

They hurried to the side of the hill. Don flung open the wooden doors of the meat safe. The stench was awful. She stared into the hole and saw it dripping with water and that the earth floor was awash with blood from the thawed meat. Her sack of ptarmigan, a large piece of caribou, and some Arctic char she had hoarded was on the left of the cache. She hauled the soggy sack into the open air.

Hilda ducked her head around the freezer door. "Well, there goes the *Rupertsland* pork roast, Don. And the caribou. And the last of the chickens I brought with me."

"How does it look?" Mike asked when he came across the compound. He stood, wringing his hands worriedly.

"Let's say," Don said, "we'd all better start doing some serious cooking. The stuff won't last for too long in the refrigerators. I'd better call Gerry so he can get his sack." Then he grinned a little wistfully at Hilda; Dorothy felt the way she had when one of her brothers had failed an exam, got into trouble for smoking, and bruised a knee, all in the same day. "*Ayonamut*," he said.

Dorothy unpacked her sack on the kitchen table. The char and the small ptarmigan were already slimy and odorous. She tossed the spoiled fish and birds into a pot for Ishawakta to feed to the always-ravenous dogs. The caribou was a problem. The piece she had traded for four cans of butter and some jam weighed at least ten pounds and she had been planning to hack a roast from it every few weeks. She cut the greying outer layer from the meat and put the haunch into the oven to roast. At least the cooked caribou would make sandwiches as long as it was edible. She checked the nursing station thermometer. The temperature had risen to sixty degrees.

Ishawakta was coming from his house with another Eskimo. She waited at the window until the Inuit were closer. It was Pudloo, she was pleased to see, the young man with the scrotum problem from Napatchee's camp. She went to the porch door.

"Pudloo," Ishawakta said. "Go Beaver?"

Pudloo grinned at her. He had probably walked from the camp. She had not been sure whether the young man would take her advice about going to Frobisher Bay, but Mike's mention of the Beaver must have intrigued him. She nodded and smiled. "We ask." She wondered about Kavavoo, the appendicitis patient.

"Ishawakta," she said, rubbing her stomach. "Kavavoo. *Nangoovok*. Kavavoo okay?"

The Eskimo nodded his understanding and turned to Pudloo. The Inuit exchanged a few words. "Kavavoo okay," Ishawakta told her. "Go *Howe* when come. Okay?"

It seemed like a sensible decision. "Okay."

The Beaver flew into the fjord just after midday. She could see the water from the melted sea-ice spurting from the runners as it landed. Three Eskimos climbed down from the cabin and stood, staring a little uncertainly at the settlement. Georgie and Sandy loaded Hilda's luggage on a small sled and dragged it through the wet snow and ice to the aircraft. She followed them with Pudloo. After clearing the trip with Don, she had given the Eskimo a note to deliver to Heather Matthews in Frobisher Bay. She looked up at the pilot. The man was sitting, the mail sack in his hands, waiting for his passengers.

"Nice summer resort you've got here," he grinned at Dorothy. He leaned out of the plane to help Pudloo inside then grabbed the trunk and suitcases. "Don't think I'll get out. I didn't bring my galoshes."

She laughed back at the man, wanting to talk with someone new from the outside world, but not knowing what to ask or say. "How are things in Frobisher?" she finally asked.

"The same as ever," he answered, handing out the mail.

The constables were walking through the puddles from the detachment side of the bay. She could see Hilda and Don with Mike close behind setting out from the glistening ridge of melting barrier-ice. Georgie said something to the three Inuit, and they nodded and started walking towards the shore. She saw they were wearing ordinary leather boots and wondered how long they had been away from their homes.

Hilda's calm had broken, and she was weeping a little when she reached the aircraft. She hugged everyone, kissed Don, and climbed into the Beaver.

"Hi Bill," Don said. "How are things in Frob?"

The man shrugged again. "The same as ever."

"Don," said Hilda, "You have Nylee cook that pork roast tonight, you hear? Ask Dorothy over."

Everyone laughed. "Don't forget to write, now," Hilda was saying. "Even if the letters never get out."

"God bless," said Mike. "I hope it's a boy."

Then the door slammed, everyone stood back and the engines coughed and roared. She could hear the runners sluicing through the water as the aircraft gained speed. *One little, two little* she thought as she waved. *And now there are only five.*

The mercury dipped to forty below during the night of the following day. She woke to an ice-rink world made even more hazardous by a stiff wind from the north. Bars of icicles hung from the roof over her windows. Oola was late and so was Ishawakta. When the Eskimo finally came through the door, he unsmilingly shook his head.

"Oola not come," he said as he lit the coal stove. *"Peongeto!"*

After he left, she cooked breakfast, then stood at the living-room window looking out at the settlement. Once again, she felt the lonely panic of Arctic imprisonment. If she ventured along the slick, hard paths of the compound she knew the wind would knock her off her feet and that she would have to crawl back home on her belly. She shuddered, remembering Don's story of the Eskimos who sailed to their deaths down the slippery fjord. She knew, too, that her neighbours were also trapped in their houses; that the settlement telephone was probably not working because of ice on the wires. She picked up the receiver to check and was surprised to hear men's voices. Don and Gerry.

"I don't know how long we're fucking well socked in," Don was complaining. "All I know is that I'd fall flat on my bloody face if I stepped outside the fucking door."

"Did Nylee cook the roast?" Gerry asked.

"It's cooked. You want to come and help me eat it?"

Gerry laughed. "You must be bloody well out of your mind. I got some magazines in the mail. I'm going to hole up with a bottle of Scotch until it fucking well starts to snow."

Dorothy listened breathlessly. She had known men used words like that. She had read them. But no one, not even her brothers, had ever uttered them in her hearing. She guiltily held the receiver to her ear.

"Who's got the Inuit?"

"Akavak and Pitsulala. It could be days before we can get them back to the bloody camps. They're not saying a damned thing, but it's a fucking shame. Akeego's been out for more than two years."

She quietly replaced the receiver. She was not shocked, only interested. It was all part of the mystique of existing in an isolated community, of course. But apart from the incident of the chaperone she had never been so obviously exposed to the way the rules worked. It was difficult to know whether she should be flattered that Don and the constables had agreed not to swear when she or the other women were around. Or simply be reassured the men were as aware of the delicate problems of survival as she was. She decided to be reassured. Suddenly, she felt a warm rush of affection for her neighbours. Later in the day, she picked up the telephone to talk but the line was dead.

The wind became stronger, massive clouds moved in, and then it began to snow. Ishawakta was smiling the first day of the blizzard. He had not bothered to explain it had been impossible to walk down to the bay to dump garbage or the contents of her toilet during the days of the ice. But now he laughed and said *"peoyook,"* adding that soon he would go to hunt seal. She had sliced the cooked haunch of caribou in half and given a piece to him, but she knew the meat could not have lasted long in his household. Besides, the Inuit probably thought the cooked caribou was tasteless, anyway.

She surprised herself by thinking seriously about another *komatik* trip. One snowy morning she asked Ishawakta if there was a camp she had not yet visited that was no more than two sleeps away.

He nodded. "Sheeookjuke's." He held up one finger. "One sleep. No igluksak," he shook his head. "Wait more snow."

While she waited, she re-read the letters that had come in on the Beaver, wrote her monthly report to Health and Welfare, and made an inventory of her dwindling drug supplies. There had been a note from the Brandon Sanatorium saying that Saa was responding well to streptomycin, I.N.H., and P.A.S., and that the Eskimo woman would be hospitalized for at least two years. She would ask Ishawakta to get the news to Utye's camp when it stopped snowing. *When it stopped snowing.* Each morning she looked out of the window, the blizzard seemed to be worse than ever. She comforted herself that it was all in the cause of *igluksak* and plunged into an orgy of letter-writing.

"I have no idea when this letter will get to you," she wrote to Sylvia. "It may never get to you at all. But I want you to know that before the snow finally buried us altogether, I was thinking of you all at home."

Ishawakta came to check the space heater. *"Igluksak?"*

He laughed. "No *igluksak.* Wait more snow."

There seemed to be no end to it. It was as though the Arctic was trying to atone for the chinook by dumping more building material and travelling snow on the land than the thaw had destroyed. After the fifth day, she simply stayed in bed. Oola and Ishawakta did their chores and left her alone. *Funny,* she thought as she padded in slippers to the kitchen and back to the bedroom with food. *This is the kind of thing we all longed to do in train-ing when the twelve-hour night shifts were coming up. Being snowed in and staying in bed.* She ate a can of pears, then went to sleep again.

The sun shone with almost apologetic brilliance the day the storm ended. She watched Georgie and Ishawakta hitch light *komatiks* and take off down the fjord. She jogged to the hospital and back to stretch her legs. Don and Mike were out in the compound. The two men laughed like schoolboys and pitched playful snowballs at each other. There was a festive air about the settlement, and she found herself humming some wordless tune. Later in the day she decided it was time to cook something extravagant. She was pulling out pots in the kitchen when Don came into the house with an Eskimo man behind him.

"Dorothy?" the Hudson's Bay manager said. "This is Akarolik from Mingeriak's camp." She recognized the young Eskimo and nodded. "He just came in by *komatik*. He says there's something wrong with his eyes."

She was concerned for Akarolik, but she smiled cheerfully. She had not dared hope there would be work to do so soon after the blizzard.

"I don't know what you'll find," Don continued. "But he can stay at Georgie's if you want to see him again. I'll tell him to go there after you've finished with him."

Akarolik's eyes were sore, red, and gummed with discharge. She looked carefully for signs of keratitis and when she found none, she checked the medical manual and decided the Eskimo was suffering from a straight conjunctivitis. The condition had probably been caused by irritation from snow-reflection, aggra-vated by scratching and rubbing.

"*Eejee!*" she nodded sympathetically and gave the man a compress to hold over his eyes while she rechecked treatment and drug choice in the manual. Antiseptic drops were recom-mended, so she sat the Eskimo in a kitchen chair and adminis-tered them. She decided to give him aureomycin capsules to swallow at six-hour intervals. Then she would see him at the same time next day for more drops and further assessment.

She thought about how she could make Akarolik understand what she wanted him to do. The Eskimo was wearing a cheap wristwatch so she pointed to the six on the dial, put one capsule on the table, moved her finger around to the twelve and added another antibiotic capsule. Her finger moved again to six and then to twelve and she handed Akarolik the four capsules he was to swallow. *"Ee,"* he nodded. *"Eejee!"*

She grinned back at him. *"Ee. Eejee!"* When the Eskimo left the house, she telephoned Don.

"It looks like conjunctivitis," she said. "I've given him eye drops and some antibiotics to take every six hours. I'll see how he's doing about this time tomorrow afternoon. Can you let him know that he's to come?"

Don promised to visit Georgie's house that evening so she went back into the kitchen to think about dinner. She had scarcely begun to read can labels on the shelf when there was a small sound in the livingroom. Akarolik came to the kitchen door.

"Akarolik," she said, surprised.

"Ee," grinned the Eskimo. *"Enooleenoon."* Medicine. The man held out his hand as though he wanted more capsules.

Oh my God, she thought sickly. *He's swallowed the lot! I've overdosed this man!*

She went quickly to the telephone. "Don? Can you come over here? I'm sorry, but I need some help with Akarolik."

The Eskimo stood, patiently waiting. She motioned for him to sit on a chair, then found one for herself. They sat, staring silently at each other until Don banged at the door and came in.

"What's up? I thought he went to Georgie's house."

"So did I. I don't know for sure, but I think he decided to swallow all of the aureomycin I gave him."

"Is that dangerous?"

"Well, it's not very good. Can you talk to him about it?"

Don spoke in Eskimo and Akarolik laughed and said *"ee."* He pantomimed the breaking of a capsule, then flung back his head, and emptied the invisible contents into an eye. He turned in a clockwise circle and did the same thing again, then again and again. *"Eejee!"* he said. He laughed some more and held out his hand.

"Do I need to explain?" asked Don.

"No," sighed Dorothy. There were some things she could manage to do in the Arctic without an interpreter, but the incident underlined how tricky diagnosis and treatment could be without adequate communication. She looked at Akarolik's eyes, but there seemed to be no change, for better or for worse. She brought four more capsules from her supplies and asked Don to explain to the Eskimo how he was to take them.

"Ee," the man nodded amiably, then wandered out of the house. Don looked at Dorothy. There seemed to be nothing else to say. They both collapsed into giggles.

The stay at Sheeookjuke's camp was busy. There were babies to be immunized and follow-up DPT boosters. There were the usual impetigo cases, ear infections, and a child who scalded her arm the evening she arrived. She cleaned the area, applied a dressing of saturated sodium thiosulphate, and bandaged it firmly. She welcomed the work. The *komatik* trip had been as cold and uncomfortable as before, and Noota's snoring was louder. The raw caribou she had used to boost her protein intake was replaced by less-palatable seal meat. Yet, the morning they packed to return to Lake Harbour, she knew she wanted to continue on rounds.

"Ishawakta," she said as the Eskimo came into Sheeookjuke's snowhouse to collect her grub box and sleeping bag. "How many sleeps to Utye's?"

He held up one finger, explaining that they could take a short-cut across land then down to the coast.

She thought. There were some cases she would like to check at Utye's. And Ishawakta had not yet brought Utye and old Adamee the news about Saa. Utye's, she reasoned, was practically on the way home. "We go to Utye's," she said. "Okay?"

Ishawakta grinned. "Okay."

There was some sun in the middle of the day, but it dipped early, the wind freshened, and the cold seemed more penetrating than ever. She withdrew into the mindless routine that always helped make *komatik* travel a little more bearable. She jogged. She nudged Noota and they studied each other's faces for signs of frost bite. She contemplated the dogs, with King now in the important lead position. She asked herself what on earth she was doing there. She stared at her mittens, then the monotonous landscape. She pretended there was actually something to see.

She blinked away the frost. There *was* something to see. Another *komatik* had come over a low hill, and the yelping team was racing towards them over the unmarked snow. She dragged herself onto the load, watching as the sled came alongside and kept pace with them. There were two Eskimos with the *komatik*. One rode the load. The other ran and steered. Ishawakta ignored them and they ignored Ishawakta. Only the dogs seemed excited. Noota showed no interest at all.

When sleds stopped for a mug-up an hour or so later, the Inuit shook hands, talked briefly, then went about the work of untangling traces and re-icing.

"That man Keemirkpee," Ishawakta said as he lit the primus stove for tea. He nodded at the driver. "Other man Atchealak. Inuit from Kooyoo's."

Dorothy sat on her grub box. King was lying in the snow close by, and she shoved her feet under his belly for warmth. Atchealak lit a pipe, leaned silently against a box, and sipped hot tea. Keemirkpee seemed to be doing most of the chores. She wondered if one Eskimo was the servant and the other the master. Atchealak's caribou suit, she noticed curiously, was handsomely made. Keemirkpee's was badly sewn as though the woman who tailored it wanted to tell the world how little she cared for him. The ears of the skinned caribou still drooped limply from the back of his parka.

The master-servant theory was unlikely, though. There were leaders among the Inuit, but there were no rulers, no politicians, no government élite. She decided that Atchealak was simply being himself and so was Keemirkpee. She saw that Keemirkpee was glancing at her as he worked with his tangled traces. *"Eekee,"* she said, pointing at her feet under King's body. Then she pointed at her cold forehead. *"Eekee!"* The Eskimo nodded. He left his work and went to a box sitting in the snow. When he came back to her, he was carrying a pair of polar bear skin slippers.

"Ee," he said. *"Peoyook."* And he put them gently over her *kamiks.* She looked down at the slippers, not knowing how to thank him. She smiled and smoothed them with her mittened hands and the man nodded. Atchealak, she saw, had also gone to a box.

"Eekee," he said, and handed her a white fox cap. Then he backed away, puffed at his pipe and stared at her.

Dorothy turned to Ishawakta and Noota, but the Inuit had their backs to her, busy with the traces. She looked down at the cap, then threw back the hood of her parka and pulled it over her cold head. It reached almost to her eyebrows. Atchealak nodded his approval and laughed.

"Ishawakta," she called and the Eskimo came to her. His face showed no surprise when he saw she was wearing the new cap. "Atchealak gave me the cap," she said, pointing. "Keemirkpee gave me the slippers." She hesitated, not knowing how to ask how she could thank the Inuit. She spread her hands.

The Eskimo shrugged at her confusion and laughed. *"Peoyook!"* he said, and went back to his work.

She wondered if she should offer the Inuit cigarettes or food, but decided the gesture could offend. Eskimos would take butter or jam in exchange for scarce supplies of seal liver, ptarmigan, or caribou, but if there was plenty, they took pride in giving. The more an Eskimo was able to give, she had learned, the greater his esteem in the community. Keemirkpee and Atchealak were probably good hunters and trappers. She patted the slippers and cap. *"Ee,"* she laughed, showing her pleasure. *"Ahaloona!"*

The Inuit laughed along with her. *"Ee."*

The *komatiks* ran together for another hour, Keemirkpee running, shouting, and using his whip and Atchealak sitting comfortably on the load like a contented Buddha. Then, without warning, the sled wheeled and disappeared over a ridge. She was sorry to see it go. She had been planning to open cans of butter and bacon that night to share with her new friends. She put up her hands to feel the fox skin cap. It was thick with rime, but her head and forehead were warm for the first time since she had started making rounds in the Arctic.

It was in the afternoon of the next day that Ishawakta began stopping the dogs, walking to the top of the hill, and staring into the distance. After the third time it happened, she knew they were lost. It was useless, of course, trying to discuss the matter. She could do nothing about it. Ishawakta would merely shrug. He might, in fact, even say *"Ayonamut."* That would make her more nervous than she was now. She sat tensely on the load, watching the Eskimo return to the *komatik* and whip up the team. They seemed to be heading confidently in a new direction. But after a few miles, the dogs were stopped again, and Ishawakta climbed another hill.

Noota got off the sled and lit a cigarette. There was no indication that the woman was concerned. But then Dorothy had seldom seen her chaperon show signs of emotion. She wondered how Noota would react if Ishawakta suddenly announced there was no way he could get them to Utye's or Lake Harbour. She shuddered. It was ridiculous. Eskimos never lost their way for very long. Or did they? She remembered with a prickle of horror that Don had an experienced Eskimo with him when he had been lost on Southern Baffin. She lit her own cigarette and watched apprehensively as Ishawakta got the team moving again.

It was dark now, and the dogs were lagging. Usually, the Eskimo would be cracking his whip to keep them running but now they travelled at a leisurely saunter. She got off the sled to jog and found she had left it behind. When she got back to the *komatik*, Ishawakta was poling into a drift for *igluksak*.

"We camp now," he said when he saw her, and went to the sled for his snow saw. She looked at her watch. It was only five o'clock.

She hesitated for a moment, biting her lip. "Ishawakta," she said, trying not to show her concern. "Why do we stop now?"

The Eskimo was tracing a meticulous circle for the igloo. "Not sure trail," he admitted without looking at her. "Better see in morning."

She wanted to ask more questions but there seemed no point. What else could Ishawakta say? Noota began carrying blocks to the edge of the circle, and Dorothy automatically began to chink. Snowhouse-building always made her hungry, but now she made a mental check of the food supply on the *komatik* and decided it might be as well to start rationing right away. There were four frozen rounds of stew. She would eat just one tonight with a pilot biscuit and leave the butter and bacon unopened. She would eat her morning porridge without evaporated milk.

When they were sealed into the igloo for the night, though, it was obvious that neither Ishawakta nor Noota had anything so practical in mind. Both consumed generous chunks of seal meat warmed in water, and Ishawakta cut himself a second helping. They made no comment when she served her own small meal. Dorothy stared at her feasting travelling companions. It was typical of Inuit thinking, of course, but she was amazed the Eskimos could eat so heartily in such an emergency. She shivered to think that Ishawakta might have rationalized that the dogs could be slaughtered and eaten if necessary. But then she had also heard that in starvation camps there was sometimes cannibalism.

It took her longer than usual to get to sleep that night. It was hard for her to forget a story Gerry once told about a stranded Eskimo who devoured his boots. Then, after the man's feet froze, he cut them off and ate them. She clenched her perspiring hands inside her sleeping bag. She was sorry she had thought about Gerry. When she woke in the dark morning, the Inuit were still sleeping. She lay, staring at the barely visible roof of the snowhouse, wondering what would happen when it was light. Ishawakta stirred, turned, and lit the primus stove. He grinned cheerfully at her, and she managed to grin back at him, wishing it was possible to say something like, "Do you think it's serious?" or "When do you think you might find the trail?" She turned the questions over in her heard, realizing how hysterical they sounded.

She watched Ishawakta carefully after he harnessed the dogs, loaded the *komatik,* then left it to walk to the nearest hill. His face told her nothing when he returned. Noota settled herself placidly on the load, and Dorothy climbed on beside her, pulling her cap low on her forehead and wrapping her scarf around her mouth.

"*Hoit!*" yelled Ishawakta and the dogs lunged against the traces and sprinted across the tundra.

"*Hraw!*" he shouted again and the animals wheeled to the left.

My God, she panicked, we're zig-zagging!

"*Hoit!*"

It was possible, she told herself at one point, that Ishawakta was travelling in circles, perhaps to spot an elusive landmark or maybe to kill time until he could figure out what to do. When they stopped for a mug-up, she waited tensely for him to climb another hill. If he did, she decided she would question him again. The Eskimo unhurriedly re-iced the runners, reloaded the *komatik,* then padded up the side of the nearest hill. He stared across the barrens. From the action of his elbows, she deduced he had relieved himself at the same time.

"Ishawakta," she said when he returned. She tried to keep her voice from shaking. "Have you found the trail?"

He grinned and picked up his whip. "Trail right here," he said. "Utye's after one, two more mug-up."

She sat on the *komatik,* feeling a little foolish. But the terror and the suspicion lingered until she heard the howl of the dogs at Utye's. Next day when they left, she was glad the route to Lake Harbour led straight along the coast and the fjord.

There were more hours of light in March, but it was as frigid as February, and the winds were more blustery. When there was sun in the middle of the day, she tried to walk the short distance to the hospital and back for exercise. But it was difficult to breathe, and she found she was spending more and more time in the house. The endless screech of the wind made her nervous and irritable. During a lone, dark afternoon, she briefly broke into tears.

One gusty March night, she woke to hear the sound of scratching at the front of the house. She sat up quickly in bed, holding her breath. The scratching continued. She thought about getting up to investigate but stopped herself. It might be one of the dogs. Then again, she told herself with a frightened gasp, it could be a polar bear. She listened intently. It *must* be a bear. There was no reason why a dog would scratch at the boards, but she knew hungry bears had been seen trying to break into Lake Harbour houses and storage sheds before.

She lay, staring wide-eyed into the darkness and listening to the awful scratching. If she got out of bed to telephone Don or Mike, the bear might glimpse her through the livingroom window. If she made any sound, it might come to the back of the house and crash through the window of the bedroom. She looked at her clock. It was four o'clock – hours yet before it would be light and the dogs might see the bear and chase it away. She tried pulling the covers over her head to shut out the sound. She pressed her hands over her ears. There was no point in crying out, but near morning, she did.

"Oh, go away!" she moaned. "For God's sake, go away!"

The scratching continued even after it was bright enough to see across the bedroom. Odd, there was no commotion from the dogs. She crept out of bed, keeping close to the wall of the livingroom. Two sled dogs trotted unconcernedly across the compound. Then she noticed a torn wire from the roof dangling across the window and scraping at the side of the house. She should have been able to laugh. But instead, she went into the bathroom and retched over her can.

She dressed to go out during the day, but before she zipped her parka, there was a white-out. She undressed again. She sat for hours in the livingroom, filing her nails and complaining aloud about her uselessness. She called Don to talk about the wire "polar bear" and telephoned the detachment to ask the constables if they would come across the bay for dinner.

She wanted so much for the evening to be a success, but the bread she baked was atrocious and the ptarmigan overcooked. She had forgotten that Gerry hated canned raspberries until she put a bowl of them on the table.

"I'll eat them! I'll eat them!" he laughed as she remembered and snatched them away.

Terry assured her that his favourite dish was overcooked ptarmigan, and Gerry followed her around the kitchen insisting that she had converted him to raspberries. She thought he was teasing and wanted to cry. Angry that the evening had deteriorated into teasing and tears, she picked up a kitchen knife and threw it at Gerry. It clattered harmlessly against the wall.

"Well, that's that for tonight," Gerry said, taking his parka from a peg.

"I'll say it is," agreed Terry. The two men quickly left. She wanted to telephone the detachment and apologize but, somehow, she knew it was unnecessary. It was. There was a canasta evening at Don Bairds a few nights later, and when Gerry laughed about the raspberries and the knife, everyone joked about symptoms of March madness. But March dragged relentlessly on. To help cope with the boredom, she began sleeping again during the day. She dreamed about fleets of aircraft landing on the fjord, and once she woke in the afternoon, hearing the drone of a plane overhead. She dressed quickly, tidied her braided hair and put on some fresh lipstick. By the time she fought her way through the buffeting wind to the shore, the sound had gone.

It was during a March snowstorm that Ishawakta's wife Leah gave birth to their child. Oola did not come that morning. Her young Eskimo helper attended to the kitchen stove, telling Dorothy that the baby was coming. Pitsulala and Oola were at his house. Dorothy nodded. She knew the midwives understood she would come if she was needed. She waited all day for news, then Ishawakta came to check her heater and to tell her with an excited laugh that he had a son.

"Name Natakoke," he said, grinning his slow grin. "*Peoyook.* Natakoke good hunter at Sheeookjuke's camp. Die in summer. Good name son."

There was no summons from the midwives so she waited until morning to see Leah and Natakoke. The Eskimo mother was sitting on a chair sewing, the baby lying asleep on the bed, wrapped in a blanket. Leah spoke no English so Dorothy pointed at her and asked, "*Akowyook?*" Healthy? Leah smiled and nodded. And Natakoke?

"*Ee. Akowyook.*"

She could see the baby was large and strong. It woke with a cry, and Leah put the naked child to her breast. "*Shengeeyook!*" the woman said proudly. Strong.

"*Ee,*" Dorothy nodded. It was warm in Ishawakta's house, but once again she wished the Inuit would cover their infants more adequately. Leah, she saw, was making new sealskin *kamiks* for Ishawakta, not clothing for her small son. Ishawakta came through the door, beating the snow from his parka and grinning when he saw she was in his home.

"Lutiapik," he said. "Soon I take Natakoke to Sheeookjuke's to show."

She was startled and a little alarmed. "When?"

"Soon. Okay?"

She did not answer. Winter travel was hazardous enough for adults but it could be dangerous for a new-born infant, especially a baby born in a more protected environment than a camp igloo. And Natakoke, she was reasonably sure, would be carried naked in his mother's *amouti* hood. She shivered, remembering the icy wind on the trail.

"You wait until spring?" she finally said. "Until ice goes out?"

Ishawakta laughed. "Lutiapik no worry. Mosesee do work. And Oola."

Good Lord, she thought, *he thinks I'm worried about the chores!*

She decided to say nothing more about the projected trip to Sheeookjuke's to either Ishawakta or Leah, but she mentioned it worriedly to Don. The Hudson's Bay manager shrugged and frowned.

"The Inuit do it all the time," he said. "Oh, I know it sounds dangerous and it probably is. But it's tough for them to change their ways. Ishawakta is proud of his first kid; he wants to show him off. There's nothing much we can do about it."

Mosesee came to the house to collect her toilet can and garbage one morning two weeks later. At least, she sighed as she looked across the compound, the day was clear. Oola giggled and nodded when she asked if Leah and Ishawakta had taken their baby to Sheeookjuke's camp. She had used every Eskimo word she could to phrase the question but there was no way of knowing if Oola really understood. Mosesee kept coming to the house for almost a week, however, then Ishawakta suddenly reappeared. She saw him walk past her bedroom door into the bathroom. When he returned, she was sitting in the livingroom in her dressing gown.

"Ishawakta," she said. "How is Natakoke?"

The Eskimo stood facing her. "Natakoke die," he said. His eyes were expressionless slits.

She clenched her teeth. "How Natakoke die?" she asked quietly.

"*Ilnee* get very *anneayoo*. Very hot. Then he die." Pneumonia, she thought.

"Why didn't you come to get me?" she asked. It was a complicated question for him to understand but she did not have the Eskimo words to ask it.

"Son die very quick," Ishawakta said. Then he padded out of the house.

Afterwards, Mike told her he had talked to Ishawakta about the trip to Sheeookjuke's camp. Natakoke had been buried under rocks near the grave of the hunter for whom he had been named. Ishawakta had said it couldn't be helped. Dorothy stamped angrily back to her house, wishing she could swear like Don and Gerry.

11

The snow buntings came back to Lake Harbour early in April. She walked in the compound, listening to their song and watching the little round birds forage for food. She wondered what they could possibly find to keep themselves alive. The tundra was still blanketed with winter snow; even though the sun was warmer, the temperature seldom rose to more than five degrees below zero. The excitement of spring was in the air, though, and the settlement Inuit were preparing for their annual *komatik* excursion to visit friends and relatives in Frobisher Bay.

"Why don't you go along?" asked Don. "Everyone else is making the trip, including Mike and the constables. As a matter of fact, you'll meet Eskimos from all the camps along the trail. You should get back in about a week. Me? Oh, I'll stay here and mind the store."

A few mornings later, six loaded sleds pulled out of Lake Harbour and headed north over the hills behind the settlement to the frozen Soper River. Dorothy had traced the route to Frobisher on the Hudson's Bay map. The *komatiks* would avoid the Grinnelle Glacier and the high Everett Mountains along the coast and stick to the inland river valleys. It would apparently be a tough climb for much of the way. The Soper rose to 1,900 feet above sea level near Mt. Moore, to 2,100 feet when they reached Mt. Joy. There would be frozen waterfalls and ice cliffs to scale, and an uphill hike to the 2,500-foot mark at the Armshow River.

No one seemed to care. She sat on the *komatik* load with

Leah and Oola, listening to the laughs and giggles of the Inuit in holiday mood. She wore her caribou skins, but she had also brought a duffle-cloth parka for the warmer hours of the day. There was less danger of frostbite in April. Now, the Arctic hazard was snowblindness, and everyone wore sunglasses bought at the Hudson's Bay.

She was glad she had decided to make the trip. The needless tragedy of Natakoke's death still depressed her; there had been no patients at her door for weeks. Besides, she was curious to see Frobisher. She had heard the Inuit in the big settlement were becoming urbanized. It would be a chance to see how it had affected them and she could see Heather Matthews at the nursing station. She slid off the *komatik* to jog, and Gerry ran from his sled to join her.

He grinned down at her. "Know what you're going to buy in Frobisher?" he asked.

"You tell me."

"I'll tell you, all right. Booze and meat."

"Meat?"

"The Hudson's Bay has a big electric freezer. You can get steak, chops, anything you want. It'll cost you the earth, of course."

She laughed, remembering she had an almost untouched bank account at the Bank of Nova Scotia in Frobisher Bay. If there was fresh meat to buy, she would not care how much it cost. She thought about other things she might want to get in Frobisher. Fresh milk? Eggs? Fresh fruit and tomatoes? She laughed again. She could only think about food. Every other commodity faded in importance when she thought about fresh food.

She wondered if this was what happened to all *kabloonahs* in Arctic isolation. At the first mug-up, she asked Mike what he wanted to buy in Frobisher, grinning when the missionary admitted he'd like to get some fresh bread to take back, and maybe some lamb chops. Terry said he was going to look around for bananas. The last time he had eaten a banana was two summers ago in Montreal. Gerry joined them, and they talked about banana splits and memorable meals until Nylee produced a football that turned out to be a seal head stuffed with grass.

Mug-ups, it seemed, were going to be parties on the way to Frobisher. Everyone who was not icing runners or eating chunks of meat kicked the ball happily around in the snow until it was time to take off again.

The caravan of *komatiks* came to the first frozen waterfall by mid-afternoon. After Akavak and Gerry held a conference, one of the sleds was partly unloaded and two teams of dogs were hitched to it. Sandy, Georgie, and Terry hooked a rope to the front of the *komatik* and climbed the falls, slithering and sliding until they hoisted themselves over the top. Then Akavak cracked his whip, and the rest of the men pushed the *komatik* from behind.

"*Hoit!*" yelled Akavak.

The dogs strained against their harness, paws slipping on the rough ice. the men at the top of the falls heaved at the rope.

"Ugh!" she heard Mike groan as he shouldered the heavy sled. Slowly, amidst shouts and laughter, the *komatik* inched to the top. Then, each of the women picked up a sack, a box, or skin bedding from the snow and clawed their way up the steep fall of ice. Dorothy tucked a pair of sleeping bags under her arms and followed Pitsulala, who was grinning broadly at her own attempts to carry a grub box. Once over the top of the ice, she lay on her back, panting. Terry grinned down at her.

"Right," he said. "There are only five more sleds to go and then we can pack up and get going."

After it was over, she sat for a long time on the *komatik*, dozing a little. The sun went down and it grew colder. She was glad she had worn her fox-skin cap. There was another festive mug-up in the twilight and two more *komatiks* caught up with them. She peered into the gloom, recognizing Akarolik and his family from Mingeriak's camp, and Mingeriak himself, with his wife and two children.

"Lutiapik," grinned Mingeriak and shook hands.

"*Eejee!*" laughed Akarolik, pointing at his eyes. She could see the infection had cleared.

They stopped to camp two hours later at the base of a hill where Akavak had poled for *igluksak*. Most of the men began cutting snowblocks, but Ishawakta unhitched the dogs, fed them, then leaned against the *komatik* smiling to himself. Oola and Leah ignored him and began to unload the sled.

Dorothy sat on a box, watching. "Ishawakta," she finally said. "Do we make camp?"

"*Ee,*" the Eskimo said, stifling a laugh. "No igloo. Have *tupik.*"

She was surprised. She had not noticed there was a tent on the sled. "Where did you get *tupik?*"

"Georgie have *tupik* at Hudson's Bay. No igloo this time."

The other snowhouses in the camp were only four or five blocks high, with canvas anchored across the top for a roof. At this time of the year, the Inuit apparently felt complete igloos were unnecessary. Even so, the wind was freshening, and the canvas roofs flapped loudly. She trusted Ishawakta's judgement, but she hoped it would not be a draughty night inside their uninsulated tent.

Ishawakta unhurriedly put up the *tupik,* and they beat their parkas free of snow and crawled inside to sit on the skins. She had brought her usual trail rations of frozen stew. She shared some with the others, then cut herself slices of seal that Leah had warmed in water. There was no attempt at conversation. They silently drank tea, then Oola and Leah smoked cigarettes, took off their clothes and got into their sleeping bags. Dorothy stripped down to her underwear and did the same thing. She closed her eyes. A few minutes later, Ishawakta blew out the lantern.

She heard the wind whistling during the night, and the *tupik* shook. She woke with a shiver. She had been dreaming of high cliffs of ice and now she realized she was staring up at the cold morning sky. The tent was sailing high like a giant kite and her clothes were blowing across the snow.

Oola, Leah, and Ishawakta were already out of their sleeping bags, chasing their pants, dresses, and parkas. She struggled out of her own bag and ran, half-naked in the sub-zero air, to catch the tumbling shapes of her skin suit, sweaters, and slacks. The rest of the camp was still sleeping, though some of the dogs got curiously to their feet to watch. She caught up with her slacks and struggled into them. Her teeth were chattering. Then she lunged for a sweater and tugged it quickly over her head. She was aware of Oola's giggles as the woman rescued her dress and *amouti*. Somewhere ahead of her, Ishawakta was standing in the snow pulling on a parka. When she got back to the small nest of skins, boxes, and sleeping bags, the Inuit were putting on their socks and *kamiks*. No one spoke, but Oola giggled again. Ishawakta simply found his saw, cut snowblocks for a windbreak, then lit the primus stove for breakfast. They never saw the *tupik* again.

By the time they had dragged their way over three more ice-locked waterfalls to the Armshow River and begun their descent to Frobisher Bay, there were eleven *komatiks* together on the trail. She shook hands with Inuit from Napatchee's and Utye's camp. During one mug-up, a sled raced over a hill; it was Atchealak and Keemirkpee, sitting and running exactly as they had when she last saw them on the way back from Sheeookjuke's.

The holiday mood was infectious. Chores became games or contests. Mug-ups were picnics. Jogging sessions developed into races, the Inuit men encouraging their wives to jog faster, the children laughing as the men outstripped the teams and stood waiting in the snow. There were giggles and bursts of chatter as the sleds came down from the hills then sped across the frozen bay towards the settlement. It was mid-afternoon when they reached the shore and the dogs came to a panting stop at the edge of what seemed to be a road.

Oddly enough, she had not talked to Gerry, Mike, or Ishawakta about where she would stay in Frobisher. Now she came to think about it, the problem of accommodation had scarcely crossed her mind. During her past trips, there had always been somewhere for her to sleep. She supposed her white neighbours and Ishawakta and his family would stay with friends. She knew she would be welcome if she wanted to go with them. She saw Mike wave, and she waved cheerfully back at him.

"You okay?" Gerry shouted as he passed her.

"I'll stay at the nursing station!" she yelled back at him, and he raised an arm.

She slid off the *komatik*, watching the other sleds peel off from the long procession and go in different directions. "Ishawakta," she said. "I stay with *aniatitsiyuk* here."

"*Ee*," he nodded.

"How many sleeps we stay in Frobisher?"

He held up two fingers. "I find and come." He grinned and pulled her suitcase from the *komatik* load. Then he cracked his whip, yelled "*hoit*" and the sled swayed down the snowy, rutted road.

She stood, watching it go. She had no idea where to find the nursing station, so she walked to a cluster of wooden shacks huddled against a rocky hill. She knocked. An Eskimo woman with a baby in the hood of her *amouti* opened the door.

Dorothy pointed at herself. "*Aniatitsiyuk*," she explained. "*Namoot aniatitsiyuk* Frobisher Bay?" She hoped she had remembered the correct word for where.

The woman shook her head and disappeared inside the house. Two small children ran to the door and stood, eyeing her. Dorothy looked into the dark little room. The woman was leaning over to speak to a man lying on a heap of blankets against the back wall. The Eskimo got slowly to his feet and came to the door to meet her. She put out her hand and he took it.

"*Aniatitsiyuk*," she repeated.

"*Ee*," he grinned. Then he pointed to the shack next door. "Come."

She followed the man across the filthy, garbage-littered snow and watched as he opened the door of the dwelling to walk inside. He emerged with another Eskimo dressed in denim pants and a heavy flannel shirt, who smiled and shook her hand.

"You nurse?"

"Yes. Do you speak English?"

"Some. I work for *kabloonahs* when ships here. Name Koolee."

"Can you show me the nursing station, Koolee?"

"*Ee*. Not far. I take you now."

He turned to take his duffle-cloth parka from a hook on the wall. The shabby hut, she saw, was as ugly as the first. She was shocked and a little sickened. Somehow, the Eskimos' spartan pattern of living seemed to be naturally adapted to snow-houses and tents. There was a feeling of spaciousness, even in the smallest camps. But transferred to crowded rows of white man's hovels, the Frobisher Bay Inuit were clearly becoming slum-dwellers.

Koolee talked more than any other Eskimo she had met. He pointed to the shacks of neighbours and told her their names, how many children they had, the illnesses they had suffered that year. A jeep came roaring down the road, and she almost fell into a snowbank with fright. Koolee laughed and said the machine belonged to a *kabloonah* who worked at the Hudson's Bay store. He identified the settlement's cinema, which he said showed very good pictures about men who killed each other with short guns. There was a cafe that was closed. Then they stopped before a long, green and white building set back from the road.

"*Aniatitsiyuk*," grinned Koolee. "Nursing station." He politely shook her hand again and walked away.

She smiled to herself. She wondered how she must look, standing in the snow in her bulky caribou suit, her hair in braids like an Eskimo woman, and with a blue suitcase clutched in one mittened hand. She remembered what Heather Matthews had said that day on the deck of the Howe. "Frobisher is only ninety miles east of Lake Harbour as the crow flies. If the crow ever flies, that is." She knew now what her colleague had meant. Then she knocked on the nursing station door.

Heather had been astonished to see her, but she and Shirley, the other INHS nurse at the post, were busy with an emergency. Dorothy was hurriedly shown to a spare bedroom and left alone. She supposed it would be all right to make herself a meal, considering the food was supplied by Health and Welfare. She hung her skin clothing in the garage, washed her face and hands, and heated some soup and a can of stew. A doctor arrived while she was eating and disappeared into the surgery. She read a month-old Toronto newspaper in the livingroom. There was nothing in it about the Arctic, and she found the rest of the news uninteresting. She wandered off to bed.

The nurses were drinking tea in the kitchen when she joined them next morning.

"Hope it wasn't serious," she said.

"Serious enough," Heather told her. "An Eskimo girl put a rifle in her mouth and pulled the trigger. We did our best. There was a doctor in town from Ottawa. But the girl died about midnight. It's the third suicide around here in a couple of months."

The information shocked her as much as the sight of the Inuit shanty-town had done. So did Heather's story about Eskimos dying of respiratory paralysis after drinking anti-freeze from Department of Transport tractors. And the fact that there were Inuit prostitutes in the settlement who were spreading venereal disease. She was beginning to tell the two nurses about the healthy Inuit she had met at Seemeegak's camp when patients began to arrive at the dispensary.

"Impetigo. Ear infections. Scabies," said Heather when Dorothy asked her about the cases. "But probably worse than what you've been getting. These people live in one hut, stuck in one place, surrounded by garbage. Your Eskimos can move around, leave their mess behind, and build another igloo."

Dorothy finished her tea. "What should I see in Frobisher?"

"Well, you can hitch a jeep ride over to Apex," said Shirley. "There are more Eskimo huts and a church there. You can drop into the mission and the school and you can walk over to the airfield. There's the Hudson's Bay store, the bank, and the cafe. Sometimes the cafe has fresh eggs. Then there's the cinema. They're showing a George Raft film called *A Bullet For Joey* tonight. How much do you bet we'll have more assault cases on the doorstep tomorrow?"

"Oh, and by the way," Heather added before she went to

work. "Pudloo came with your note. We sent him to Montreal General for a biopsy. It wasn't a malignant tumour. Just simple orchitis. Inflammation of the scrotum."

"Where is he?"

"Staying here with friends. He'll probably get wind of the fact that *komatiks* are going back to Lake Harbour and hitch a ride."

Dorothy decided not to go to Apex. She had seen enough of Eskimo huts. Instead, she walked to the Hudson's Bay store to ogle the frozen steaks, roasts, and chops and to gasp at the prices. Pork chops had cost thirty-five cents a pound in Toronto. Here, a package of four was priced at a dollar, and a medium-size sirloin steak was $1.50. She decided she would withdraw some cash from the bank next day and buy some chops to take back to Lake Harbour. She felt a wave of homesickness for the remote little settlement on the fjord. Frobisher Bay, after all, was just another small Canadian community with all of its faults and few endearing qualities. Despite the loneliness of her life in Lake Harbour, she was suddenly grateful she had been posted there.

She crossed the road to look through the window of the unattractive cafe and was almost run down by another jeep. *Heavens,* she thought, *I've forgotten how to look to the left and the right before crossing.* There was a menu pasted to the inside of the window, but it did not mention fresh eggs. She looked at it for a moment. Baked beans. Sardines. Soup. The restaurant food in Frobisher was about the same as she would serve herself in the settlement. She went back to the Hudson's Bay store to choose some records and found Ishawakta riffling through the country-western section.

"Lutiapik," he grinned.

She grinned back at him, waiting for him to speak. Interesting that she no longer bothered with polite chatter. If the Eskimo wanted to tell her something, he would do it in his own time.

"Simeonee is friend here," Ishawakta said. He shook his head sadly, then struggled slowly for words. "He say Hudson's Bay store closed tight when boss away. Inuit here take things from store, so door closed tight."

She did not reply. The store was never locked in Lake Harbour and neither were the houses. In Ishawakta's part of the Arctic, a starving Eskimo could always take meat from another man's cache provided he told the owner. But to take it for any other reason would be unacceptable. There would be no punishment, and the owner of the cache would never complain, but the disapproval of the community would haunt the thief for the rest of his life. She understood Ishawakta's feeling of shame.

"Simeonee say," continued Ishawakta, "Inuit here not hunt much. Live on money *kabloonahs* give for *nutarak* . . . children and old Inuit."

Welfare, pension and family allowance, she translated in her head. There was nothing she could say. She bent to look at the records. It was a poor selection, but she picked out some Wagner and Beethoven that she would buy when she made her withdrawal from the bank. Ishawakta said nothing more. He took a record from the rack and went to the cashier.

The morning Ishawakta came to fetch her for the return *komatik* trip to Lake Harbour, she heard on the nursing station radio that the Ihalmiut Eskimo woman Kikik had been found not guilty of murder and criminal negligence at a Territorial Court of the Northwest Territories trial in Rankin Inlet.

"Of course," nodded Heather as they drank a last cup of tea together. "What else could they decide?"

Dorothy agreed. The story of Kikik was an epic tale of Arctic survival. The woman had been charged with the killing of her half-brother Ootuk and for criminal negligence because she had abandoned her daughters Annecatha and Nesha during a February trek to the Padlei Hudson's Bay post with her five children. Don Baird had picked up details of the case by radio from Southampton Island. Ootuk had murdered Kikik's husband Halo, and crazed with hunger, the Eskimo had tried to shoot Kikik as well. The woman stabbed him to death.

Without a husband to catch the few fish that had kept the family from dying of starvation, the woman then decided to walk forty miles to the nearest post with her children. Eight days later, she left the weakest two in a trail igloo and went on with the other three to Padlei. Nesha, one of the abandoned daughters, died in the snowhouse. But Annecatha was rescued by a search party, and the other three children also survived.

The two nurses quietly listened to the news broadcast then Heather switched to some music. That was something Dorothy had enjoyed in Frobisher Bay. Instant music.

"I don't suppose," she said, "I can return your hospitality in Lake Harbour?" She realized there had not been very much shop talk with Heather, but what could they really talk about? Talking could not replace training.

Heather laughed. "The crow doesn't fly too often in that direction," she said. "But you never know. Don't forget your pork chops." She took the frozen package from the kitchen refrigerator, and Dorothy put it in her suitcase. Outside in the snow with Ishawakta, she almost walked away without saying good-bye, but then she remembered it was the *kabloonah* custom to do so. "Good-bye," she said to Heather. It was the first time she had used the word in months.

There were two *komatiks* standing near the shoreline – the Health and Welfare sled with Oola and Leah on board, another with two men and a young boy perched on the load and an Eskimo man smoking in the sunshine. She supposed Mike and the constables had decided to stay longer in Frobisher. Heaven only knew why. There was probably unfinished business at the Anglican mission and the RCMP detachment. She shrugged over the whereabouts of the other Lake Harbour *komatiks*. They would probably catch up somewhere along the trail.

Ishawakta had kept a place for her suitcase on the sled. "That man Simeonee," he told her, "he come to Lake Harbour for stay. Speak good English."

Later, at the first mug-up in the hills beyond the bay, Simeonee told her he had represented the Inuit at Queen Elizabeth II's coronation six years before. Now, he worked as a helper at the Hudson's Bay store in Frobisher. The Eskimo was intelligent, his English was certainly polished, and she wondered if she would have a chance to talk with him. She would like to know, for example, how Simeonee felt about Eskimos with ability being trained to do other than menial tasks in the Arctic. There were already some special RCMP constables like Akavak. But why not special health aides, special teachers, and Eskimos who were systematically upgraded to become store managers rather than stock assistants and floor sweepers?

She wondered why Health and Welfare had not instructed her to find a bright young Eskimo to learn some of the basics of nursing and perhaps equip him or her with a first-aid manual in syllabics. After all, the Bible had been brought to the Inuit in this way. Then she laughed. Health and Welfare had even forgotten to pass out manuals to their own northern nurses.

That afternoon at another mug-up, she approached Simeonee and asked him if he thought the Inuit would like to do the jobs for themselves that white men and women did in the Arctic. The Eskimo took several long drags of his cigarette and looked thoughtfully over the tundra before answering. "Lutiapik," he said slowly, "how do we know until we try?"

It was difficult finding another opportunity to talk to Simeonee. The trip to Frobisher Bay had been a backbreaking uphill push. The way back was a nightmarish slide. On the first steep hills, she quickly learned she would have to ride the swaying *komatik* or be left behind. She watched, terrified, as the dogs sprinted faster on the sharp grades to keep ahead of the heavy sled. On one hill, the traces became so slack, the runners of the *komatik* almost caught the heels of the nearest animals. She had no idea how Simeonee and his family were faring. Somewhere on the trail, Ishawakta had left them behind.

The sun was setting when they came to the top of a long, sloping curve of the Soper River. As soon as they slid over the lip of the snow-covered ice fall she knew they were in trouble. The *komatik* skidded, wildly out of control. Ishawakta shouted *agai!"* and dragged desperately at the pack-thongs, trying to brake the runaway sled. He shouted something more in Eskimo, and Oola and Leah jumped off the load to help him. Dorothy did the same thing, but her caribou *kamiks* slithered on the river-ice, and the sliding *komatik* pulled painfully at her arms.

The dogs were clearly in panic. They yelped and quickened

their pace. For a moment the traces tightened. But halfway down the grade, the *komatik* slipped away and plowed through the screaming team, dragging the dogs behind it and crashing in a jumble of boxes, sacks, and skins on the bank of the curve.

She followed the Inuit down the treacherous slope. Once, she lost her footing and skidded helplessly on her back until she clawed herself to a stop. The sled, she saw, was shattered beyond repair. Two dogs were dead. Another lay howling. She could see its back was broken.

"*Peongeto!*" hissed Ishawakta. He found a rifle among the scattered boxes and bundles and shot the animal in the head.

The other dogs were standing, shivering and yelping, their snarled traces dangling in the snow. King had survived the accident with only a superficial wound on his flank. The Inuit seemed to be in a state of shock. Oola and Leah stood motionless. Ishawakta put down his rifle, crossed his arms over his chest, and stared impassively at the wrecked *komatik*. She was shaking a little and sat on her grub box to steady herself. The question, of course, was how they would get back to Lake Harbour without a sled. She remembered a story told around the canasta table one night about a smashed *komatik* – how the owner had used the dogs to carry the load and walked back to camp. It seemed like a reasonable solution. She had walked or jogged for most of the trip, anyway.

There was a sudden shout and she turned her head. Simeonee's sled was negotiating the ice fall. He had eased his *komatik* over the lip, keeping the dogs behind to brake the sled's descent. The two women and the boy tugged at the load-lashings while Simeonee cracked his whip. The dogs backed, slid a foot or two, then backed again until the heavy *komatik* was eased down the slippery slope to a halt.

She wondered why Ishawakta had not known about this sledding technique. Perhaps he did, but had misjudged that particular grade. She watched Simeonee unhitch his dogs and stow away his whip. Then he came to meet them. She knew there would be no comment or recriminations about what had happened. The men would simply discuss the problem and what to do about it.

214

It was growing dark and cold; the wind whipped icily around her parka hood. Ishawakta nodded his head and murmured, "*ee . . . ee,*" as Simeonee spoke. The older Eskimo grinned calmly, then walked to speak to her.

"We will take your load on my *komatik,*" he said. "Then we will hitch all the dogs to pull. But now I think we camp here. Good snow near hill."

She wanted to thank him, just as she had wanted to thank Atchealak and Keemirkpee for the gifts of cap and slippers. But she could see the Eskimo was satisfied that he could help in the same way the two hunters from Kooyoo's camp were satisfied that they could give.

"Yes," she said, and that was all. Then she went to help Oola, Leah, and Ishawakta as they silently sorted the load.

She had thought she would be happy to settle down again after the Frobisher Bay expedition, but still no patients came to the nursing station. Soon she was fretting again to be on the move. A visit to a camp was impossible unless she wanted to borrow a *komatik* from a neighbour. Besides, Ishawakta was spending all of his spare time building a new sled. Mike Gardener sledded back into the settlement, and one night she invited the missionary and Don Baird to share the feast of pork chops she had brought from Frobisher.

"Why don't you go fishing?" Don suggested when she asked where she could go at that time of the year. She cleared the dishes from the kitchen table as the two men lingered over their coffee. "The Eskimo women go up to Tasialujuak Lake all the time. Sometimes the men go along, too. Oola and Pitsulala will take you."

Mike clattered his cup. "It's a nice walk. Only about five miles from here. Marg and I went there when we first arrived."

The idea of a fishing excursion appealed to her, but she did nothing about it until Oola came back to the house after blacking and lighting the stove one morning. The woman giggled, showing Dorothy a string and a hook with a piece of red wool tied to it. Then she pointed at the door. Dorothy glanced out of the window and saw that Leah and Pitsulala were standing near the porch and Sandy was coming across the compound with three sled dogs loaded with backpacks. She checked the outside thermometer. It was ten degrees below zero. She nodded, *"ee,"* at Oola and went to dress in slacks, sweaters, and her duffle-cloth parka. It was not cold enough for skin clothing, though she wore her caribou *kamiks* and socks.

She put pilot bisuits, butter, and some cans of meat into a sack, and Sandy stowed the picnic lunch into one of the backpacks. She felt a sudden surge of excitement. This was like the times in Toronto when she would take some sandwiches and wander under the newly budding trees of the park near the house. *"Opangaksha!"* she laughed. It was the Inuit word for spring.

"Ee," said Pitsulala. Her smooth brown face broke into a smile. *"Opangaksha."*

There were gulls soaring over the white fjord that morning, and she saw the shapes of ravens in the northern sky. As they climbed the round hills, she glimpsed the tracks of lemmings and ground squirrels. Moss and lichens were beginning to show on the surface of grey rocks blown bare of snow in the March gales. Far off, there was the shrill bark of foxes. Sandy, carrying fish and bird spears, brought down three ptarmigan on the trail. After a while, she unzipped her cloth parka in the warm sun. It was the first time she had not needed the fur cap outdoors since Atchealak had given it to her.

Tasialujuak Lake was a wide, flat desert of snow-covered ice, ringed with high hills. She knew the water must be crystal-clear and wished there was no snow so that she could see into it. She explored while the Eskimos made tea, then Sandy took a steel ice-digger from a pack and began punching fishing holes.

Everyone was assigned their own place. Pitsulala handed Dorothy a string with a wool-baited hook at the end of it, and she crouched over the hole, jigging the line into the water below. The Inuit began catching char almost at once. Within an hour, the three women had each pulled three or four large fish from the lake. Sandy had hooked or speared even more. Dorothy caught nothing. She was disappointed, but the April day was so glorious she decided it scarcely mattered. At midday, Oola heated a pot of snow over the primus stove and warmed some of the char in the bubbling water. They all took pieces of the still-raw fish in their hands and gnawed at the red, delicious flesh.

She tried jigging again, but it was hopeless. Surrendering her line, she walked alone around the shore of the big lake and sat on the warm rocks to stare at the stocky figures of her Inuit friends on the ice. The sun was waning when she made her way back to the spot where the dogs were lying in the snow. She was hungry again, and she hoped the Eskimos would wait to eat another meal before hiking back through the darkness to the settlement.

She watched as the women came from the ice-holes, carrying their afternoon's catch. They seemed in no hurry to leave. Leah foraged around the shore collecting flat stones. The Eskimos layered the char with the rocks until they had made a cache. They fed some fish to the dogs, then lit the primus stove again and warmed more for Dorothy and themselves. It was twilight by then, and there was a moon. Dorothy took pilot biscuits from her sack, opened the butter, and shared the food with the Inuit. They licked the butter from their fingers, nodding and giggling as she reached for more chunks of the fish they had caught. Then there were tea and cigarettes. The Eskimos unlashed another of the packs and spread out their sleeping bags.

Dorothy was astonished. It had not occurred to her that they would be spending the night at the lake. Again she wondered why no one ever told her anything. She rummaged in the pack. Perhaps Ishawakta had thought to put her bag with the other bedding. She sighed. It was not there. She sat on a rock, unde-cided what she should do. The Inuit ignored her until they had finished more cigarettes and put out the primus stove. Then Pitsulala turned her head and laughed. There was a short exchange of words before Dorothy saw Sandy and Leah scurry-ing in the gloom. They came back with armfuls of soft moss and lichens.

Leah pointed to a wide ledge in the rock on which the moss was spread and piled until it was a foot thick. Pitsulala patted the bed and giggled. *"Peoyook,"* she said, and left her. The Inuit took off their clothes without speaking and got into their sleeping bags.

Dorothy tugged the hood of her parka around her face and stretched out on the ledge. She stared across the frozen lake. The surface glimmered under the moon. It must have been well below zero, but there was no wind, her clothes were warm, and the moss was comfortable. She slept soundly, woke when she was cold to stamp her feet or to move her arms and legs. Then she slept again. She sat up when it was dawn. The stars were very large in the brightening sky. One of the dogs raised his head to look at her, then whined lazily and buried his nose in his tail. There was no movement from the peacefully sleeping Inuit. At last she felt she had met the Arctic.

12

Oola and Leah traded half a dozen char for some jam and butter. After putting some in the hill freezer, Dorothy invited her four white neighbours to dinner. The constables contributed some Scotch they had bought in Frobisher Bay, and the party was quite lively until Mike got to his feet and announced it was time to leave. She yawned contentedly after the men closed the door. It had been one of her most successful evenings. The poached fish was superb; the bread was actually edible. Gerry had been relaxed and charming, and she knew she had looked her best in a skirt and blouse she always liked. She undressed and slipped into her robe, then went into the livingroom to get a paperback Don had loaned her.

"Hi," said Gerry. He was standing just inside the door.

There was no point in trying to hide her astonishment. "Hi! Anything wrong?"

"Well . . ." he hesitated, throwing back the hood of his parka. "I forgot my lighter. And I didn't tell you about next Saturday night. Annie shot some ptarmigan. You're invited."

"Fine, Gerry. I'll be there." She looked up at him then turned away. "Goodnight."

She sat on the edge of the bed waiting to hear the door open and close. There was silence then the click of a lighter. Gerry came to the door a few moments later.

"Hi," he said again. He had taken off his parka.

She was surprised, but fascinated. He gently pushed her down against the pillows and lay beside her. *I don't believe it,* she thought. *It's really going to happen!* She said nothing. He moved as though he was about to take her in his arms but apparently changed his mind. He cleared his throat and sat up, his boots thudding against the floor.

"Why don't you go home, Gerry," she said quietly. "We both know we're not right for each other. It's not going to work." *And Lake Harbour is no place to try,* she thought.

"I'm sorry."

"Don't be sorry. I think we've both been expecting this for a long time."

He stood up. "I suppose you won't come to the detachment on Saturday?"

"Sure I'll come. This doesn't make any difference. Maybe it's better for both of us that it happened, anyway."

"Yes," he said. He walked into the livingroom. Once again she heard the click of his lighter. Then the door opened and softly closed.

She had some work to do that week. Mike had a stomach upset so she brought him bismuth and visited throughout the day until he was better. Two Eskimos travelling from Shaftsbury Inlet to Cape Dorset to find wives came to the nursing station for aspirin. One complained of toothache. She showed the other how to steady the man's head while she pulled a badly decayed molar. She was so pleased to see the Inuit, she fetched her special china and served them tea and cookies in the kitchen. She learned a new Eskimo word as they sipped and munched. *"Eelkeeanain!"* They rolled their eyes appreciatively to the ceiling. Good to eat.

Georgie arrived to tell her that Mingeriak, who had been staying at his house, was very sick.

"No." The Eskimo replied to her questions, Mingeriak was not hot. He was not vomiting. Fetching her medical bag, Dorothy followed the young Hudson's Bay employee across the compound.

Mingeriak was lying on some skins on the floor of Georgie's plainly furnished livingroom. He was conscious, but he rolled his head weakly, groaning a little.

"How long has he been this way?"

"Not long. Yesterday he came with me down the fjord to hunt seal at the breathing holes."

Georgie was right; Mingeriak's temperature was almost normal. She brought her sphygmomanometer from the medical bag and took his blood pressure. The reading was 70/50. She stared at the abnormally low reading. Mingeriak seemed to be in shock. She sat on a chair studying the patient. Yesterday, he had been strong and healthy enough to go hunting on the ice. There had been no accident, no trauma. There was no sign of a respiratory problem.

She was suddenly scared. She had no idea what was wrong with Mingeriak, so there was really nothing she could do for him. Perhaps he would die. She told Georgie she would be back soon and went to see Don Baird.

"How's the radio working?" She stood at the door in her parka.

"It's not!" Don put down the book he had been reading. "Any problems?"

"Mingeriak's very sick at Georgie's house. I've no idea what's wrong, but it could be terribly serious. I thought we might try to get through to the doctor at Pang for advice."

"No way. But I could send a May Day if you think it's that bad."

She thought, weighing the possibilities of an improvement in Mingeriak's condition with the responsibility of calling for help. "I'll let you know," she said.

She sat with Mingeriak for the rest of the afternoon, leafing through the medical manual's section on shock and agonizing about what to do. Each time she took his blood pressure it registered the same as before. In the evening, Georgie and Nylee cooked a meal of seal liver. She ate some from the pot. Near midnight she got to her feet and paced around the little room telling herself she would wait another hour to see if Mingeriak regained his senses. Then, if he were no better, she would ask Don to send the May Day.

Mingeriak muttered something inaudible. She went quickly

to him and knelt on the floor. The Eskimo's eyes were open and he grinned at her. "Lutiapik."

Dorothy smiled back at him. She brought her bag and once again took his blood pressure. The reading was now a normal 120/80. She was puzzled but she sighed with relief. The Eskimo sat up and sniffed the air. *"Tengo,"* he said. Liver.

"Okay," she said to a grinning Georgie. "Give him anything he wants to eat. He looks fine now."

The next time she would think about that anxious day in Lake Harbour was more than a decade later when she read the memoirs of northern circuit Judge Jack Sissons. Mingeriak was arrested for the knife-slaying of a six-year-old Frobisher Bay child in 1963. Doctors consulted by Arthur Maloney, the defence lawyer, found the Eskimo was an epileptic. Mingeriak pleaded guilty to the murder and was sentenced to life imprisonment.

Thinking back, though, Dorothy still puzzled about his condition as he had lain on Georgie's floor. There had been no epileptiform convulsions. Yet epilepsy was a symptom, not a disease; it was possible that whatever caused the epilepsy also cause the disturbance to the Eskimo's central nervous system. Perhaps it was also a factor in the mental derangement that had caused him to kill.

The detachment party on Saturday was a success. The ptarmigan was a treat; the three-handed bridge game was more fun than usual. She realized now that there had always been some tension in the air when she had been with the constables. Gerry threw back his head to laugh, and once again, she was glad the incident in the bedroom had happened and was over. That night, there was not the useless banter about one of the men seeing her home. When she was ready to go, she thanked them for the dinner, pulled on her *kamiks* and parka and headed alone down the slope to the barrier-ice.

The April twilight had darkened into night. Dorothy was annoyed she had stayed so late, especially when she realized she had left her flashlight on the kitchen table at the detachment. The opposite side of the fjord was not visible, but she knew by now she would get there in about twenty-five minutes if she walked straight ahead. She amused herself by wondering who would win the bet on the date of break-up – the day the ice would sail out of the bay into the strait. Her dollar was on July 10, but Gerry thought the ice would leave earlier this year. Mike was pessimistic enough to feel it might stay all summer. Poor Mike. He had hoped Don might have some news of Marg from the Southampton Island post by now, but nothing had come through.

She stopped dead, feeling vaguely disoriented. Funny. She should have been close to the opposite barrier-ice. She looked at her watch, then realized she had not checked the precise time she had left the detachment. She tried to remember how long she had been walking. Twenty minutes? A half hour? It was difficult to tell. She peered through the inky gloom, hoping to glimpse the hummocks along the shore, but there was nothing to see but the white glow of the sea-ice. She began walking again, her heart thumping. The black-out of the night was as frightening as the white-outs of the winter blizzards. She was definitely not lost, of course. But if she were, she wondered if anyone would hear if she shouted for help. Or if they could find her.

She looked again at her watch. She had been walking for another five minutes. This was ridiculous. The barrier-ice had to be dead ahead. She stopped to stare, taking off her glasses, rubbing her eyes, trying again. For moment, she thought she saw a hummock in the darkness. She started to jog. But then there was nothing at all.

"Where am I?" she said aloud. Her voice was hoarse. She peered ahead, then to the right, and to the left. She turned quickly to the left. Good Lord, her parka hood was as effective as a pair of blinkers. She had not seen the light, far ahead and to the right. It was probably a porch light, though she sickly remembered she had not switched on her own. But a light and to the right? "For God's sake, Dorothy," she gasped in panic. "All this time, you've been walking down the fjord to the sea!"

She had no way of knowing just how far she had strayed, but she began to run back the way she had come, keeping her eyes fixed on the light. "Come on," she panted. "Oh come . . . on . . ." She rechecked the time. Only ten minutes. Surely she could not have been running for only ten minutes! Twenty minutes. "Come . . . on . . ." She was abreast of the light now and began jogging towards it. In a few more moments, her *kamiks* scraped against the rough outer ice of the barrier.

The slabs and hummocks were more slippery than she remembered; she fell, catching at the corner of a jagged block to save herself from sliding. She lay on her stomach, breathing hard. This was awful. But at least she had reached the barrier and there was not much farther to go. She adjusted her glasses, and propped herself on her elbows. It was then she heard the grind and screech of slab against slab as the tide rose slowly under the ice.

Dorothy scrambled to her feet. The shoreline barrier was frozen fast during the winter months, but for nights now she had been aware of the slams and thuds as the spring ice loosened at the turning of the tides. The sound was frightening enough but she never realized the barrier had been moving as crazily as this. Slithering around a slab as enormous as an elevator, she was thrown against a hummock as the ice shifted. Her skin mittens clawed desperately at the slick surface of the next slab. There was an ice-valley on the other side. As she fought her way over it, it shifted to become a mountain. She cried out in her terror. If she climbed the high, glassy slabs, they could overturn with her clinging to them. Unless she got around them, another slab could crush her from above or behind.

She glimpsed the light again and hauled herself over a groaning ice-chunk, shouting to herself that it was only a short way now; she had to keep going. With a grinding crash, two slabs slid together. She lunged ahead, stumbling across a low hummock. Then, incredibly, she was kneeling in the packed snow on the shore. She looked up. The light that had saved her was shining from the porch of the Hudson's Bay post. Don must have noticed she had not come home during the twilight and switched it on for her.

She staggered up the slope to her house, feeling sick and ashamed. She thought she had learned that mistakes were costly in the North. But she had almost paid with her life for the errors she had made that night. Her neighbours might have been killed trying to find her. And how could they have explained what had happened?

"Thank you for the light," she said to Don in the compound next day.

"You were late," he said crisply, and that was all. She was glad she was wearing gloves. Her hands were taped. When she had come through the door last night, shaking with cold and terror, she had seen that her caribou mittens were torn by the ice and her fingers were lacerated and bleeding.

There was a two-day snowstorm early in May, but somehow, it was not as depressing as those that had imprisoned her in the house during the dark months of winter. It was light now until well into the night, and she could see the walls of her bedroom if she woke at five o'clock in the morning. The day the storm cleared, the thermometer hovered at twenty-five degrees above zero, and the sun shone blindingly on the fresh snow.

She dressed, put on her sunglasses and walked into the hills behind the house. A pair of lemmings scurried out of her path, and there seemed to be more buntings around than before. She reached a favourite rock where she could survey the settlement and the fjord. After a while, the sun became so hot, she pulled off her parka, her sweater, and finally her shirt. The mild air was soft against her bare skin. She closed her eyes, listening to the sound of running water in some secret channel under the snow.

Down in the compound again, she stopped to look at the side of the nursing station. She had not noticed until now, but the white paint had worn away as though it had been sand-blasted. She remembered the brittle rattle of snow during the February blizzards. The snowblock windbreak around the house had become spongy, like old foam rubber. She poked experimentally at a piece, and it slid away with a wet thud. *Opangaksha*, she smiled to herself. Spring had never been as exhilarating as this in Toronto.

She crossed the wet snow to Ishawakta's house. He had been hunting at the *agloos* the seals kept open with their flippers all winter. There was fresh, bloody meat in a tub, and Leah was scraping a skin which she would probably sew into summer *kamiks*. The new sled was lying, overturned, near the door. It had been fitted with painstakingly-carved whalebone runners that Ishawakta kept for spring trips when the sun could melt the runner-ice.

Ishawakta came around the corner of the house carrying an armful of walrus-hide harness. *"Ee,"* he said when she saw she was inspecting the sled. *"Komatik* finished." He shook his head, probably at the memory of how the other sled had been wrecked. "Sometime soon Inuit go to floe edge. Hunt many *neche*. Maybe whale. Nice time. *Peoyook*. Everyone go."

The floe edge, she knew, was a place about fifteen miles down the coast where the winter shore ice slowly crumbled against the pounding of the open sea. Sun and water were irresistible lures in the spring, and the Inuit packed tents, spears, rifles, and topped their *komatik* loads with boats and sewing machines for the annual holiday. She wanted to go with them, but there was always the chance she might be needed in the settlement. Besides, she argued to herself, the hospital should be put in order for the summer invasion of the Eskimos. It would be her birthday in a few days, though, and Health and Welfare would surely not disapprove if she took a short vacation.

"After you have been to the floe for seven, eight sleeps, will you come back to get me?" she asked Ishawakta.

"Ee," he said. The tips of his fingers touched the whalebone runners. It must have taken some Eskimo an entire winter to fit each sculptured strip of bone into place in the long, graceful jigsaw. No wonder the runners were used for just a short time each year. "I come," Ishawakta nodded.

The Lake Harbour Inuit left the settlement with the blessings of their *kabloonah* employers a week or so later. As usual on such occasions, the chores were left in the hands of Mosesee and other Inuit who were asked to come from the camps. She tried to keep busy, returning most of her medical stores to the hospital and asking Mosesee to clean the floor. She made the ward beds and stacked the fresh sheets and blankets that Oola had laundered and hung to dry in the attic.

She made out requisitions, remembering her confusion and

disappointment when they had been overlooked the previous year. This time, she ordered extra supplies of cortisone ointment and a croup tent. She had not needed crutches or canes since she had been there, but there was always the possibility of accidents when the Eskimos came in from the winter camps. On the food supply list, she doubled the order for canned butter, bacon, and jam. Her successors would find they were the best items for barter.

She wished she could ask for some radio equipment to pass out to the Inuit in the camps. Transmission and reception would always be spotty but at least it was a chance of getting through to the nursing station in an emergency. She wondered if she should ask for a microscope. She had read and re-read the section on tuberculosis in the medical manual and had learned it was possible to diagnose and treat the disease in the Arctic if one had a microscope, some laboratory materials, and anti-tuberculosis drugs.

She shrugged over the idea of suggesting to Health and Welfare that manuals should be supplied to all of the northern stations. The real need was for orientation courses and a knowledge of public health nursing – plus some feedback from Ottawa about what was happening in research concerning INHS programs in the Arctic. She decided to write the suggestions in her final report.

Mike was at the hospital door when she got up to go home for lunch. Don had picked up a message from Marg, relayed to Nottingham Island. "It's a daughter," the missionary told her. "They're both well." He smiled, then hugged her around the shoulders. She went into the Quonset hut kitchen and poured two glasses of canned grapefruit juice to toast the occasion. Then they walked back across the compound.

Incredibly, the settlement seemed to change in appearance from hour to hour. Now, there was sun or twilight around the clock, and the waterfall behind her house had begun to flow. At midday, the thermometer had risen above freezing. The snow on the paths was spongy underfoot. Protected places behind the building were green with new grass, and in one spot, she had glimpsed a clump of ground birch and saxifrage.

Ishawakta came to collect her the next day. She gave him her medical kit, grub box, and sleeping bag to pack on the *komatik* before telling Don Baird she would be at the floe edge for about a week.

"Great idea," he said, standing at the store door in the sun. "It's about the last chance for sled travel this season. Then we'll get the June fogs and the rain. I might even hear I'm a father in a few weeks. A message came this morning, you know, that Hilda's fine. She sends her love." He walked into the store and found something on a shelf. "Here's a going-away present. You'll need it." She saw to her surprise it was a bottle of suntan oil.

Ishawakta had fitted the sled dogs with skin boots tied with thongs. Once they began their fast run down the fjord she could understand why. At the bottom of the pools already forming on the ice there were sharp icicles. She relaxed in the sunshine on top of the light *komatik* load. Although the day was cold, there was less need to jog to keep from freezing. And, unlike the mind-numbing hours of winter travel, there was so much to see. A formation of geese honked high overhead, and the air seemed to be filled with gulls. The once bare and sombre cliffs were tinged with emerald. A seal pushed its head out of a breathing hole, heard the *komatik* and quickly vanished.

"Neche!" whispered Ishawakta. A few moments later, the dogs came to a stop, stood in their traces, then sat quietly on their haunches. Another seal was basking in the sun not far ahead of them. Ishawakta reached beside the steering box and brought out his rifle, a white cap, and a canvas shield stretched on crossed sticks. He pulled on the cap, then padded a step or two towards the seal, his body sheltered by the canvas. The seal looked up, listened, then put its head down again. Ishawakta took a run forward, then froze. The seal again inspected its surroundings and returned to basking. Ishawakta was within twenty feet of the seal when he shot it neatly through the head. The dogs promptly got to their feet and sprinted towards the dead animal, yelping excitedly.

"*Peoyook!*" grinned Ishawakta. He stowed his equipment on the *komatik* and hauled at the heavy seal until it hung over the back of the load. When it was safely lashed, they were off again.

There was smooth running for another mile or so then they were travelling over ice slashed by blue leads of open water. At first she was not alarmed. The *komatik* was longer than the leads were wide. Ishawakta simply drove across the cracks and the dogs leaped them easily. Soon, though, the leads became wider, and the front of the sled runners scarcely crossed to the next stretch of ice before the back-end hit the water. There was a howl as two dogs at the rear of the fan hitch fell into the sea and the *komatik* slid over their heads.

She looked back. The animals were dragged out and over the ice-pan, screaming and protesting until they regained their footing and their place in the team. The harness tangled but it was clearly too dangerous to stop for long. One lead that seemed narrow as they raced towards it suddenly gaped wider. Four dogs splashed into the water and two were almost strangled when their harness caught under the edge of the jagged ice. Ishawakta stopped the team, and she helped him pull three shivering animals to safety.

She wanted to ask Ishawakta how long the awful conditions would last, but she knew he would either soothe her with some vague comment or shrug and simply say it would last until it was over. Then the ice stretched out before them, flat, white, and unbroken. Then the dogs flung themselves against the harness, quickening their pace.

"Floe edge," said Ishawakta, pointing and laughing. "Camp!"

She peered again. Suddenly she could see the angular shapes of icebergs jutting above the horizon and there were more birds than she had seen in the fjord. Tents materialized with people sitting or walking around them. The sound of the dogs grew louder. Ishawakta yelled "*hraw!*" and the team wheeled to sprint parallel to the lip of the floe-edge. Dorothy caught her breath at the sight of the dark, restless expanse of Hudson Strait with its sun-silvered parade of floating ice-turrets and jagged pans. Sandy paddled by in a skin kayak, a seal slung over its prow. The team came to a yapping stop between two of the tents and she slid off the load. Pitsulala was sitting in the sun making duffle socks at her hand-powered sewing machine. The woman looked up and smiled, and Dorothy knew the Inuit were glad she had come.

The week at the floe edge was a celebration of sun, water, and glittering ice. No one bothered to consult a clock. She slept in Akavak's tent whenever she felt the need. She ate when she was hungry. She rubbed her face with the suntan oil and basked like a lazy seal. She shared her canned provisions with the Eskimos, and they shared birds they speared and chunks of seal. She ran far along the edge of the ice with King dancing beside her, marvelling again at the contrast with blue water and white, shining icebergs.

It was the kind of time she had always dreamed about. There were friends who never questioned what she wanted to do. There was freedom. There was inner privacy without loneliness. There were new things to touch, taste, and do. She went hunting in the strait with Akavak one calm day and watched as he shot a bobbing seal in the throat, gunning the motor so he could gaff the dying animal before it sank. She helped Pitsulala slice the carcass and flense the skin, and she gorged on the meat as extravagantly as the Eskimos always did. She drifted in a boat with Annie and Nylee and the three women sat silently and at peace in the crisp, sun-drenched air.

Ishawakta took her to explore the sailing ice sculptures. She put out her hands to scoop some of the turquoise water from an iceberg's pool. She laughed when she discovered it was as clear as the drinking water in her kitchen barrel.

She sat on the skins near the *tupik* watching Georgie unhurriedly mend a harness and Sandy patch his kayak with sealskin. Work merged with leisure and leisure with work when the brothers peeled off their shirts to wrestle. She spoke as little and as economically as the Inuit did. Words became useless. There were no queries, no answers, no seeking of permission. Understanding came from experience and observation. No one told her when it was time to leave the floe edge. The Eskimos took down their tents and loaded the *komatiks*. She simply pulled at the hood of her parka and went with them.

Epilogue

Dorothy Knight returned to Toronto in 1958 and became assistant head nurse at the East General Hospital. Duty on the ward was a challenge, but she still wanted to work in the community as she had in the Arctic. In September 1960, she applied to the Ontario Department of Health for a bursary to study public health nursing and, one year later, graduated from the University of Toronto. Under the terms of the bursary, she was sent where the ministry felt she was needed most: northeastern Ontario, based in the town of Kapuskasing. She practised there, as chief of a generalized public health nursing program, until 1964.

In that year she was offered a position with the World Health Organization as a public health nursing expert in Basutoland (later Lesotho) in southern Africa. She stayed for four years, eventually becoming adviser to the government on basic health services, shaping health policy, and administering the public health nursing service. When she returned to Toronto in 1968, she earned her Bachelor of Science in Nursing at the University of Toronto and worked as professional standards officer for the College of Nurses of Ontario. Since then, she has studied public health law and graduated as a Bachelor of Arts. She is now continuing with her work as a public health nurse with a special interest in health legislation.

Lake Harbour changed slowly as a community since 1958. The nursing station was closed in 1959 and the mission in 1960 after many of the Inuit drifted to Frobisher Bay and Cape Dorset.

For ten years, the settlement was almost deserted. But in 1970, the Lake Harbour Eskimos began to come home. In response to the trend, the federal government built frame houses, and the Inuit abandoned their nomad life to live close to the village where there were communal oil bins and electricity. Dog teams were replaced by snowmobiles. The Eastern Arctic Patrol was discontinued in 1969. First, there was an RCMP lay dispenser in Lake Harbour, then the Department of Health and Welfare re-opened the nursing station.

Dorothy Knight never went back to Lake Harbour. Neither did the white neighbours she knew there seventeen years ago.

The Reverend Mike Gardener is now a Canon and pastor of St. Luke's Anglican Mission in Pangnirtung on the east coast of Baffin Island. He and Marg have three daughters. Don and Hilda Baird never did decide to live in a large metropolitan area. They returned to Newfoundland, and today their home is in Labrador City, population 12,000. Hilda's first child was a boy, Don, Jr., who spent his infant years in Lake Harbour. The Bairds now have two more boys and a girl.

Both of the RCMP officers stayed in the force. Gerry Heapy is now a sergeant and lives with his wife and four sons in North Battleford, Saskatchewan. Sergeant Terry Jenkin is married, with a son and a daughter, and is stationed in Ottawa.

Notes from the Protagonist

When I left the Arctic in 1958, I was invited to talk about my experience in the Lake Harbour area and to make any suggestion that might help improve the nursing service.

I remember saying that it might be a good idea to consider supplying each Eskimo camp with simple short-range radio equipment for communicating with the nursing station. It seemed a fundamental change for the better. Not only would it serve an obvious purpose and save a great deal of time, money, perhaps lives, it would also be the beginning of what I considered essential – a time when the Inuit would become responsible for their own health care. I felt that northern nurses should long have been working themselves out of jobs. We could have started by giving certain responsibilities to Eskimos who showed an interest in health matters or who exhibited a flair for leadership. The midwives, for example. We could then encourage those persons to do as much as they felt capable of doing and give them total responsibility and accountability in a limited area of nursing practice once a skill had been demonstrated.

The program might have been very elementary at first. We might have expected, perhaps, that the individual concerned could learn to operate a radio and report signs and symptoms to the nurse. But we could have built on that. The important thing, in my mind, was to start – like the nurse who converted the abandoned Quonset hut into a hospital. She had the imagination to see the possibilities of the hut, just as the Inuit saw potential bears and seals in their rough lumps of soapstone.

From a simple beginning, we could have gone on to train Eskimos on the job in all kinds of health-related activities and, in particular, in tuberculosis control. Was it absolutely necessary to take sick Eskimos away from their homes and families for years at a time? Was there, as I once asked Dr. Sabean on the *C. D. Howe*, no other way?

I have since learned that the Canadian government did a superb job in lowering the incidence of TB in the Arctic in a remarkably short period of time. But I wonder if all possible alternatives to sanatorium treatment had been fully explored throughout the world before the decision was made that "the natives were not good candidates for the latest ambulant routines" (1957-58 INHS Directorate report).

Later, I worked in Africa where the natives lived much as the Inuit did as far as inadequate housing and sanitation were concerned. But they were treated at home. It was found that hospitalization made little difference to the cure rate and that one need not remove the average TB case from his home to protect his family, because most household contacts had been infected by the time the cases were diagnosed, anyway.

The whole program depended totally on the natives themselves. One person in each village accepted the job of seeing that the TB patients and suspects took their pills. These pills contained drugs found to be effective against tuberculosis in the early fifties.

An adjunct to the treatment of TB was the use of preventive vaccination – not only for tuberculosis but for other dangerous childhood diseases. All official reports said there had been systematic vaccination since 1945 and that anti-tuberculosis BCG vaccination has been carried out since 1933 among our Indian population. Yet there was no officially directed immunization program, either in Arctic nursing stations or the Inuit camps, so vaccination was not as "systematic" or as thorough as it could have been. I wonder if it would not have helped reduce the incidence of TB and therefore prevent some of the hospitalizations south if a permanent vaccination service, particularly of newborn babies, had been organized using nursing stations instead of waiting for the Eastern Arctic Patrol.

We could also have given individual Eskimos the task of keeping track of the ages and immunization requirements of their children. In this way, we could have introduced the Inuit to a vital area of health care – the keeping of simple records. We could have built on that experience and begun to train some natives as vaccinators.

They could have been diagnosing the cases, as health aides had been doing in Africa, by examining sputum through a microscope. Cases detected this way could have been on treatment for a year by the time the *Howe* came around.

Did we miss the boat by shouldering all the responsibility ourselves and depriving the Inuit of the one thing they badly needed – the opportunity to develop a competence – however small – in which they could take pride?

If that is so, I am sorry, because it has amazed me how strongly individuals respond to the expectations of others. I am sure that by now those Inuit who exhibited an initial interest would be in positions of authority. By now, there might be Eskimo aides, registered nurses, public health nurses, doctors and administrators. After all, I rose beyond my own initial competence through education. Why not the Inuit?

It does not seem, in retrospect, too much to have asked at that time. Other countries, long before 1958, were doing much more. Fifty years earlier, Denmark was training the Greenland Eskimos to lead their people. By 1945, the country had a significant percentage of native-born professional personnel.

A few years later, my own personal experiences with the World Health Organization in Africa reinforced my feelings about health care education. I worked there with native practitioners who had been encouraged upwards through the health heirarchy. When I left Lesotho after four years, I was replaced by an African.

The major health problems that we faced in Africa were identical to those we dealt with in the Arctic. Strangely though, WHO strategy was the reverse of that chosen by Canada. In assisting developing countries (and Canada's Arctic was certainly underdeveloped), WHO spared no money or effort in sending native people out of their home country for years at a time to be educated. The problem of tuberculosis, on the other hand, was handled in the patient's home. Canada spared no money or effort in sending Eskimos away from their camps for treatment in southern sanatoriums. But there was no interest in spending a similar amount to help educate the Inuit in health care. Perhaps we needed, and still need, WHO to advise Canada with its problems of developing peoples.

These notes may only demonstrate that hindsight has 20/20 vision. Things have improved in the Arctic – there are X-ray units in the nursing stations, better communications, special courses for nurses. But until 1970, northern health services were still manned essentially by non-natives. As Diamond Jenness, writing for the Arctic Institute of North America stated in his 1968 book *Eskimo Administration, Analysis and Reflections*, "Why have the government's strenuous efforts ... proved so ineffectual? Why has the situation deteriorated?" To which I would add my own question – why does it always take twenty years from the time we know something needs to be done, until it is done?

Dorothy Knight